Feb 2014

THE AX MURDERS OF SAXTOWN

THE AX MURDERS OF SAXTOWN

*The Unsolved Crime That Terrorized a Town
and Shocked the Nation*

NICHOLAS J. C. PISTOR

LYONS PRESS
Guilford, Connecticut
An imprint of Globe Pequot Press

Lyons Press is an imprint of Globe Pequot Press.

Project Editor: Lauren Brancato
Layout Artist: Maggie Peterson

Library of Congress Cataloging-in-Publication Data is available on file.

ISBN 978-0-7627-8697-8

Printed in the United States of America

10 9 8 7 6 5 4 3 2 1

To my mother and father

CONTENTS

Contents

PREFACE

I HAD STOPPED SLEEPING DURING THE SPRING OF 2003.

A conversation with a Jesuit priest had triggered a childhood nightmare.

Father Francis X. Cleary taught a class on evil and demonic Christianity at Saint Louis University, where I was a student. Cleary was stern—to put it mildly. The snow-haired man walked with a cold shuffle that accentuated the white priest's collar around his neck and the scowl on his face. When I first met him, he used a cane, which he would rap on the floor or the desks of inattentive students.

He specialized in the mythology of exorcisms. In particular, the exorcism of the young boy who inspired William Peter Blatty's book *The Exorcist*. Cleary's Jesuit brothers at the university had performed the ritual on the possessed boy in the late 1940s. (Blatty said he changed the sex of the possessed child from boy to girl out of deference to one of the priests.)

All of that had been turned to legend by the time I walked the statue-lined pathways of the university. Talk of ghosts and evil spirits had supplanted the true story. Folklore said that a room on campus at Verhagen Hall served as the site for the exorcism—near where Cleary once had an office. "The kids gather outside on Halloween and look up at the window," Cleary once said. "I suppose every school has its ghost stories. Ours just happened to become a best-selling book and movie."

The real exorcism took place in the psychiatric unit at Alexian Brothers Hospital in St. Louis.

Cleary was a young student at the university when the exorcism happened. One day I approached the aged priest, as had so many others, to talk about it. I was nervous. I made sure to watch my words. (Cleary was obsessed with good grammar.)

To my surprise, he was engaging about the whole affair. We spoke about how a fourteen-year-old boy in suburban Washington, DC, had allegedly become possessed by the devil. About how and why he came to St. Louis. About the process Father William Bowdern used to allegedly expel his demons.

Believers and nonbelievers argue over whether it was a case of demonic possession or mental illness. I look at it with a skeptical eye. But the mythology that took hold after the event—of twisting heads, shaking beds, scratching noises, changing voices, flying vomit—is frightening.

"Some of the Jesuits living with me at Saint Louis University at the time were conversant with some of the events of the case and, as often happens, as the story was passed on, it became more fanciful and inaccurate," Bowdern was said to have written to Blatty.

But Bowdern cautioned, "I can assure you of one thing: The case I was involved with was the real thing. I had no doubts about it then, and I have no doubts about it now."

I discussed those details with Cleary. Our conversation turned to my own story. My major. My background. My future. I told him I was interested in becoming a journalist.

He asked me where I had been raised. I told him I was from a small town in Illinois called Millstadt. Surprisingly, Cleary had heard of it. He said there had been a bad murder there more than a century before, and that the event gave way to mythology. I knew immediately that he was talking about the Saxtown murders—the unsolved killing of a five-person family on an isolated farm. My childhood had been filled with stories about how the German immigrant family had been hacked to death with an ax in the middle of the night.

It had often kept me awake as a boy. I was afraid that someone would storm into our house while we were asleep and kill us all.

Nobody really had the straight story. It had been embellished through the years. The family was said to have netted a gold fortune from Germany and had been killed by someone hoping to steal it. From there, fact had turned to fiction. Locals often repeated fragmented details of the case and then said this person or that person knew the "real story"—although no one ever did. Of course, everyone was sure that the farm where the murders occurred was haunted.

My parents owned a copy of a short, fictionalized account that had been published in the local newspaper by a dentist in 1974 for the centennial of the murders. The story was frustrating because names had been changed and events distorted. It didn't tell you what actually happened. But it was still scary. As a kid I would remove the copy tucked away in a dresser drawer, half in a fright, and look at the red cover with dread. Then I would slowly turn the pages to read the story. A sleepless night almost always followed. I often clung to my covers in bed, lying there with one eye open while hearing noises and fearing shadows—even though nothing was there.

Years later, after having talked to Cleary, my childhood nightmare had been reawakened. I searched online late at night for more information on the Saxtown story. But it was largely fruitless. The case, which had made national headlines for weeks, had been forgotten. Almost like it hadn't really happened at all.

But I couldn't stop thinking about it. I wanted to know the details of the family that was killed. Why someone raised an ax over their heads. Why their murderer was never caught. I wanted to feel the drama. I wanted to be thrown back in that world and learn about my roots. About the Germans who had immigrated to the Midwest in the 1800s.

That story didn't exist in one place. It was scattered in libraries across the country.

So, being an aspiring journalist, I decided to seek out the truth. I walked into the Pius XII Memorial Library and requested microfilm rolls from the newspapers of 1874. I slipped the flimsy celluloid through the machine and turned it on. Now the case seemed alive. There before me blared the headline from the *St. Louis Dispatch:* SAXTOWN. THE TERRIBLE SCENE IN THE STILLZENREIDER FARM HOUSE.

I made copies of the original newspaper stories and walked home to my apartment to read them. I locked the doors, turned on every light— and stayed up all night.

Prologue: The Murdered Family

The Saxtown farmers hurried to Freivogel Cemetery to make their stand.

They were older men now. Wrinkled and gray. Their creaky limbs could barely hold steady a pitchfork or a lantern, much less a gun or a knife.

But they were ready for battle. Their aged bodies and fragile memories could not forget what had happened all those years ago—and they were still willing to do whatever it took to avenge it.

Under the barren grass beneath their feet in the tree-wrapped graveyard were the wooden coffins they had made in March of 1874. In them were the five bodies of the murdered Stelzriede family—three adults, two children.

The mostly German-American mob remembered those days from years ago. When the detectives came. When the newspapermen came. When more than a thousand people had tramped the lonely Southern Illinois cemetery's lawn the day the Stelzriedes were lowered into the ground.

There was so much drama, with neighbor suspecting neighbor of cutting throats, that few people knew exactly where the bodies were. The Stelzriedes, after all, had been buried in unmarked graves.

But Sexton Joseph R. James knew. And now the men were ready to protect the bodies from him.

Walking into the cemetery, amid gloomy woods and wheat fields, James was charged with opening the graves, digging up their bones, and moving them eight miles from the small farming community to the sprawling Walnut Hill Cemetery in Belleville, Illinois, where a stone obelisk had been erected to honor the German immigrant family's memory. Chiseled into the monument's surface were the words Zum Andenken am der Ermordete Familie.

In English: "To the memory of the murdered family."

The memory was frozen in the minds of the Saxtown men who were standing in the cemetery. They could see the Stelzriedes' horror-stricken faces. See them like it was yesterday.

And they could picture an ax in the hands of a faceless killer, glinting in the moonlight as it approached the Stelzriede cabin.

They had mythologized what happened on the night of the murders. Their minds buzzed with a frightening sequence: The killers approached the small farmhouse and knocked on the front door. Fritz Stelzriede, sleeping on a lounge near the door, asked who was there.

"The answer reassured him," it was reported. Fritz put on his trousers and opened the door.

With a foot on the threshold, one of the "midnight callers" slammed an ax down on Fritz's head. But it only staggered him. There was a brief, desperate struggle. He fought for his life. The ax came down twice more. Fritz dropped to the ground.

"His brains were oozing from the three great holes in his head, but to make the work complete his throat was half severed with one sweep of a keen corn knife," the *St. Louis Post-Dispatch* reported.

The eyes of his wife and children opened. But not fast enough. The ax slammed their heads and the corn knife slashed their throats.

In the next room old man Stelzriede awoke to the commotion and ran out. As he approached through the doorway, a misguided ax swing missed the patriarch's head and bore into the doorjamb. Another swing missed, too, and took out another hunk of wood. The third swing hit its mark. Square in the head. The corn knife swept across his neck and finished him.

At least that's how the men imagined it now as Sexton James and his hired hands ambled through the cemetery amid the white tombstones jutting out of the ground, looking for the Stelzriedes' unmarked resting place.

News of James's arrival had spread through Saxtown. Fast. The farmers dropped everything and headed to the Freivogel Cemetery. They feared that James was going to try to raise the bodies.

That's exactly what he intended to do.

James, a grave-digging Englishman, had buried bodies at the Walnut Hill Cemetery in Belleville since 1855. Through the years, he had converted Walnut Hill from a "bramble-grown wood to a well-kept modern park of the dead, with shaded drives and walks and vistas which would be pleasing if they were not dotted with the marble signs of homes bereft and hearts broken."

He had even lived in the cemetery for a time. Then across the street, looking out at the headstones with flowers and evergreens—but not ghosts.

"I have been through it all hours of the night," James said. "I have dug graves at midnight by the light of the moon. But I have never seen a ghost or anything that looked like ghosts are supposed to look. There may be such things as ghosts, I can't say there ain't, because I don't know. But if there are any I think they are about as careful as most people are to avoid graveyards at night."

He continued, "I'll tell you what I think about ghosts. People who expect to see them and think they see them, do see them—in their minds. It's all in their imaginations."

James had buried thousands and thousands of corpses. Or, as he called them, "live ones." "A live corpse is a fresh one—one buried for the first time, you know," James once said. "Dead ones are those which are handled a second time."

In Saxtown James was looking for dead ones.

He had been asked to dig up dead ones before. Mostly by imaginative mothers who had convinced themselves that their dead children really weren't dead.

"I say to all of them: 'If the child was not dead before, it is certainly dead now.'"

"Some have had so strong a feeling that a person had been buried alive that nothing I could say had any effect on them and I have had to open the graves. In no case, however, did I find anything to indicate that consciousness had returned after internment."

James wasn't expected to chisel open the Stelzriede coffins to check if the inhabitants were alive. He was expected simply to raise them up, place them on wagons, and take them to his cemetery in Belleville, where a Stelzriede relative had erected the handsome nine-foot-tall monument.

The farmers of Saxtown stood in his way. They believed the removal of the bodies would prevent efforts, which had been ongoing for years, to find the killers. Suspicion being what it was, perhaps the unknown killers stood among them.

The crime had hung over the community for too long.

The farmers declared that the bodies should not be removed. And that they would use force to prevent it.

The exhumation was abandoned. James turned around and left without putting the bodies on the back of his wagon. One more attempt was later made to remove the corpses. The farmers prevented it again.

A monument that marks no grave remains in Walnut Hill Cemetery. The Stelzriedes remain in Saxtown. And some say so do their ghosts.

CHAPTER 1

Escaping Tragedy

CARL STELZRIEDE WAS AN OLD MAN ESCAPING TRAGEDY. A SIXTY-FIVE-year-old German immigrant farmer evading God's vengeance.

Death was near, he surely knew. Weathered and pocked by the marks of age, he had shaky hands, weak legs, and cloudy eyes. A German farmer did most of his work with his hands. Carl Stelzriede (pronounced *stilts-ZEN-reeder*) was no different. He had split his own wood, milked his own cows, and hunted his own meat. For decades he had plowed the Southern Illinois soil and fetched buckets of water from a creek. Now the hellish labor was evident to anyone who bothered to notice. He was bent, his back hunched like the stem of a wilting sunflower.

And yet his hair was still black—a remarkable jet black deep enough to reflect the fearful elegy frozen in his mind. Carl had been running from death his whole life. First from fire, then from fate. At least now his anxiety was calmed by the probability that it would be natural.

The old man had lived well beyond the life expectancy of the time. In 1874 the average man could expect to live to age forty. About 2 percent of the United States population made it to sixty and beyond. Carl was reminded almost daily that his time was almost up: Maria Christina Horstmann Stelzriede, his wife, had been dead for eight years.

Carl lived in a countryside hamlet of German immigrants east of St. Louis, Missouri, on the Illinois side of the Mississippi River. He had given up farming his sixty acres. Instead, he roamed the land like a lost soul, with a forlorn hope to avoid whatever bad thing God had in store.

The economic disaster catalyzed by the Panic of 1873 was in full force—and it was brutal. The post–Civil War boom, fueled by railroads and land speculation, had ended with a hangover.

"As the nation emerged from the civil war and 'got its breath,' as it were, after that great struggle, it leaped into the task of upbuilding which had been temporarily abandoned in the four years preceding," the *New York Times* wrote. "Railroads were projected and laid out, new territory opened up and settled, the roads themselves built, and all on credit that was freely extended."

The credit dried up. Panic set in. Cotton and iron mills threw thousands of laborers, many former Union and Confederate soldiers, onto the streets and into unemployment. The terms *tramp* and *bum* became commonplace as relief rolls exploded.

The Long Depression, as it was later known, terrorized bottom lines for the rest of the decade. Grizzled laborers headed to farms where they begged for work. The men who had fought the war and the cowards who had avoided it were willing to do anything for money. Anything.

None of it mattered to Carl. The honest, Christian man had finally found prosperity. He had his land, which the Germans had coveted in the old country. And now, after his years of struggle, locals were gossiping that he had just received a legacy fortune of cash and gold from Germany. He had money at a time when few did. Carl only fretted that God would notice.

There was reason to worry.

Carl had spent his early life in the farming village of Hille, Germany, amid war and political unrest, in a land that was constantly being carved up by nobility and kings. Against the backdrop of the Napoleonic Wars, he had performed much of the same grueling farm work he later did in America—just without success.

He lived a desperate life in Germany. The newspapermen were more kind with their assessment. "Life in the old country had not prospered with him," one wrote.

Carl owned a vine-clad cottage there. That is, until someone burned it down. The cruel flames came at the hand of an incendiary. The perpetrator was unknown.

Carl's spirit, though, was unbroken. That was the German way. He rebuilt, albeit a smaller house, simply remembered as a "less imposing domicile."

It didn't stand for long. Soon the wooden house was struck by a bolt of lightning and destroyed. Carl and Maria were stunned by the electric shock and barely made it out alive. They were able to recover in time to save a small amount of their household belongings. Not that there was much to save.

His children added to his dread. Between 1838 and 1841 three of Carl and Maria's children had died. Four-year-old Friedrich Christian in 1838. Thirteen-month-old Christian Friedrich in 1840. One-year-old Christian Heinrich in 1841. Only one son, Fritz, made it to adulthood.

Carl was disheartened by the death and destruction and felt that the ominous recurrence of misfortune was somehow representative of God's displeasure. A devout churchgoer, he surely heard the words of Job: "When I looked for light, then came darkness."

Carl's life in the old country mirrored a Jobian struggle. His kids were gone. His house was gone. God seemed to have taken away more than he could handle.

So Carl Stelzriede escaped.

In 1844 he and his wife boarded an immigrant sailing ship and headed for America, where many Germans either sought refuge from the turmoil of Europe or ran away from their past. The trip across the Atlantic wasn't easy. A New York newspaper called these immigrant vessels "damned plague ships and swimming coffins." The Stelzriedes carried little with them from the old country other than a green chest of dry goods and a small trunk of "trumpery usually to be found about a German cottage."

The average journey across the Atlantic took about two months. Aboard the ship, the Stelzriedes lived in close quarters with practically no fresh air. There were few toilets. Meals consisted largely of salt meat, custard, and plums. Most of that was passed back up from stomach to wood floor. Seasickness reigned.

After weeks at sea avoiding disease—and surviving the pungent smell of urine and vomit—the couple docked in New Orleans. They immediately went up the fabled Mississippi River, which looked remarkably different than the great rivers of Europe. The Mississippi was the color of clay and clogged with tree trunks, ripped by the river's strong current. The Stelzriedes landed at St. Louis, a boomtown bustling with steamboats and troublemakers perched above the river like a terrace. "If you send a damned fool to St. Louis, and you don't tell them he's a damned fool, they'll never find it out," Mark Twain once wrote. The Stelzriedes headed into the foolish abyss and never looked back.

Founded by the French in 1764, St. Louis had cultivated a vast German-speaking community that offered the prospect of a safe harbor for the Stelzriedes. They could hide from their angry God in a foreign land but still speak their native tongue. The couple, however, wasn't interested in city life—particularly in St. Louis, where residents drank muddy water and breathed coal dust.

"The coal smoke turns it into an antiquity the moment you take your hand off it," Twain wrote of the city. "The smoke used to bank itself in a dense billowy black canopy over the town, and hide the sky from view."

Disease was rampant. Cholera and bilious fever, acquired from drinking river water, killed whole sections of the population.

"The funeral bells were ringing nearly all of the time in St. Louis," wrote Gustave Koerner, a German immigrant passing through the city. "Everybody expected to be taken down any day."

Still, St. Louis was on the rise. Steamboats lined the river wharf, where merchants battled for customers. The streets were full of immigrants, the barrooms crowded with Irish, Germans, Swiss—and fistfights. The city was an international stew of newcomers, businessmen and wayward souls headed out west.

One thing shocked some of the visiting rural Germans, like the Stelzriedes. The streets were also packed with black people (roughly equal to the number of whites). The courthouses conducted slave auctions, and public lashings were common.

"From the second story of our residence we could see into the neighboring house, where we once saw what appeared to be an American lady, lashing a young slave girl with a cow hide. Had there still been a lingering disposition . . . to settle in Missouri, these scenes would have quenched it forever," Koerner remembered.

The Stelzriedes had the same outlook. They stuck with their farming vocation and disembarked to the nearby prairie uplands of Illinois, where German encampments had sprung up around cheap farm ground. The swath of land pinned above the American Bottom in St. Clair County was their destination.

Saxtown was pronounced by locals with a short *a*, which put special emphasis on *ax*. It sounded like a frightening place to outsiders, especially when barbed with a thick, Low German accent. The Stelzriedes didn't mind. They had decided it would be their home.

To get there they likely paid the Wiggins Ferry Company to shuttle them eastward across the Mississippi, where steamboats swarmed the muddy channel "like ants in their labyrinthian cities." The crossing was dangerous at times. The river was infested with bold pirates who weren't afraid to steal or murder.

Once safely across, the Stelzriedes headed through the American Bottom, a stretch of floodplain below the river bluff. A path of black mud led through the wilderness and up the bluff, where the bright gas lamps of St. Louis, muffled by coal smoke, faded behind the treetops.

Saxtown wasn't easy to find. Traveling the path there was a bit like wearing a straightjacket. The way out was clear. Movement was difficult. Perseverance was a virtue.

The path was called a *cut*. The word *road* would have been too kind. "On either side of the track, if it deserve the name, was the thick 'bush;' and everywhere was stagnant, slimy, rotten, filthy water," Charles Dickens wrote of his trek through a nearby area. Horse carriages often drowned in the mud during wet seasons. The sound of frogs and wild pigs echoed everywhere, creating a strange cacophony of noise in almost all seasons. (Dickens described the swine as "a course, ugly breed, as unwholesome-looking as though they were the spontaneous growth of the country.") Flecks of limestone jutted through the hills and marked the route. The yellow rocks appeared to smile at those who left and grimace at those who came.

About twenty miles in on the way to Saxtown was Millstadt, a small town fueled by coal mining and flour manufacturing. There wasn't much of note other than a large mill, steep with swollen grain elevators. There was no bank or police station. All of that was in Belleville, about eight miles northeast. That meant most people policed themselves and hid their money at home before they could make a day's journey to a bank—sometimes a dangerous task in later years as people grew desperate for money.

Millstadt was a German town, which meant there were lots of funny-sounding German names like Valentine Brenfleck (a brewer and tavern owner), Henry Oldendorph (a wagon dealer), Herman Bruggenjurgen (a grocer), and Adolph Schlernitzauer (a doctor). Small wooden homes were arranged neatly about the blocks. Chickens were known to tramp in the front yards and cluck a sort of disjointed waltz.

About three miles south was Saxtown, which sat almost invisible in the countryside. Stitched together by a patchwork of adjoining farms, it was divided by split-rail fences and woodlands. Saxtown, much like the neighboring hamlets of Boxtown, Bohleyville, Darmstadt, and Herr Gott's Eck (God's Corner), was "strictly rural in all its character." There was no town center or municipal government. Unless a person spoke German, he or she wasn't welcome. Saxtonites had created a closed German society separate from the surrounding English world. They kept their own land and bought out neighbors of other nationalities. Almost all of them were congregants at the Zion Evangelical Church in Millstadt on Sunday. None of them enjoyed any social standing.

Sometimes the neighbors would gather and play music. They used backcountry fiddles, not the violins of the great German composers.

The Stelzriedes liked the area because it reminded them of home. They wrote to relatives in Germany, who later moved nearby. Carl and his wife bought land with their savings and built a small cottage made of squared logs. Split pieces of hickory were dipped in mud, wrapped with straw, and slapped on the house as insulation. The frame house was one of rugged austerity. It had just three rooms—a sitting room, a small bedroom, and a kitchen. The house fronted eastward about twenty yards off a broad county highway. There was an open porch in the rear, not far from a rocky stream.

Life prospered for Carl. His son Fritz appeared to have survived the ills that had wiped out the other children in Germany. His farm grew with the boy. Soon, the place had a rich wheat field, not to mention oat and corn fields. It was stocked with cows, bulls, mules, horses, and pigs (which were surely just as ugly as the ones Charles Dickens bemoaned).

Farming wasn't everything. The German-Americans often adopted a thrifty way of life to benefit their farms, which meant a standard of living much lower than the native population. They made their own clothes, tools, and food. With the money he had saved, Carl liked to play part-time banker. Lending out money (at interest) was a good way to generate extra cash, especially because he was landlocked by larger neighboring farms, which stunted growth.

And that was that. Life remained unremarkable and made its inevitable circle. Maria died in 1866. Fritz married Anna Tatje, also from the area, two years later. The couple took over the farm from the aged Carl and soon produced two children—a boy and a girl.

It was a matter of German pride for Saxtonites to keep their farms in their own families generation after generation. The German immigrants welcomed children as a joy, and as an asset. Hired labor was used only during harvest time. Carl had relied on it more than most and often had two men on payroll at any given time. Fritz continued the practice. Hired hands had reputations for being menacing folks with little intelligence, downtrodden people capable of anything. Sometimes they were violent or just plain mad; their tempers were quick as they passed from farm to farm. Most were tolerated, though, because they were strong and willing to work—important resources for a productive farmstead.

The Stelzriedes had to use such rough-and-tumble paid labor. Illinois was a free state that barred slavery. The question of slavery had sent violence coursing throughout the new nation and proved more vexing than the Mississippi River's tricky current. In 1837, just a few miles north of Saxtown, in Alton, Illinois, a mob had gathered to destroy the printing press of newspaper publisher and abolitionist Elijah P. Lovejoy. The angry throng killed Lovejoy and dumped his printing press in the Mississippi. Across the river in St. Louis, the courts had sorted out the lawsuit of Dred

Scott, the Missouri slave who said he should be emancipated because he had lived with his master in free states, including Illinois. The courts decided against him, which hastened the Civil War.

The gunfire and cannon blasts were evidence that the Stelzriedes couldn't escape the political unrest they had fled in Europe. Just as the war ended, President Abraham Lincoln was shot in the head while watching a comedic play in Washington, DC. Old man Stelzriede saw headline after headline detailing the assassination, the great conspiracy to cripple the fragile government, and the inevitable trials that followed. For years the event dominated column inches in local newspapers.

Carl's own murder would soon fill the space.

It was March of 1874. It seemed like nothing but good fortune was within the family's grasp. The hard winter had turned to a soft spring. Money was in surplus for the family despite the ailing economy. The farm's hens were laying the best eggs. And each evening knitted stockings grew underneath Anna's hand. They fetched good prices at the market.

But beneath the surface, the springtime rain-heads foreshadowed a different future.

The old man couldn't shake the tragedies from his days in Europe. He had become a drunk, driven to alcohol by fear of God's inevitable retribution. Oftentimes he sauntered about the land like a ghost, mumbling incoherent German expressions. His bitterness led to arguments with friends and family members—and even his own son. Earlier in the month, Carl had quarreled with his brother over a relative's inheritance. The hard-minded Germans often carried such feuds to the grave. The two brothers broke off all contact and never spoke again.

Carl also had frequent quarrels with anyone who owed him money—especially Fritz's brother-in-law, who farmed nearby ground. Carl held a chattel mortgage on the property and was often frustrated with slow payments.

Fritz and Anna weren't worried about the old man's fragile state or constant arguments. They had greater concerns. A cold snap earlier in the week brought a suspected whooping cough to their eight-month-old daughter. Disease could kill her young lungs at any moment.

All eyes were on the family. In hushed conversations Saxtonites gossiped about rumors of a sizable inheritance the Stelzriedes had netted from Europe. It was the sort of thing you'd expect from a small frontier community. Everyone whispered about the suspected fortune—friends, neighbors, distant relatives, hired hands. It was already well known that the old man lent sums of cash for interest. Now word was that a package of gold, much desired amid the country's economic woes, had arrived in Millstadt from Germany. The package, according to local lore, was addressed to the Stelzriedes of Saxtown.

On Thursday, March 19, 1874, Fritz went to Millstadt to retrieve the package. He then headed to a farm auction at the old Eyman place in High Prairie, another farm community not far from Saxtown, quilted with deep woods, rich soil, and quiet houses. Just about every farmer from Saxtown was there.

Farm auctions were a rural, social version of a stock market. Folks from surrounding areas would gather to sell farm stock and trade tools; family, friends, and even strangers would attend. Women cooked food because the event normally lasted all day. People eyeballed one another with shotgun glances meant to instill the appearance of toughness. In those days you had to scare people into doing business the right way. This was still very much the frontier.

Fritz was remembered to have appeared in this bristly milieu with a covered willow basket hanging from his neck. It made him the focus of wild stares. The auctiongoers suspected it was the inherited gold, but no one asked. They just whispered.

Fritz was watched with the kind of careful attention a passerby would give to a rattlesnake. He didn't have any trouble doing business, though. He sold some potato seedlings to Ben Schneider, a neighbor, and told him to pick it up the next day. Then he offered to loan anyone at the scene up to eight hundred dollars cash, which he kept stashed at home. It was well known that he had the money at his farmhouse. He stated to all within earshot that he'd keep the money at his house until the following Monday.

Rumors of a legacy fortune had put the Stelzriede family name on the locals' thick German tongues. Now the windfall was all but confirmed.

Not one soul had an interest in borrowing the money—but someone did have an interest in taking it.

Fritz clutched the wicker basket close to his chest, climbed his horse, and headed home. It was the last time he was seen alive.

Because banks weren't nearby, the Stelzriedes' wooden shack had become a storehouse for hard cash. Two days earlier, a local mill had paid the family one hundred thirty dollars. They kept it tucked away with hundreds of other dollars, possibly along with the gold, according to legend. This was risky. In an apparent acknowledgment of the danger, Fritz had vowed to make a day's journey to Belleville, the St. Clair County seat, and put the fortune in a bank.

He never made the trip.

That night, Monk, the family's recently acquired dog, roamed the outside of the house. As on most nights, the old man went to sleep in his bedroom. His son and daughter-in-law slept in the house's main room. There, Anna placed the sick baby in bed with her, instead of in the crib on the other side of the room. Three-year-old Carl Jr. joined her. Fritz would sleep on a lounge at the foot of the old-fashioned bed so his wife could care for the children. The eight-month-old baby girl clasped her arms around her mother's neck and nestled against her bosom. The family fell into a deep slumber.

That warm night seemed like all of the others out in the Saxtown darkness, where a springtime cadence of tree frogs lulled everyone to sleep. If only the Stelzriedes knew that someone was watching, waiting, looking for the right time to strike and disrupt their ordinary routines.

The house was still but filled with the music of five beating hearts that planned to greet another sunrise. The old man had hung his coat by the door. Fritz had laid his boots and stockings out to dry in preparation for another day of hard labor. A child's toy was abandoned in the middle of the floor, awaiting a return to playtime in the morning—playtime that would never come.

CHAPTER 2

Death House

THE CLEAR SKY WAS STREAKED WITH ORANGE AND BLACK. A SOUTHERN wind collided with the cool air blowing in from the northern high plains. It was winter's last murderous struggle, but spring was winning out. The weather mirrored the range of human emotion that would be traversed that day, from calmness and serenity to madness and horror. Something terrible had happened.

It was Friday, March 20, 1874. The temperature was unusually high, begging to be knocked out by a thunderstorm. It was the kind of day that drove mutts to run in circles. The wind was still, but the old folks could feel something coming. They always did.

The rivers of the Mississippi valley were swollen, nourished by melting snow and heavy rains. The stagnant water brought all kinds of bugs and flies and rats. Most of the area surrounding the Mississippi looked like a swamp—and felt like one. Humidity wreaked havoc on the bone joints of young and old.

Ben Schneider's legs must've felt the pain. But he ran. Hard and fast with no hesitation. It was instinctive. He *had* to run.

Ben wasn't running *to* somewhere. He was running *from* somewhere.

His heavy leather boots, breaking apart with age, clogged deep into the mud and left footprints that would later be questioned by dozens of wannabe sleuths.

It was about five o'clock in the afternoon, most newspapers would later agree. That's when his screams were first heard, or at least when someone took note of them.

His panic had caused him to revert to his native German tongue. He couldn't think straight enough to even stutter in English.

Ben screamed deeply from his stomach with a windblown holler that some within earshot could have mistaken for a Confederate war cry, that war still hanging in the background. The local boys, who had worn Union blue a decade before, heard the sound only in their nightmares. Until now. It was the kind of shout that happened naturally and couldn't be re-created without a shock of horror or a cattle prong.

Horror was in Ben Schneider's wake.

Five minutes before, ten at most, Ben had gone to the nearby Stelzriede farm to pick up potato seed he had bought from Fritz Stelzriede the day before. Germans were funny about potatoes. The vegetable triggered bad memories. The Irish had their potato famine—and so did the Dutch. In 1840 the German population had grown large; it relied on the potato to sustain it. When a disease struck potato crops across the land, rural Germans swelled into a panic that still played with their minds. Several agrarian crises ensued. Many people fled the country.

Potato planting must be done with care and attention. Ben knew that. Superstition scared everyone into planting potatoes before St. Patrick's Day. But the wet weather had left Ben at the mercy of the gods. It was already three days past, so he reckoned he'd pick up the seed on Friday afternoon.

Ben later wished he'd never gone.

Barrel chested. Average height. Strong. Hunched back. No education. He was not a patrician farmer who milled about the land drinking bourbon. Nor was he a famed "Latin farmer" who debated the merits of agricultural theory. Ben worked the land himself like a slave. His body, at just twenty-eight years old, was assaulted by life on the farm. He had lost most of his teeth, and his hands were so badly calloused they looked like the belly of a snake. Today, he intended to carry the sacks of potato seed a mile home on foot by balancing them on his shoulders.

Ben was from the Alsace-Lorraine swath of Germany, the turf later lost in the First World War and quickly "annexed" back by Adolf Hitler. His fatherland was constantly in turmoil. So, a few years before, he had made a go of it in the United States.

He loved America. Except on this day.

The Stelzriede family—Fritz, his wife and two children, and Carl, the family patriarch—were Ben's neighbors. As in, they were the people who lived closest to him, about a mile away from the rented ground Ben occupied with his wife, Kate.

It was a long walk. The path to the Stelzriede farm was muddy, which made it hard to walk. Ben passed creek beds, blackberry briers, wheat fields, and white dogwood trees. Things were starting to bloom, but the glimmer of death was everywhere. Soon the purple trumpeted foxglove would be ready to cause nausea and jaundice. The green-leafed poison ivy would afflict anyone who touched. The brown castor bean, with its white ricin, would be ready to destroy anyone with a single whiff.

Ben marched to the Stelzriedes' farm like a caveman. The Germans here didn't take their time.

He paused as he approached the small Stelzriede house.

The animals on the farm were in a panic. Chickens pounced at his tattered homespun trousers. The cows hunched in distress. They hadn't been milked. Crows and buzzards circled up in the sky. No smoke was coming from the house's chimney.

Something was wrong. There was a strange stillness.

Monk, the Stelzriedes' Newfoundland dog, howled in the unseen background. The big dog sounded like he was penned behind the house.

"Fritz!" Ben yelled from the road.

He listened. No answer.

Everything seemed strangely quiet at the house. Ben wondered why.

Ben approached the house with caution and stepped across an old, creaky, wood-planked porch. He rapped at the front door with his left hand.

Silence still.

He checked the door to see if it was locked. It tipped open; he peeked inside like an intruder. Darkness. He swung the door open and allowed the fading sun to flood the house's front room, where the Stelzriede family slept. It was a sight that made his blood run cold.

Observers would later say the place looked like a domesticated slaughterhouse, with its inhabitants struck down and butchered like hogs.

Three severed fingers were scattered on the floor like spent gun shells. A head, nearly severed from its body, lay three steps from the doorway. A few feet away, a woman lay dead with her two children, whose heads were pounded so hard they looked like raspberry jelly.

Blood was everywhere. Brains were spattered on the white walls. And the house had been ransacked.

Ben ran out.

Soon, his screams summoned the world to Saxtown. And soon, Ben's left hand would make him a suspect in the biggest crime to happen in America since the murder of Abraham Lincoln.

Murder had happened here before, but nothing like this. A vagabond on the loose killing a passerby? Sure. A crazy man killing for quick sex? Yes. Just a month earlier, a German farmer riding in the fields had been shot and killed in broad daylight. Days later, another farmer was beaten and assaulted in his wagon. But those crimes were standard fare, representative of the Reconstruction era, not blood feuds or love triangles. "These brutal affairs," the *St. Louis Dispatch* reported, "were attributed to a gang of negroes." Arrests were made.

But now men would come from far away. From places named Belleville, Waterloo, and Maeystown. From St. Louis and its gritty neighbor, East St. Louis. And from even farther. Men boarded trains in the smoky dins of Chicago and Kansas City and bolted to tiny Saxtown, a place unknown to them just days before. Sleuths and police and newspapermen couldn't stay away. The simple details of the terror commanded attention—and attracted the brave and curious and downtrodden by the wagonload.

Saxtown was easier to find than when the Stelzriedes had first arrived all those years ago. Railroads now crisscrossed Southern Illinois, a symbol of progress and the present economic malaise. But travelers still lacked one convenience. A technological marvel, a bridge longer than any in existence using steel, was rising over the Mississippi at St. Louis. The Eads Bridge was a stunning symbol of the coming industrial age, a beautiful hulk of limestone arches crossing the river and connecting the western and eastern railroads in St. Louis. But those wanting to use the structure to get to Saxtown would have to wait. The bridge wouldn't open to traffic until July 4—almost three months away.

Still, against the violent, nasty black of the sky, the men came at once. They had heard what happened. Now they just needed to know who did it and why. Rumors wafted that the German family had been butchered over a secret fortune—some in their sleep, others in a death struggle.

Dead. Dead. Dead. Dead. Dead. All of them.

CHAPTER 3

Help!

AS THE SUN DROPPED IN THE EVENING SKY, BEN SCHNEIDER STOOD IN the barren fields and told neighbors of what awaited behind the wooden facade of the Stelzriede home. In his breathless German, Ben painted a gruesome picture of blood-spattered walls and dead children.

George Schneider, his brother, was the first to hear the news. He immediately became shaken. He knew the Stelzriedes. They were German immigrants just like himself who struggled daily to make a better life in Saxtown, a shared experience between neighbors. George, who lived about three-quarters of mile from the Stelzriede home, had seen the family often and knew their daily habits. He had spent most of the winter with some friends chipping at a coal bank near their property. He could recount when young Fritz Stelzriede fed his animals and when the old man left the house for one of his rambling walks into the wilderness that surrounded them.

A few days before, Fritz had bought a dog named Monk from George Fritzinger, one of George Schneider's mining buddies. The Stelzriedes were looking for extra protection. A dog known for its giant size and strength helped. The massive Newfoundland was found at the crime scene penned into an interior room of the Stelzriede house.

George Schneider's grief was questionable. Coal miners didn't bear the cleanest character, locals noted, and Schneider boarded a number of them on his property. They were hard-drinking men unfazed by bloodshed. The newspaper columns of 1874 showcased violent tales of labor riots and worker uprisings. This image was best characterized by the

Molly Maguire Men, a roving gang of Pennsylvania miners who used murder as a bargaining tactic. The Irish-American miners did anything to preserve power and were known to kill their own. "When a miner is to be put out of the way, a member is chosen by lot for the dark deed, and it is performed without flinching," wrote *Harper's Weekly*.

The poor men who boarded with George Schneider weren't that extreme—or industrious. They were said to take out just enough coal "to pay for their winter's whisky." For sure, they were capable of killing one another. But would they slaughter innocent children for plunder?

George was skilled with a knife. When he wasn't mining he was a butcher. He killed pigs and cleaved cattle. For years his steady hands had turned livestock into food for supper. But now they trembled when his brother repeated the news of a human slaughter.

The police were needed. Fast. A fiendish killer was on the loose and likely watching the events unfold, pretending to be unaware of the crime. Help was needed to unmask the killer and prevent the horror from happening again.

The first clue was the sodden ground beneath their feet. The roads to and from Saxtown consisted of a heavy mud that would have required a massive drawbridge for a quick exit. Saxtown might as well have been a moated castle. The ground served as leg irons. The murderer had to be among them.

"The roads are in almost impassible condition, and as the news spread like wildfire, it seems almost impossible for the murderers to get away with any rapidity," affirmed one written account.

Everyone agreed on that. The dirt pathways were soaked by an abnormally wet season that swelled the rivers and threatened the idea of easy transportation. Countless headlines had told Saxtown residents the tale of punishing river levels that swallowed whole villages like a muddy monster. Anxiety increased daily in the downstream river towns of Memphis and New Orleans as the Mississippi would rise with suddenness and rapidity, like a night stalker.

"The calamity surpasses in extent and ruinous consequences any that has occurred from fire, storm or flood on this continent during the current century," one man wrote from New Orleans.

The Germans didn't care. River levels were of more concern to the Irishmen who flocked to East St. Louis and the Mississippi River floodplain. The Irish took land that was well-watered, near the big rivers. The Germans preferred ground that grew the best trees (such as oaks), which was found above the river bluffs. Saxtown was on high ground. Only travel was hindered by heavy rain. But on this night, they were reminded that man was more dangerous than nature.

The Schneider brothers notified others nearby, mainly farmers and laborers who were finishing up their daily work. Locals learned in rapid-fire succession that one of Saxtown's original families had been wiped out. Fred Eckert Sr., a farmer who was one of Saxtown's largest landowners and who lived a quarter mile north of the Stelzriedes, was told. As were George and Charles Killian, two of the miners who boarded at George Schneider's house. All greeted the news with disbelief.

The news spread as fast as a man could run or a horse could gallop. Distraught voices interrupted the cool dusk. Men quit work in the fields to understand the fuss. Women abandoned their preparations for supper. Children, ignorant of the mayhem, played and laughed after school until the adults struggled to explain what had happened. Then the fear began to sink in.

People ran about in different directions, as if they were taking shelter from a sudden summer storm but still wanting to keep an eye on the sky. The St. Clair County sheriff was headquartered in Belleville. It would take hours to get the news to him, and still more hours before law enforcement could arrive. For the time being Saxtonites were on their own. The investigation was up to them. And so was their safety.

A group of men—including Eckert, George Schneider, and the Killian brothers—agreed to go to the murder scene and keep vigil. They went together, likely traveling across the same muddy path of the unknown assailant. Certainly they thought about that. And certainly they thought about each other's circumstantial peculiarities. The young Killians had bad reputations. Eckert was the murdered family's closest neighbor and would become an administrator of old man Stelzriede's will. And, of course, there was the trembling George Schneider.

As they marched along the soft dirt path to the Stelzriede home, George Schneider grew nervous and excitable. His whole body convulsed, which drew sharp glances from the group. His miner friends helped calm him down.

The men pressed forward. There wasn't time to wait. Soon, the Stelzriede farmstead appeared in the dark distance. Its large gray barn resembled a giant tomb.

The Stelzriede house was set up close to the road that sliced through Saxtown and stood square in the ghostly shadow of the three-story barn. It looked like the house of a practical German farm family. It was small and spartan and much less prominent than the nearby barn. The house was simple and rustic—like the frontier birthplace of Abraham Lincoln.

The group stopped and stared at the house, but no one would enter it. Not one man would step over the limestone slabs that led to the front door and cross the threshold to verify Ben's account. Questions rushed through their minds. Would the killer strike again? Was the murderer walking among them? Was some evil force at work?

The fear prevailed until the area's well-respected schoolteacher approached. Isaiah "Esquire" Thomas was considered the most educated man in Saxtown. He was thirty-one years old but had the visage of a man much older and wiser. He spent his days in a small schoolhouse teaching the young farm boys about the outside world, from history to horticulture. Thomas had an air of sophistication. He was tall and known to carry a thick and shiny silver-headed walking stick, which he often used as a prop to punctuate his speech. On special occasions he was known to wear a long coat and top hat. Intellect wasn't the only thing that set him apart from the others. He had been born in Ohio, not Germany or St. Clair County. He had bought a small plot of forty acres in Saxtown in 1869.

Thomas was passionate, independent—and a natural leader. Just the kind of man needed to take control of the extraordinary situation. He was also a local justice of the peace.

Ben had told Thomas of his discovery. At first Thomas didn't believe it. The men gathered outside swore that Ben was telling the truth, and after some back-and-forth, he took their word. Thomas agreed to enter the house and make sure the Stelzriedes were all dead. Several other men followed, just so long as they weren't leading the way.

But not George Schneider. He remained outside, struggling to keep his composure. With the house in his view, he staggered up against a wood fence and fainted. The Killian brothers rushed to help. They took him off to the side and splashed water on his face to revive him. He regained consciousness but remained on the ground.

Isaiah Thomas was undeterred by the commotion. He walked over the Stelzriedes' front porch and into the crime scene. Several others peeked from behind. He was on a mission.

Dead bodies were scary enough to view in full daylight, but a lantern's firelight provided something more haunting and sinister. The flicker played tricks with its ever-changing shadows. Points of light unequally distributed—just as the horror before him. Thomas counted the bodies. Five of them. Three in the bed and two on the floor. No survivors.

Stillness reigned. The air was heavy with the smell of dead flesh. A playful young boy, a sick baby girl, a devoted mother, an ambitious father, and a tired old man had all been rendered lifeless. Three decades of their laughs, their cries, and their screams were now nothing more than faint whispers soaked into the bare, blood-drenched floorboards.

The men could barely look at the bodies. They covered them with bed sheets as a sign of respect for the dead. The act disturbed the crime scene. It was now tainted.

George Killian stood outside the house and watched his friend George Schneider gather himself. Killian was a man small in stature and red in the face. He wasn't known to care for others; his eyes often displayed an uninviting expression. Killian decided to leave Schneider there. His friend was too distraught.

Killian walked into the Stelzriede house at dusk. It was so dark inside that he could barely see his way. The faces of the dead were covered. Killian motioned to the other men to remove the cover over Anna, witnesses remembered. He remarked, "Let me see how bad her head is hammered out of shape and if that eye is sticking out yet."

The comment drew curious glances from the other men and reinforced what they already knew: Suspects were everywhere.

CHAPTER 4

The Bride

THE MEN LOOKED LIKE OUTLAWS CHECKING THE EXITS BEFORE HOLDING up a bank. But they were eyeing one another, then looking away in attempts to mask their thoughts.

They stood on the front lawn of a brutal crime scene as night fell. Isaiah Thomas had ordered everyone out of the house to preserve the crime scene until the sheriff arrived. He wanted everything watched, and nothing disturbed. They had stayed in the house only a matter of minutes. Few would have wanted to stay longer. The place smelled awful.

Ben Schneider had gone to Millstadt to notify the constable and summon law enforcement help.

Suspicion built like a symphony. Slow and steady to a loud crescendo. Minds raced. Thoughts flashed here and there and back again. Who did it? Why? How?

As time passed they began to spin theories. The first one—and the only one that gave them brief comfort that the killer wasn't among them—was that the Stelzriedes were killed by an unknown passerby.

"The theory of the murder," the *St. Louis Democrat* reported, "is that some traveler had been given lodging in the house that night . . . and had cruelly abused the kindness shown him by killing and robbing his benefactors."

Then, they remembered the story of the bride. A tragedy like the Shakespeare plays they had never read.

Her name was Mary. She was attractive and lively and once sought-after by all right-headed young men in St. Clair County. Three years back, in 1871, the men who stood at the Stelzriede crime scene would have killed to be her husband. Although it would have done them little good to have wooed her. Marriages weren't forged out of love or looks. They were arranged unions of like-minded fathers. Women were treated like property, chained to their masters just like the chickens and cows.

In Mary's case a young man would have done quite well. Her father was a wealthy, aged farmer. The type of man who could dote on his daughter by lending support to her husband. By custom, a young German woman came with a dowry.

The lucky suitor was a young farmer named Christian Peter. After a brief courtship the two married and followed German customs. Weddings weren't weekend affairs. The ceremony was on January 31, 1871—a Tuesday, the day Germans in the old country preferred to wed. By tradition a morning church service was held, followed by a breakfast for close family members. Later, friends were invited to the home of the bride for supper, followed by music and dancing on a wooden platform in the yard.

Soon after, the newlyweds moved into a small, one-story house near Millstadt along the muddy road leading to Belleville. It was a wedding gift from Mary's father. The dowry was already paying off.

A hard life awaited Mary. She would soon be expected to have children. Perhaps one or two of them would die during birth. Then she would spend years cooking, cleaning, taking care of the children, sewing and stitching clothes and quilts. Mary would be required to raise chickens and sell their eggs—an important job because it was how farm families made most of their money to buy household things like flour, sugar, and coffee. She would also, by custom, be in charge of the livestock and the curing of meat on butchering day.

Mary's young, trim body would soon take the shape of a weathered, old woman through hard physical labor. German women were demanded to do farm work. This wasn't the antebellum South. Women weren't showpieces in pretty dresses; they were rag-wearing extra hands on the farm. Court cases of the day questioned whether women even had the right to "hold property and act for themselves independent of their husbands."

The German immigrants benefited from their hard-driven ways. While many American-born farmers failed, German farmers were able to survive the hard economic times because they used women for more than just sex and procreation. Rural German-speaking women weren't likely to bring "gender conflict" into the home. If Mary had any thought of seeking the kind of independence some of her American-bred sisters desired, she had best keep it to herself. German women were expected to obey their men and to support the language and cultural traditions of the Old World through their domestic duties on the farm.

And that's what Mary was prepared to do. But not right away. The short time after marriage was the good time. The carefree time. The happy time.

One Saturday in April, about three months into their marriage, Christian left the house to pick up some corn from his father-in-law. He traveled on a wagon pulled by a team of horses. The journey on the country paths took several hours round trip, maybe more.

He returned before sundown. Everything appeared normal on the farm. But something surprised him as he approached the house. His new wife didn't come bounding out of the front door to meet him. That bothered him. The honeymoon was over, he worried. Christian cracked his whip loudly, and it still failed to summon his wife to the front door.

Christian left his wagon and raised the latch on the front door to his house. As he entered the back door vibrated as if someone had just left. Christian looked down and saw his wife. She was lying on the floor gasping for air as warm blood squirted from three cuts on the left side of her neck. Her hands were clutched to her hair. She stopped breathing within a half minute of her husband's arrival.

Christian paused for a few moments and then bolted from the house. He screamed and called attention to the crime scene, a replay of what the men witnessed with Ben Schneider and the Stelzriede family.

The one-person body count had not caused the fever that currently enveloped Saxtown, but it still had shocked the area. The *St. Louis Daily Times* headlined: ANOTHER FEARFUL CRIME. ATTEMPTED RAVISHMENT AND BRUTAL MURDER OF A YOUNG WOMAN IN ST. CLAIR COUNTY, ILL.

The *Missouri Democrat* put it in context of the violent era: "The prevalence of crime in various parts of the country is becoming quite alarming. Not a day passes without bringing news of some diabolical murder of daring robbery. Almost every neighborhood has had its tragedy, and the large cities a succession of them. The latest horror that has come to our notice occurred on Saturday afternoon . . ."

The chief suspect was a stranger. A man unknown to Saxtown or any surrounding community. He was seen wandering the area around three o'clock in the afternoon, going from farm to farm asking for work. The Germans assumed he was an Irishman, but no one really knew. His profile was described as such: heavy set, broad shouldered, five foot seven inches tall. Someone got a good look at his face. It was reported to be thin, with a sharp nose, short hair, dark complexion and eyes, large nostrils, and beard of about three weeks' growth. The stranger was guessed to be approximately thirty years old.

His clothes made him stand out. He wore a red denim jacket and worn-out pantaloons. His head was covered by a slouched wool hat with a four-inch brim and low crown. His shoes symbolized his hardscrabble state: Civil War–style heavy-duty brogans, the right one torn at the toe.

In that garb the stranger ambled from farm to farm and begged for work and food. He eventually stopped at a store in Millstadt and asked for matches. The store's owner told him where to find them. The stranger slipped the matches into his pocket and walked out the door. The store's manager took note of the odd man but then returned to his business.

Soon after, the stranger sauntered about town until he saw a small house posted near the open country. It was the house of newlyweds Christian and Mary. He was seen loitering on the Peter farm the afternoon of the murder. One theory supposed that he knocked on the door of the Peter home that afternoon and asked for work. Mary, known for her feistiness, most likely told him to go away—and in less cordial terms.

It was an epic encounter. When the stranger realized a defenseless woman was the only person on the property, he decided to kill her for plunder. The specifics of the struggle are unknown, but Mary definitely fought back. The marks on her body and the blood on the walls told the tale. Her face was hacked and bruised. Her hair torn from her head in clumps. Her clothing thrashed. Her front teeth knocked out. The back of her hand burned, indicating she had been thrown against the hot stove.

The stranger tore apart the bride's small house as she bled to death on the floor. He had time to change clothes. He put on Christian's brand-new, dark brown beaver frock coat, a vest, and steel-mixed pantaloons. He left his own clothes on the floor. Garments thoughtlessly discarded on the ground just like the young man's wife.

One other memento of the crime was left behind. A bucket of red-tinged water was found next to Mary's body. The stranger had used it to wash up.

There was one minor consolation. A doctor examined Mary Peter's body and found that she hadn't been raped. (That didn't stop the newspapers from insinuating otherwise.)

The stranger left the house with a bundle of loot: two finger rings, two breast pins, and two sets of earrings bearing the initials of the dead woman. Some schoolchildren playing near the house said they saw a man fitting the stranger's description run from the home in a northeasterly direction. From there he faded into the wild countryside.

The slaying made news in St. Louis for several days as authorities hunted for the murderous stranger. But St. Louisans quickly became focused on a more celebratory matter. President Ulysses S. Grant made a "hurried visit" to the city as the news of the murder spread. Large, enthusiastic crowds gathered along the Republican president's train route to Carondelet, the city's burgeoning southern neighborhood. It was familiar territory for the former Union general. He had once lived in St. Louis.

The big city's streets bustled with the excitement of a presidential visit. Veterans lined the streets to get a glimpse of the general who had helped save the Union. The old confederates in the half-and-half state of Missouri didn't bother. They just stayed home and went about their lives.

Across the river an organized effort to find Mary's killer didn't materialize the night of the murder. It was too dark. That gave the assailant a head start to escape. The next morning, Sheriff James W. Hughes and his deputy sent investigators across the region. Neighbors, fifty men strong, joined in the pursuit.

A one-thousand-dollar reward was offered for the stranger's capture, but it wasn't claimed. The stranger vanished. Sheriff Hughes couldn't solve the crime. And he would soon struggle to solve another.

"The whole community betrayed intense anxiety to catch the brute," wrote the *Missouri Democrat.*

That fearful community included the Stelzriede family, which soon suffered the same fate as Mary. Everyone watched things a bit more closely. They sized people up and looked at them square with suspicion. Strangers were unwanted outsiders. Although it relaxed suspicions that the biggest threats could come from within.

For years the bride remained a cautionary tale about the dangers of the frontier. Above all, it signaled that rough-and-tumble farmhands could turn at once, like wild animals.

Mary Peter's story gave the Saxtown men a quixotic hope that the Stelzriedes were killed by a crazy man passing through town. Not one of their own. But deep down they knew that wasn't true. It was evident that someone wanted the entire Stelzriede family dead. Every last one of them.

As the men waited for the sheriff and struggled with what to do next, they heard footsteps in the distance. A man's silhouette appeared to the soundtrack of boot heels padding the young grass.

The man who came into view was John Afken, someone they all knew. He was a fellow German who had worked in the area for years as a farmhand, passed from farmer to farmer like a bottle of strong whiskey.

Afken stood tall and firm with the hulking form of a steam engine. He was a powerful 180 pounds, with a long, muscular frame. The newspapers said he seemed as "strong as a giant." He had bright blue eyes that looked at the men "fierce and straight." He had light hair and skin so pale that it appeared unaffected by the sight splayed before him.

Make no mistake: Afken was an ugly customer. His face was so scary a newspaper wrote that "on first sight [it] would condemn him as a criminal."

Not surprising. Farmhands were among the scariest-looking folks around—and the most dangerous. They were essentially field laborers scarred by the outdoors. They often slept in barns, outhouses, or packed with several others into a farmhouse's cramped spare bedroom. Just like the miners at George Schneider's property. They drank heavily, had little education, and didn't own property. They would do anything for money, ranging from backbreaking labor to murder.

One only had to glance at execution records to realize their danger. The death penalty was in heavy use in 1874. Across the nation male heads were wrapped in black cloth and hanged from courthouse squares like lollipops in candy store windows. And that year farmhands were hanged for murders in all parts of the country, from New York south to Georgia and west to California on the Pacific coast.

Marshall Martin, a farmhand who worked in Contra Costa County, California, murdered his work supervisor with an ax. He had been put up to it by the supervisor's wife. Martin, of course, was convicted and sentenced to death. His hanging in 1874 was particularly gruesome, at a time when such things were public spectacles. The noose was so tight that it snapped Martin's head off. *The Alta California,* a San Francisco–based newspaper, recorded it this way: "Although there was a drop of only six feet, the body dropped headless to the ground. His head rebounded a distance of six feet."

Also hanged that year was farmhand Joseph Waltz. He had worked on ground for his parents near Catskill, New York. One day in 1873, a male passerby was given lodging at Waltz's house. Waltz entered the visitor's bedroom during the night, smashed his head several times with a hatchet, cleaned up the crime scene, and buried his body on the farm. Waltz later confessed to the murder by saying "an evil spirit came over me." He led police to the body and was eventually sentenced to death by hanging. Before the ultimate sentence was rendered, Waltz killed again. Confined to a jail cell, Waltz ripped an eighteen-inch iron bar from the flooring and used it to beat to death a policeman who stood guard.

"Joe won't hurt me," the policeman had told others when asked why he allowed the farmhand to roam the cell without leg irons.

He should have known better. Across the nation bitter, nasty farmhands were killing over the most minor of things. Some of them killed just because they were hired by someone else. Some killed over jealousy. Others killed simply because someone gave them a funny look.

But despite their misdeeds, they were physically strong. That was their asset. Farmhands were necessary. They knew the terrain well because of the nature of their work. And in most communities, just like Saxtown, farmhands were a common thread. They knew almost everyone because they worked for everyone.

Afken was thirty years old. He was born in the Lower Saxony town of Oldenburg, Germany, a land that didn't treat him well. It was a feudal society that didn't have much to offer someone with little intelligence and a bad family tree. He eventually packed up his things and left. He showed up in St. Clair County in the 1860s and earned his bread working odd jobs on farms. His hands were his asset, not his brain. For a time he lived in Belleville, before ambling to the farms of Saxtown.

Afken wore on his face the staid facial expression of a Methodist. He was calm and quiet. He looked at the Stelzriede house and listened to everything the men said. His ear turned to one conversation and then to another as the men gossiped about who might have killed their neighbors.

Afken said nothing . . . for the whole night, in fact. But his body did the talking.

He didn't flinch when hearing the descriptions of the hacked body of Fritz Stelzriede. Not once. The others noted his lack of a reaction. Mainly because Afken knew the family well. He had once lived with and worked for them.

Then his body language turned "taciturn and scowling." It appeared he suffered from an "unrest of mind."

Soon, everyone's eyes drifted from analysis of his mannerisms to subtle glances at his muscular frame. Afken's body was the product of his work. He spent long hours plowing soil in broiling summers and biting winters. Sometimes his muscled arms would spend days plucking apples from the trees. Sometimes his knees would be bent all afternoon as he pulled wild strawberries from a patch.

Afken lived a few miles away on a farm owned by Henry Boeker, a longtime resident of Saxtown. Boeker employed Afken and boarded him at his house.

Afken was a grubber in the weeks and months before the murders. His main tool was an ax.

Illinois farmers didn't have heavy machinery in 1874. On the untamed frontier they often needed help with the grubbing (or removal) of tree stumps, a common chore on tree-heavy German farms. Grubbers like Afken could swing an ax from any direction.

They could work fast to destroy brush, tree roots—or people.

CHAPTER 5

Sheriff Hughes

Saxtown was just plain scared.

The grounds of the Stelzriede farm glowed with the orange light of oil lamps and handheld torches. A few hours had passed since the Stelzriede bodies had been discovered. The tough Saxtown farmers arrived one by one, and then in groups. Some on horseback, others on foot. Many showed up on the property with their families. They were too afraid to leave them home alone.

Isaiah Thomas worked to calm the frenzy. First the lawn was filled with dozens of people. Then fifty. Then one hundred. They spilled out from the hinterland the moment they heard the news, like animals running to higher ground from a flood.

Horror. Panic. Fear. Worry.

The tension filled the cool March night air and hung on sad faces. It was compounded by the fact that no one knew what to do. The only thing that seemed right was to keep vigil until the sheriff arrived.

Thomas knew it was only a matter of time before people asked to enter the house. He knew a riot could break out if they did. The horror was too gruesome. Worse than even the darkest imagination.

How long would it take before the sheriff arrived? Before order could be restored?

All they could do was wait.

William G. Bangert, the constable, had heard the news that evening. It was his job to get the sheriff in Belleville, the county seat. He was based out of Millstadt, the closest town to the farms of Saxtown and where nearly everyone did business. Bangert knew everyone in Millstadt, where in addition to his minor powers of police he was also a butcher.

Public awareness was important in solving crimes. An eyewitness could crack the case open before it began. Detective work relied heavily on what other people saw, a distinct challenge in the remote and lonely woods of Saxtown, where farms were spaced by miles and miles.

The news arrived at George Kern's saddlery shop, at the southeast corner of White and Monroe Streets, which also served as Millstadt's general legal headquarters. It then swept to Valentine Brenfleck's brewery and tavern, the main social meeting point in town, built square at the corner of Washington and Main Streets. Friday night brought a good crowd; Bangert knew that. He was an immigrant from Nassau, Germany. Germans loved Brenfleck's place because they loved his beer, which he stored in a coal bank just outside of town. He brewed it just the way they did back in Germany, and in warm months allowed them to swill it in his outdoor beer garden. And this was a night Germans needed alcohol. Something. Anything to remedy the news.

In the dimly lighted tavern, the beer-drinking men greeted the news with disbelief, and soon the alcohol in the pit of their stomachs was joined by fright. They could no longer continue their card games of pinochle and kloepper. Even the drunks grew sober. The news spilled out to the town's other taverns, and then to individual homes. Men took it upon themselves to be messengers.

Having set off a panic behind him, Bangert rode his horse from Millstadt to Belleville, slowed only by a tough hill along the way. He hit the city limits about eight o'clock.

Although Belleville shared the customs of the farm villages surrounding it, the city was much different than the rural atmosphere of Millstadt and Saxtown.

Belleville was a bigger, wealthier city fast on its way to becoming the capital of Southern Illinois. Located on high ground near the center of St. Clair County, it had doctors, lawyers, teachers, and educated men. Not just farmers with missing teeth. The city had made progress from when Charles Dickens visited in the 1840s, describing it as "a small collection

of wooden houses huddled together in the very heart of bush and swamp
... [its main street] a forest path nearly knee deep in mud and slime."

One of the new educated men was Gustave Koerner, a revolutionary
German immigrant who had studied law at the University of Heidelberg.
Koerner gave Belleville an air of sophistication as he became a political
boss who controlled German immigrant votes.

German immigrants flocked to Belleville, and Koerner brought
them into Illinois politics. It's hard to overstate his political importance.
After all, he helped found the Republican party. He was president of the
Republican State Convention in 1858, the convention where rising GOP
star Abraham Lincoln said the words, "I believe this government cannot endure permanently, half slave and half free." Koerner witnessed the
"House Divided" speech.

Koerner, along with the German immigrant wave, helped put Belleville on the map. The town enjoyed a building boom. Soon, railroad
tracks were slammed into the ground and a new progressive spirit dis-
placed the city's image as a rough frontier outpost. Big, hulking brick
homes overshadowed wooden shanties. The Germans had built a library,
stocked with the Greek and Roman classics, as well as markets, banks,
schools, and their own newspapers—some written exclusively in German.

But most important in March of 1874, Belleville had the most needed
man in Saxtown: Sheriff James W. Hughes.

If anyone could find the Saxtown killer and exact justice, it was Hughes.
St. Clair County's top cop was a lawman of unquestioned integrity and
intellect, but one also of incredible stubbornness.

Hughes believed in swift, tough justice. The vengeful farmers of
Saxtown wanted that, and they took solace in knowing of Hughes's law-
and-order pedigree. Sheriff Hughes knew St. Clair County well—and
nearly all of its crooks and crannies. He had grown up there during its
earliest days as the son of John D. Hughes, who had come to the wild
frontier from Virginia. John had served as a saddler in the Black Hawk
War of 1832 and became county sheriff soon after. At a time when kids
still played cowboys and Indians, the young boy Hughes had been witness to the real thing. His father presided over St. Clair County when

it still used the whipping post as punishment for minor crimes. Back then, the sheriff would strip an offender to the waist, tie him to a walnut tree in Belleville's public square, and inflict the appropriate number of lashes. The elder Hughes later had the practice abolished in the Illinois state legislature. He went on to become a respected judge.

Law enforcement was in the Hughes blood.

Some said James Hughes stood as high as six feet three. His broad chest made him look even taller. His face was boyish and intense. His blue eyes had fire. His clothes fit him well, as did the trimmed mustache that sat just above his lips.

That facial hair was a sign that Hughes wasn't an ordinary man. Or an ordinary cowboy sheriff like people were reading about out west. His looks made it clear that he was a politician. A man who commanded respect.

Hughes was one of the most politically connected men in the State of Illinois. But he differed from Koerner in two major ways: He was from an old American family, and he was a Democrat. His politics were honed during feisty public-square speeches and smoky backroom deals. At forty-seven years old, he had already been mayor of Belleville for three years, been appointed postmaster by President James Buchanan, and was now the elected sheriff—a designation that he considered an honor. His real power didn't come from the offices he had held, however. It came from his connections across Illinois, forged by extreme loyalty.

In 1860, as the nation slid into civil war, James Hughes was a delegate at the Democratic National Convention in Charleston, South Carolina. There he was a staunch supporter of two things: slavery and the Democratic party. Hughes arrived in Charleston to the whiff of war: the sound of frequent drumming, military parades, and martial ceremonies. Frederick Law Olmsted, the famous journalist and landscape architect, wrote of Charleston that "the numerous armed-police, which is under military discipline, might lead one to imagine that the town was in a state of siege or revolution."

The convention was a disaster. Democrats argued for days over slavery, in a city that was perhaps its most fervent supporter. It ended in a so-called rump. No candidate garnered the two-thirds vote necessary to win the nomination.

Illinoisan Stephen Douglas got the nomination at a second convention in Baltimore and went on to lose the general election to Abraham Lincoln. Many feared the Democrats had been mortally wounded over infighting, that the party of Jefferson and Jackson was dead. Not James Hughes. He was loyal. He stood firm with the Democrats, and as the Civil War slogged on, he encouraged local boys not to enlist. Hughes didn't want one drop of blood spilled for the Union.

All of that is to say, Sheriff Hughes knew drama. And he always acted the part.

Hughes now embodied his office with a theatrical appearance. From top to bottom he always looked immaculate. He wore a white coat and a white vest, which accentuated the lace of his gold watch. A Stetson sat on his head, a .44 colt on his hip, and shiny boots on his feet. He cared so much about his footwear that inmates in the county jail were ordered to keep them at a high shine. Always.

The sheriff was at his home on South Charles Street in Belleville when a deputy told him of the Saxtown murders. Under his roof was his wife, Sarah Scott Hughes, and their six children—Julius, Virginia, Loulou, Elizabeth, Whitfield, and Emma. His oldest son, twenty-two-year-old Julius, served as a sheriff's deputy. While it's unknown how the sheriff reacted to the news, it's almost certain that his first action was to dress.

Hughes was said to have marshaled his staff like a "general would call upon his troops." He gathered supplies and a few deputies (including his son), telegraphed the coroner in East St. Louis, and left Belleville at about ten o'clock on a wagon pulled by two horses. The race for justice was on. Belleville residents saw the sheriff's hurried departure into the cool mist and wondered what was amiss. They would find out in the morning. A messenger in town had slipped a telegraph to the *St. Louis Daily Globe* newspaper.

The sheriff and his deputies plodded through the wet pathway to Saxtown and stopped for a brief respite in Millstadt, as did most travelers.

The horses needed water, and the lawmen needed to prepare themselves for what they were about the see at the end of their hastened voyage. In Millstadt they found the townspeople in a panic. Hughes had no words to calm them—he himself knew only the basic details. As the sheriff's horses and wagon departed south for Saxtown, a group of folks spilled out of the taverns and houses of Millstadt and followed Hughes.

The landscape supplied natural drama. The gaslit caravan plodded through the wet mud and methodically crossed a creaky wood bridge across Roos Creek, the final barrier to Saxtown. The murder scene appeared as a flashpoint of firelight. Almost no one spoke.

The crowd waiting for the sheriff was made up of neighbors and Stelzriede friends. Smoke from fire and torches hung over the crowd like a canopy of death. They needn't be reminded that the killer could be among them.

The sheriff's arrival calmed Saxtown's nerves like a stiff drink. Finally, help had arrived. Finally, an investigation would begin.

Hughes arrived to a big audience—like one of the large crowds to whom he was used to hollering political speeches. But this group was devoid of the pomp and circumstance of the political stump. It was made up of dozens and dozens of scared farmers. Isaiah Thomas greeted Hughes almost immediately and told him the basic particulars of what he knew: five people, all dead, bodies inside the house, very gruesome, no suspects, discovered by Ben Schneider.

Hughes wanted to speak with Ben. The person who finds the crime is often the person who did the crime. It was quite common for murderers to show up at crime scenes while unwitting detectives attempted to solve cases. They liked to assess their bloody work from a close distance. Little is known about what Ben told the sheriff, other than that he had found the bodies and they appeared cold.

Ben had already caught the attention of Isaiah Thomas. He had found the bodies, and his brother, George, had been acting unusually strange. Deputy Julius Hughes surveyed the crowd and asked questions, searching for anything that could crack the case or provide motive. When did you last see them alive? Did they have any enemies? Did you see anything unusual in the days before the murders? Do they have any relatives living nearby?

The young Hughes gathered answers as best he could from a crowd still struggling with the shock of what had happened. The torches placed around the farm grounds were said to have created an eerie scene of "flame, smoke, and faces." Those faces included the nervous Schneider brothers, the watchful Isaiah Thomas, the grim-looking George Killian, and the quiet farmhand John Afken.

Hughes entered the dark death house with his deputies. Their oil lamps illuminated the draped windows so their movements could inadvertently be seen by the large crowd outside—a shadow play as the lawmen methodically inspected the scene. They catalogued each body, going from one part of the room to another.

They moved nothing, other than the sheets that covered the dead, wanting to keep things as they were for the coroner. The position of the bodies would be an important clue in determining who was the first to die. Anna was still in the bed with her two children, indicating she may have been killed first. The yellow-haired infant daughter's hands were still clasped around her mother's neck, and her split-open head was on Anna's bosom. Anna's skull appeared to have been crushed, as did the children's. The young boy's head had been smashed with such repeated hacks that he no longer had a human form.

Fritz's body was also in terrible condition. His head was nearly detached, his body soaked in a pool of blood. Three of his fingers had been cut off and laid nearby. Carl's body had also taken a beating. His clothes were pocked with marks of blood and "congealed gore." The sheriff took note that the old man, whose body was on the floor, had his coat in his hand.

The interior of the home presented what was called a "sad scene of confusion." The murderer had opened bureaus and closets. Their contents were strewn on the floor, creating a mess of blood and clutter. Everything had been at least partially emptied, from the closets to wooden boxes and suitcases.

Hughes remained focused, although he surely was affected by seeing two young children, one an infant girl, hacked and cleaved to death. After all, he had an infant daughter, Emma, waiting for him back home.

Hughes examined things like the locks and the doors.

At first the evidence matched the early theory of a murderous lodger. It was noted that the rear door was found locked, and the front one appeared to have been unlocked from the inside. The murderer had either lodged with the Stelzriedes or been secretly concealed inside the house.

The wooden doorjamb bore another clue. Deep cuts and indentations were found in the entryway to the old man's room. Possibly misguided swings of an ax. The marks indicated they came in at a particular angle, as if an ax had been swung left to right. Meaning the murderer may have been left-handed.

Police work wasn't scientific. It was largely based on emotion and observation. On what someone saw—or, at least, what someone *thought* he or she saw.

Hughes eventually walked out of the house and back into the crowd. Legend grew that he spent considerable time observing the neighbors of Saxtown to see who was left-handed—even going as far as to hand them something, like his cigar, to see what hand they would use to retrieve it. That apparently brought his attention to Ben Schneider, the lefty who had discovered the bodies.

But if Hughes did that, he never said so.

Later, as he stood among the frightened folks of Saxtown, he was asked what he had witnessed inside the house. Hughes didn't mince words.

"I think it is the most revolting crime that I have ever seen or heard of," Hughes said.

Someone asked, "What is your belief as regards the manner in which the murders were committed?"

Hughes responded with some early details to satiate the onlookers' curiosity.

"It is my honest belief that the crime was committed by one man, and that that one man completed his work inside of ten minutes," Hughes declared. "I think he entered the house, in some way to me unknown, and killed the mother and her children first. One blow was sufficient to kill her, because if it were not she would have moved in bed, or changed her position in some way; as she lies now, she laid when she was struck, with the baby pressed closely to her breast. The man used an ax or a heavy hatchet. When he had dispatched the mother and little ones, or before he had got through, I believe that the woman's husband, Fritz, who from all appearances, was lying on the lounge there, was aroused from his sleep. He must have fought for his life, for you see he has changed his position on the floor once or twice. The noise awoke the old man in the next room, and as he opened the door he was struck in the forehead and knocked down, then his throat was cut. The whole thing was done so quick that there was no chance for anyone to escape or give an alarm."

Then, with the investigation still fresh, Hughes made a startling revelation.

"The murder was certainly committed by someone who did not care for money, as two pocket books were picked up containing greenbacks, and the drawer in which the old gentleman kept his notes and money was opened, but neither the notes nor money were touched. The man who committed this murder did it simply because he wished to clean out the entire family. He wanted none of them, and he has left none of them."

The crowd chattered and gossiped all night. Hours passed. The spectators were tired but too afraid to shut their eyes and sleep. A brutish killer was on the loose. Perhaps the attacker would strike again.

In a daze of excitement and fear, the residents of Saxtown watched the sun rise. They had lived to see another day, but there was much work to do. The bright light would help the investigation. Now all of the grounds could be seen.

A search party fanned out looking for anything to help solve the case. Everything needed to be looked at: creek beds, wheat fields, haystacks, footprints.

It was now March 21, 1874. The day after Saxtown residents had learned their neighbors had been slaughtered by an unknown assailant. The search soon uncovered a major revelation. Blood and bloodstained tobacco leaves were found on a road about a mile north of the Stelzriede house.

Tobacco was commonly used to stop bleeding and to treat wounds.

The killer may have been injured.

CHAPTER 6

Demonism!

DEMONISM! WHOLESALE HUMAN SLAUGHTER! A CRIME UNPARALLELED IN A CENTURY! ONE OF THE MOST HORRIBLE CRIMES ON RECORD! ONE OF THE DARKEST DEEDS EVER RECORDED! THE ILLINOIS HORROR!

On the following morning, the headlines hit everywhere men could read and women could cry. New York, San Francisco, Chicago. Newspapers hammered readers with the frightening details from Saxtown, Illinois. All of it was enough to make even iron-stomached farmers sick.

The *St. Louis Daily Globe* got the news of the Saxtown murders by telegram from Belleville at 10:55 p.m. on the Friday night of March 20, 1874. The newspaper had the barest of details, but competition meant they had to go with what they had. They went to work—editors and composers and printers jumped to break the story. Metal letters were quickly arranged together in a press to showcase a bold headline: A BLOODY TRAGEDY.

Under the headline, in the Saturday morning edition, the paper printed the telegraph verbatim. As a morning paper the *Globe* didn't have time to investigate further. That would have to wait. The messy ink-stained business of putting out a newspaper came first. Paper streamed through a giant press in the dark of night and was prepared to tell thousands of the news. Drama came from two simple paragraphs.

"News of a horrible murder was received by the Sheriff late this evening, brought by a special messenger from Millstadt, in this county," the *Globe* declared. "The victims consist of a family of five persons, by the name of Stiltzenreiter, who resided on a farm about three miles south of Millstadt, on the road leading to Saxtown. The discovery of the crime was made by Isaiah Thomas, who happened to be in the neighborhood about six o'clock this afternoon, and it is not known at what time it was committed, but it is supposed to have been sometime this morning."

It continued: "The two men were found with their throats cut, and the wife and children had their skulls broken. The youngest child was an infant, and was found lying on its dead mother's breast. The other child was about three years of age. Who committed the horrible crime, or for what purpose, is not known. Everything was left as found, to await the arrival of the officers."

The dispatch shocked local readers and left them wondering what would happen next. And then it streamed on the wire to other cities, sweeping across the nation like a disease: Chicago, Indianapolis, Little Rock, Denver, and everywhere else.

Horrible Murder of Five Persons in St. Clair County, Ill., headlined the *Chicago Daily Tribune*. Its story credited the *Globe* special from Belleville with the basic details of the "Stiltzenreiter" murders.

Forget accuracy. Ben Schneider had found the bodies, not Isaiah Thomas. And names were hard to spell, especially when the events involved rambling German consonants. It was Stelzriede, not Stiltzenreiter or any other version that was later used. Phonetics were good enough. Breaking news trumped everything. Competition was fierce. Editors couldn't be timid. Newspapers came and went like gypsies.

Only two years in existence, the *Globe* was already considered one of the best newspapers in the country. And it was duking it out daily with its older rival, the *St. Louis Democrat*.

The *Globe*'s coverage was directed by a man who could cuss "like a seven-foot pirate." Few loved a gruesome story more than Joseph B. McCullagh, the managing editor who had seen death up close on Civil War battlefields. The Saxtown news was fertile ground for his ongoing process of transforming the *Globe* into a sensational, snappy read. He wanted stories that readers would talk about. Stories that would command attention. He knew that an entire family being mysteriously killed promised to produce copy that everyone would want to read. In this case it wasn't hard to sensationalize a story that was already sensational by nature.

McCullagh was thirty-one years old and on his way to becoming a pioneer of modern newspapers. Born in Dublin, Ireland, McCullagh was as fearless as he was independent. He had come to the United States at age eleven. Alone.

McCullagh was short and stocky with a cherubic face. Novelist Theodore Dreiser said his body was "so short, so sturdy, so napoleonic, so ursine rather than leonine, that he pleased and yet frightened me."

McCullagh wanted to be a great newspaperman, and that's what he became. His persona was fueled by his old Irish ways: He was a genial fellow, a great joker, and a grand storyteller. McCullagh learned his craft in battle. As the United States sank into civil war, he headed for the front lines to be a war correspondent for newspapers in Ohio. He wasn't even old enough to vote.

That's where he saw the bloodshed. The torn-off arms and legs, sliced with bayonets. The piled-up bodies, stacked like dirty laundry. The wounded men dying, with no one to care about their cries.

In April of 1862 McCullagh went to a peach orchard in Tennessee and witnessed one of the bloodiest fights of the entire war: the Battle of Shiloh. His dispatches (signed "Mack") from there and other Civil War battlefields became nationally known—especially for the vivid images he drew of the war's greatest generals. He described General Ulysses Grant as "slouched on his horse, whittling pieces of wood."

Later, McCullagh printed an interview with President Andrew Johnson during his impeachment. It cemented his reputation as the father of the personal interview—although he often disputed it, saying the real father was Moses. Newspapers back then relied on short dispatches that often excluded a writer's voice or a subject's own words. McCullagh changed that.

Despite the accolades, the hard-charging reporter wanted to be an editor. In 1870 he was approached by Chicago businessmen who wanted him to take charge of their *Chicago Republican* newspaper. McCullagh did. A year later, warning bells broke out all over the city. Legend had it that a cow tipped over a lantern and sent flames spreading over three square miles. The wooden homes of the lakeshore city were a tinder box and burned over parts of three days. This event became known as the Great Chicago Fire; it killed more than one thousand people—and changed the young editor's life.

The *Chicago Republican* was burned out. McCullagh lost a valuable library and everything he owned. After McCullagh gathered his thoughts and dusted off the ashes, he headed for St. Louis.

McCullagh took a job as editor of the *St. Louis Democrat*. Within a short time he had a falling out with its ownership and headed to a new upstart.

The *Globe* printed its first issue in 1872. McCullagh assumed his position as managing editor a year later in the fall of 1873. Instantly, the two papers were bitter rivals, and it was McCullagh's job to put his old boss out of business. With McCullagh at the helm, the *Globe* was uniquely aggressive and sensationalistic, hurling headlines that readers couldn't ignore.

"There was a snap in its editorial comments that St. Louis had not been accustomed to; there was an air of sensationalism about its news departments that was new in that field," wrote *Harper's New Monthly Magazine*.

Of McCullagh, the magazine said he "is what the western people call 'a rustler.' . . . He was said to be sensational, but if he was, it was a sensationalism that was popular and everyone read what appeared with his initials attached, and liked to read it too."

McCullagh believed in muscular reporting. He said his secret to success was "guessing where hell will break loose next." In March of 1874 it was breaking loose in Saxtown.

McCullagh, who worked in the *Globe*'s St. Louis newsroom at 118 North Third Street every night until past midnight, often sitting for hours at a rolltop desk piled with papers, knew that other newspapermen would soon be on the story. During the night he dispatched reporters to make the trek across the Mississippi and up the bluff to Saxtown. Timing was everything in the nineteenth-century news business.

By Saturday morning the *Democrat* had the same essential information as the *Globe*, but it left readers wondering what would happen next with the small additional information that Sheriff James W. Hughes was headed to the crime scene. The *Democrat* was once a solid newspaper, but its finances and circulation had dropped as the *Globe*'s McCullagh spent heavily on news gathering instead of wire copy from the Associated Press. McCullagh routinely accused his rival paper, operated by former friend George W. Fishback, of stealing the *Globe*'s information and simply reprinting it.

The *St. Louis Dispatch*, an evening newspaper, had an advantage over them both. It was able to cobble together more details because its staff had all night and morning to follow the news. The *Dispatch* transfixed evening readers and told of Sheriff Hughes's arrival at the panicked farm.

"Hughes and his deputies found the neighborhood in a state of great excitement, but suspicion points in no direction with any certainty," the *Dispatch* wrote.

The story quickly became a whodunit—serialized by the press.

Across town at Fifth and Market Streets, the *Westliche Post* couldn't leave the story alone. The *Post* was a German-language newspaper for the city's growing class of immigrants.

It had been co-owned by a Hungarian named Joseph Pulitzer, who had come to the country a decade before and began transforming himself into a Democratic politician and visionary newspaperman—often learning from the iconic McCullagh, who had little aspiration for money. McCullagh's greed was fueled only by circulation. The more newspapers that hit the dirty streets, the happier he was.

Belleville's only daily newspaper was the *Stern des Westens*, which also was printed in German with highly stylized lettering that made everything look a little more terrifying. The paper had a huge influence over the crime investigation. It served St. Clair County and told stories in the language Saxtown farmers could read. Many, if not most, struggled with English.

GRAUENHAFTER MORD punched one headline. German for "gruesome murder."

The *Stern des Westens* laid out the details of the crime. The blood. The dead bodies. The struggle in the house. And it reported that Fritz Stelzriede had told many neighbors about getting one hundred thirty dollars from a mill in Millstadt. That was the first acknowledgment that cash was in the house—and indicated that neighbors knew about it.

"Whether the murderer had knowledge of this or even had been able to steal the money can only be determined by further investigation of the body," the *Stern* wrote.

The paper described Saxtown's anger. The brimming vitriol. The building call for vengeance: "There is terrible anxiety amongst the inhabitants all around the house where the murder occurred. If the murderer or possibly murderers are caught—there is sadly no trace of them—it is quite possible that the people will not ask for any help from the judge to try them."

Its follow-up edition took it one step further as the intensity heated up. Old-fashioned justice was necessary, the paper editorialized. An eye for an eye wasn't good enough. The punishment for this crime had to be harsher—if that was even possible.

"The guilty person will not be able to escape the punishment for the crime, for which the German language has no sufficient words of description," the *Stern* declared. "Nothing will be left undone to achieve this goal of getting results. Just punishment for the crime cannot be named, because our law books do not mention a punishment that would suffice for such a terrible crime. The torture pole of the native Indians would be a punishment too mild for the crime that these cruel and heartless murderers committed."

Meanwhile, McCullagh's *Globe* reporters were on their way to "the scene of blood." As they thrashed through the woods to Saxtown, they found no one who could confirm the news in the telegram. Not a soul had heard of the horror. Then the reporters arrived in Millstadt.

"Here, groups of excited men were found on every corner, and the subject of their conversation blanched the cheeks of both young and old," the *Globe* reporters observed. "The telegram was not only confirmed, but the particulars of the affair were added, making it, if possible, more thrilling than the first announcement."

The arrival of newspaper reporters in Millstadt added to the excitement. The fast-talking city boys with their pads of paper and rapid-fire questions weren't a common sight there. The presence of newspapermen reminded the local Germans that whatever had happened in Saxtown was big news—and it would likely get bigger. Ink would amplify the horror. The *Globe* reporters were aware of their disruptive appearance, writing that they added fuel to a fire "already burning white."

Constable William Bangert showed the reporters the way to Saxtown. About halfway there, on the snaking dirt road through untamed woods, the group stopped at Freivogel Cemetery, the final resting place for the area's dead Protestants—and the future resting place of the murdered Stelzriede family.

"We passed the cemetery where the bodies were to be buried, and found a number of German farmers already at work digging the graves of the five victims," a *Globe* reporter noted.

The German men plunged their old shovels into the soft ground and removed piles of wet soil from three manmade rectangular holes. It was unmistakable—and all the more heartbreaking—to notice that one was smaller than the rest.

"Three graves were being dug—one for the old man, one for his son and wife, and one for the children," the *Globe* reporters observed.

The sight was depressing and evocative of what was yet to come. The reporters went on their way and "rolled slowly toward the house."

Daylight reigned, but the sun didn't appear to be that bright.

"Every face was pale, and every head hung low, as if a blight had come over the entire settlement, and all realized it fully because it had come so suddenly," the *Globe* reporters remembered.

Sheriff James Hughes had left the crime scene to set the foundation for a long investigation. In Belleville he took the unusual step of appearing before a judge on a Saturday afternoon at the St. Clair County Courthouse on the city's public square. Hughes found the place enthralled by the bare-bones details of the Saxtown case, which had been reported in the morning newspapers and spread by word of mouth. The Stelzriedes had numerous friends and acquaintances in Belleville. "Everybody was anxious for details," the *Globe* wrote. Residents buzzed about town swapping gossip with this familiar refrain: "I heard . . ." I heard it was a neighbor. I heard it was a farmhand. I heard it was a relative. I heard it was a jilted lover.

Despite the gossip and unfounded whispers, Sheriff Hughes had to deal with the facts—as bare as they seemed. Hughes laid them out and persuaded a judge to issue a one thousand dollar reward for the "discovery, apprehension, and conviction of the murderers." The reward notice was printed in newspapers that afternoon. In some cases it even made the headline, which caught the attention of sleuths across the country. This was the era of gold digging and silver panning and bounty hunting. The bad economy coupled with the rough frontier meant people would do anything for a buck—and hunting for a murderer seemed like reputable, if dangerous, work.

With the money secured, Hughes prepared to return to the crime scene for the coroner's inquest, an event he hoped would bring him closer to solving the crime. The *Globe* reporters remained at the Stelzriede farm, where ten to fifteen wagons were hitched on the property. About fifty men, young and old, walked around the yard and premises of the farm. Most of them in a state of fear. Coroner John N. Ryan still had not arrived.

The *Globe* reporters took matters into their own hands.

"The sheriff had left explicit orders not to allow anybody to enter the dwelling during his absence, as he was then in search of some clue that might lead to the detection of the murderer, but, our business being known, we gained admittance," they wrote.

"It was a trying moment. Although a horrible sight had been lured up in our fancy, and although we were determined to fulfill our mission, yet when the door opened and the air was made pregnant with the smell of blood, our nerves failed, and it was some time before we could enter. At last courage was mustered up, and the party, consisting of the Constable, a friend, and the *Globe* reporters, entered."

Upon entry they shouted or murmured the same words almost all at once: "Oh my God!"

CHAPTER 7

The Crime Scene

"It was indeed a sight that would make the stoutest heart stand still."

The bodies had decayed fast. Rigor mortis appeared gone. Hour by hour the Stelzriede family had withered in their own death.

It was common for reporters to be allowed inside a murder scene in the nineteenth century. Their presence, of course, provided little good other than to satiate the appetite of interested readers, but perhaps on a good day they could point out some clues for detectives who lacked manpower and science. But they weren't trained investigators, and could perhaps complicate the crime scene

They wanted to paint a picture of the murder scene—but they also wanted to help reveal who was responsible for the carnage. It was the morning after the bodies had been found. The killer was loose, perhaps in the crowd outside watching them, or perhaps long gone. Every detail mattered, and reporters could help put together the puzzle.

Daily Globe editor Joseph McCullagh's reporters, known for their vivid writing, walked through the wooden front door and found a room full of bodies. There were so many it was hard for their eyes to fix on anyone in particular. Looking down at their own boots was perhaps the easiest. But maybe not. At their feet was a pool of blood. Time had turned it into a congealed mess. Everyone almost stood still as they took in the scene, but if they hadn't watched their step, they would have gotten their feet wet. Less blood would have dried fast, but there was too much of it, which created a big puddle of red muck.

The blood source was Fritz Stelzriede, whose body lay nearby with gaping wounds on his head, face, and neck. Fritz was lying on his left side, they observed. His head dangled on his arm. Head and arm were surrounded by a thick pool of blood. Nearby lay three decaying fingers that had been torn from his hands. They looked like darkened nubs. His white skin no longer had the color of flesh. Fritz's face had turned black. A lot of blood had lodged in his head.

His throat had been cut from ear to ear. This was no accident. Someone wanted to make sure he was dead. Fritz was the strongest, ablest member of the family. The most likely person to fight back to stave off the rage against his family and protect their fortune.

Fritz wore a pair of denim pants and a blue shirt. He didn't bother with real sleeping clothes or fancy pajamas. Fritz was always ready to work, even while asleep.

The *Globe* reporters theorized that "he had evidently been lying on the lounge from which he arose to meet the assassin's instrument of death." Within seconds he was hacked to oblivion.

He fought back, for sure. The missing fingers were a sign of that. His hands were no match for sharpened metal.

The reporters' eyes wandered to the doorway of the adjoining room, which was Carl's bedroom. The door was open. The dead old man lay on the ground. It was said to be "the most terrible sight that ever a human being looked upon."

The man who had run from death his whole life—surviving harsh winters, hot summers, fires, death, and everything else—looked like butchered meat. He did not meet the saving grace of Job. His body had been mutilated even more so than his son. Many thought that was a clue to motive: The murderer appeared to hold the most animosity for the old man's bones.

Who were his enemies? the investigators wondered.

His throat was cut and chopped a little below the chin and his head was crushed. Pounded and pounded with the force of something very strong. Still, his old skull held up better than the soft bones of his grandchildren.

"From all appearances he had been first struck with an ax or some heavy weapon and knocked down, and then butchered in the awful way in which we saw him," a *Daily Globe* reporter observed. "His bed was still unmade, and seemed as if he had just left it. He was dressed in a white shirt and a pair of drawers. Both on the shirt and drawers were clotted drops of blood, and, like the picture in the other room, congealed gore was seen all around him. The old man's hair was jet black, and, strange to tell, not a sign of blood was noticeable in his locks."

The centerpiece of the murder scene was the large four-post bed. The wooden frame, which normally held the exhales of tired breath, displayed "the most heart rending scene of all." Anna and her two children lay in it. Their faces of death unforgettable.

"The mother's face was a complete mass of blood and hair, and was, in fact, scarcely recognizable," a *Daily Globe* reporter wrote. "In her arms she held a little infant, pretty even in the bed of death, and its little arms were closely clasped around the neck of its mother. It was a little girl, [eight] months old, with light flaxen hair and blue eyes, which were open and seemed to beg for mercy. The mother's bosom was exposed, and close to it she held the babe. Both looked as if they had sunk in sweet sleep and never afterwards awoke. On the inside of the bed lay little [Carl], whose head was also crushed in, and whose features were not to be seen because of the blood and bruises which disfigured his little face. The mother had a deep gash in the throat, but the children were killed by a single blow each. Little Anna, in fact, could not have been struck with an ax or hatchet, but rather with a club. There they lay, all huddled up together, as they had gone to rest, and God only knows whether they ever awoke to see the weapon raised above their heads, and, if they did, whether they looked only once and then all was over."

The reporters scribbled notes as fast as they could (mistaking some facts, like the baby's age and boy's name). At first it was hard, because of the terrible scene, but soon they got their wits about them. The first-person details they were getting would please their boss, McCullagh, and their readers.

What was most difficult for the reporters to look at wasn't the bodies, but the things. Real people lived in this house and real people had died in it, the reporters were reminded. Anna's clothes hung on a chair by her bedside. A cough syrup and spoon were on the bedside table—a reminder that the young Stelzriede baby had been sick. It appeared that the baby had thrown a toy on the floor near the foot of the bed. Several trinkets belonging to the children were scattered about the room. Their little boots and stockings were hung neatly.

"The whole scene bore a likeness to a bed chamber where the family group had sought shelter, never thinking it would be their last night on earth," the *Daily Globe* wrote.

The clock on the wall drew a lot of attention. It had stopped at eighteen minutes after six. "A number of those inclined to be superstitious pronounced it the time the murderer was at work."

The identity of the murderer was now on everyone's mind. The sheer harshness of the crime had settled in. Thoughts quickly turned to who.

"Who was the murderer, and can he be caught?" the newspapermen wondered. What clues within the dead family could lead to the perpetrator?

The reporters exited the crime scene and began the process of getting their story back to St. Louis for the next day's paper. They would compare notes, and one man would remain behind to catch any new details. An inquest, which would push the investigation along and provide the first public legal proceeding in the case, would begin as soon as the coroner arrived.

As time passed the gossip flew. Everyone suspected this person or that person. John Afken was on the list. As were the Schneider brothers. And George Killian's mysterious comment the night before was being repeated, and most likely embellished, as Saxtonites performed their own investigation.

Isaiah Thomas escorted the reporters around the front yard and continued his own investigation. Rumors began to swirl of a family feud. One of the Stelzriedes' distant family members must have wanted them dead, some supposed. That would be the only reason to snap off an entire branch of a family tree.

But everyone disagreed about which side of the family was to blame. Curiously, none of the family's relatives had yet come to the house. Not Anna's sister or her brother-in-law, Fred Boeltz. Not Carl's brother Charles, who had moved away from Saxtown several years before after a feud with the old man and never returned.

But a new clue soon materialized. Investigators, intrigued by the talk of a family feud, put together that the bloody tobacco leaves, found about a mile north of the Stelzriede house, were dropped on a road headed toward the home of Boeltz—the man who had not even bothered to come to the Stelzriede farm when news spread of the murders.

Faint drops of blood appeared to point in the direction of Boeltz's house. Investigators followed the lead at once.

CHAPTER 8

Wanted

"ONE OF THE MOST TERRIBLE AND REVOLTING MURDERS EVER COMMITTED in the history of this or any other country has taken place in this county."

The cursive handwriting in the Western Union telegram was the screed of St. Clair County Sheriff James W. Hughes. His message was addressed to John L. Beveridge, a former lawman and the current governor of Illinois.

Hughes needed to get Beveridge's attention. At once. The governor was one of the few people in the state who could marshal resources—money or manpower—to help smoke out the unknown killer of the Stelzriede family. Reward money, Hughes knew, was an easy way to get people to come forward with criminal information, or enlist private detectives to help investigate.

Law enforcement agencies were a new concept. Extra help was badly needed, even if fueled by greed.

The promise of money in criminal cases was fast becoming the norm. In 1874 "wanted" posters with big, bold lettering were going up throughout the West, announcing searches for outlaws and thieves. Perhaps most famously that year, "wanted" posters for Missouri bank robber Jesse James hung throughout the land. In January James and his gang had held up the St. Louis Iron Mountain & Southern Railroad train at Gads Hill, Missouri, and made off with up to six thousand dollars. A few months later, days before the Stelzriede murders, a Pinkerton private detective had arrived in Missouri and attempted to infiltrate the James gang. Instead of collecting reward money, the detective's family collected his body, which was found discarded with three bullet wounds.

The reward notices for James and other suspects all included dollar signs and offers of cash.

Hughes didn't need posters. He had newspaper headlines, all of which were printing the news of the Saxtown murders and the money being offered to anyone who could help solve it.

St. Clair County had already offered a staggering sum of one thousand dollars. Saxtonites had cobbled together an additional thousand. That was enough money to grab the attention of thrill seekers and wannabe sleuths all over the Midwest. But Hughes wanted more—and he sought it from the state of Illinois.

The problem: Beveridge, an inch over six feet tall with gray hair and gray eyes, was a Civil War veteran and no stranger to blood or death. It would take a lot of both to get his attention, especially because the murders happened hundreds of miles south of Chicago, the governor's political base.

While there is no question the Stelzriede murders were terrible and revolting, many in Illinois, and most in the state's capital city of Springfield, would have placed it second to the murder of Abraham Lincoln—now almost ten years past. Perhaps Hughes was being a little dramatic with the words in his telegram. The steadfast Democratic sheriff, who cared little for Lincoln, might have disagreed.

The telegram arrived on the governor's desk as rain fell on Springfield, a city that looked like it was still mourning Lincoln's death.

The statehouse building that held the governor's office reminded everyone of Lincoln. It was the last stop of Lincoln's long funeral train procession. His body had lain in state there for twenty-four hours in the same room where he had delivered his "House Divided" speech.

Outside the statehouse windows was Mather Block, the highest point in the city and the place where locals, led by Beveridge's predecessor Governor Richard J. Oglesby, wanted to bury the former president. The location was central to Springfield's downtown and close to many railroad lines, which were transforming the city from a dusty outpost to a bustling capital. The people of Springfield knew early on that they needed to capitalize on Lincoln's image, and building a memorial in the center of town would bring people from all around. Mary Todd Lincoln refused and had him buried in the Oak Ridge Cemetery north of town.

Now, instead, stone slabs were slowly stacked together to build a new Illinois state capitol on the site. It wasn't good enough to house the slain president's bones, but it was good enough to house the state legislature—a body known for its raucous debates. The building would take decades to complete, and in 1874 it was still a work in progress.

Construction was altering the Springfield landscape. The city was slowly being transformed into a giant Lincoln memorial. Literally. At the time of the Saxtown murders, a giant obelisk tomb was being constructed at the Oak Ridge Cemetery where Lincoln was buried; it was just months away from being dedicated. Meanwhile, Lincoln's image was everywhere in the city, from government buildings to shop windows. It seemed like almost everyone in town was trying to take advantage of the former president's popularity.

Even William H. Herndon, Lincoln's former law partner, was getting in on the action. Herndon was busy arguing that Lincoln admired deists and wasn't a Christian when he died. The lawyer was setting the foundation for a book he would write about Lincoln's life, saying that the other titles in print showed the "real Lincoln about as well as does a wax figure in the museum."

In Chicago the sculptor Leonard Volk was busy crafting statues of the long-dead Lincoln and Stephen Douglas, statues that would adorn the new state government headquarters. Volk had known Lincoln. In 1860, shortly before he received the Republican presidential nomination, Lincoln went to Chicago and sat in Volk's studio so the sculptor could make his "life mask" using a plaster casting process.

"My studio was in the fifth story, and there were no elevators in those days, and I soon learned to distinguish his steps on the stairs, and am sure he frequently came up two, if not three, steps at a stride," Volk later remembered.

"It was about an hour before the mold was ready to be removed, and being all in one piece, with both ears perfectly taken, it clung pretty hard, as the cheek-bones were higher than the jaws at the lobe of the ear. He bent his head low and took hold of the mold, and gradually worked it off without breaking or injury; it hurt a little, as a few hairs of the tender temples pulled out with the plaster and made his eyes water . . ."

That was for a life mask. Now Lincoln was dead and almost every politician in the state paled in comparison to his tall and lanky shadow. Governor Beveridge was no different.

Beveridge, a lawyer by trade and a veteran of Lincoln's war, had served as a second major of the Eight Illinois Calvary, which fought at the battle of Gettysburg; was commissioned colonel of the Seventeenth Illinois Cavalry; and rose to the rank of brigadier general by the time he was honorably discharged. During the war Beveridge had led a battalion that was later nicknamed "the Avengers." Jeriah Bonham, who wrote a recollection of the Civil War years, said Beveridge "followed in such quick succession in the battles of Chancellorsville, leading his regiment at Gettysburg, Williamsport, Boonsboro, Funktown, Falling Waters, and five times over the ground between the Rappahanock and Culpepper, either chasing the enemy or beating off their attack. Such was life with Major Beveridge in the Army of the Potomac."

A Republican from Chicago, Beveridge quickly entered politics after the war, serving stints in the Illinois state senate, in the US House of Representatives, and as lieutenant governor. Despite his battlefield success, Beveridge lacked Lincoln's homespun charisma. When Governor Oglesby resigned to take a seat in the US Senate in 1873, Beveridge became governor for almost a full term without ever having to run for the position.

Leader by default.

Beveridge, at forty-nine years old, lacked gravitas and was leading a state in the middle of a nationwide economic crisis. Times were tough. Money was tight. All of that meant difficult choices for the governor and lots of political debts that went unpaid. There wasn't enough cash to be the chief executive that everyone wanted.

On top of that, Beveridge was no friend of the Germans in Southern Illinois. In 1874 Beveridge supported the state's Dram Shop Act, which made it harder to sell alcohol.

"Beveridge was, on account of his prohibition views and religious bigotry, very unpopular among the German element," wrote Belleville Republican Gustave Koerner. "Besides, a great many Americans would never have voted for a Chicago man as governor. No one from that city had ever filled the Governor's chair, and those who had been candidates for the office had been always defeated."

Also, Beveridge was no friend of Sheriff Hughes. Politics made sure of that. One was a staunch Republican, the other a Democrat. Hughes's telegram to Beveridge was straightforward. The sheriff asked for five thousand dollars—a hefty sum considering budget constraints and the economy.

After the dramatic opening line, the telegram read: "The County offers one thousand dollar reward, the administrators [of the estate] one thousand. The state should offer at least five thousand or more. Telegraph me at once what the state will do so I can get out my bills. Don't delay."

Hughes did have some reason to hope Beveridge would offer a helping hand. The governor was the former sheriff of Cook County. That law enforcement past, Hughes hoped, would help Beveridge understand the severity of the situation. Hughes was bolstered by the *St. Louis Times*. On March 24 the newspaper reported, "Governor Beveridge has also been telegraphed to by the sheriff on the subject of offering a reward, and although no answer has as yet been received, it is thought that [Beveridge] will increase the amount of the award two thousand dollars."

Despite his unpopularity, Beveridge had crafted a law-and-order image, one that Hughes was sure he'd want to burnish. In February the governor had stood firm and refused to save Christopher Rafferty, who had been convicted of killing a cop, from the gallows. News accounts had depicted Rafferty in his cell on his knees, praying to be saved. Word spread that Beveridge would consider a reprieve. But when asked by reporters, the governor simply telegrammed from Springfield: "I have not consented to reprieve Rafferty." The man was put on a scaffold near the courthouse doors and hanged.

Beveridge's response to Hughes would be just as simple. The *Stern des Westens* reported that Beveridge rejected Hughes's request, saying he couldn't provide the incentive money "because there are no appropriations made for such cases." Beveridge simply offered moral support.

The news was a blow to Hughes, who thought it was a blow to the investigation. A bigger reward could only help. Or so he thought.

Regardless, in Saxtown the existing reward money was already luring sleuths looking to make a buck during tough economic times and contributing to a frenzy of finger pointing and distrust.

Hughes started dealing with the accusations minute by minute. One neighbor gossiped about another. Everyone seemed to suspect each other.

Hughes was in Saxtown on Saturday afternoon in preparation for the inquest. The area burned with excitement, even more so than when he had left. While Hughes awaited the coroner's arrival and the inquest's beginning, he started sifting through the tips.

One from a railroad conductor caught his attention.

Conductor Fleischert, who ran a train on the Cairo Short Line, had read the early news accounts of the murders. Fleischert, whose route traveled from Belleville to St. Louis, reported that a strange man had gotten on his train the morning of the murders.

Fleischert eyed him closely and said the man "had a guilty look upon his face."

The *St. Louis Dispatch* later reported: "Around the roots of the man's finger nails there were blood gatherings, and though his clothing showed no signs of blood, the impression was so deeply made in Fleischert's mind that no sooner had he heard of the awful murder of the Stelzriede family than his thoughts naturally reverted to this unknown passenger."

The tips created a puzzle. And Hughes was struggling to put it all together. Did the railroad conductor come face-to-face with the murderer of the Stelzriede family? Was it a neighbor? A stranger? A friend? A relative?

It was too early to tell. The inquest was soon. All of the suspects would be there.

Fleischert gave a vague description of the man but confidently said he could identify him among "ten thousand convicts."

CHAPTER 9

The Inquest

FRED BOELTZ ARRIVED AT THE STELZRIEDE FARM AGAINST HIS WILL and faced a crowd that wanted him to die a brutal death. He was said to look "like the most wretched looking man that probably ever stepped outside a lunatic asylum."

He had been told early that morning that his wife's relatives—Carl, Fritz, Anna, and the kids—all had been murdered the previous night. Boeltz, who lived in a ramshackle house on a nearby farm with his wife and five children, appeared to have shown little concern—for anyone. Even if he didn't care about the Stelzriedes, neighbors thought he would have at least been concerned that a killer was on the loose. The neighbors had pleaded for Boeltz and his wife, Margaret, to go to the crime scene. They had refused.

Boeltz first said he couldn't go because he could not get on his boots. He said they were too wet from "wading in water the night before." Newspaper reporters called it the "lamest of excuses."

With Boeltz's claim about his boots not passing muster, he pleaded sick. He said under no circumstances could he look upon a dead man—much less five of them.

Sheriff James Hughes was startled when he heard of the refusal. Why would a relative not come to the murder scene? Only if he had something to hide, Hughes suspected.

Everything was pointing in Boeltz's direction. His boots were wet. The bloody tobacco leaves had been found along the road in the direction of his house. For a space of about 150 yards, drops of blood appeared as if they had dripped from wounds or a bloody garment. And now Boeltz's uncaring behavior did little to reduce the suspicion.

Tobacco was often used to draw blood from wounds. The sheriff wondered, was Boeltz wounded? He would soon find out.

Hughes, who liked his orders to be obeyed, called upon Boeltz by having his deputies tell him "that as he and his wife were the only living members of the family, it was nothing more than their duty to go to the house and attend to matters."

Hughes was wrong. Boeltz and his wife weren't the only living family members. Carl had an estranged brother who lived hours away. But that side of the family seemed to have slipped from the sheriff's mind as he began to narrow his focus on Boeltz. Hughes tended to be very myopic. He overlooked less obvious things in favor of what was most prominent.

When officials arrived on Boeltz's farm, he was found hidden away having a discussion with John Afken, the grubber and former hired hand of the Stelzriedes. The two were said to have been in an intense conversation. That detail commanded attention as detectives wondered why the two were together. Afken was already rumored to have been keenly interested in everyone's conversations at the murder scene and known as one of the best locals at swinging an ax.

At first Boeltz rebuffed Hughes's request, saying he didn't have time to go to the murder scene. Hughes responded by serving him with a subpoena and had his deputies bring him to the Stelzriede house by force. Boeltz, who was agitated, cautioned that he wouldn't look at the dead people.

He could scarcely recognize the Stelzriede farm. People were packed on the grounds like they were attending a cattle auction. Old men and young men walked in all different directions looking for clues and discussing the case's sordid details. By the time Boeltz appeared, the crowd numbered three hundred and growing.

The group resembled a small town lynch mob. Word had spread through the crowd about the tobacco found near Boeltz's farm, about his wet boots, about his disinterest in coming to tend to his sister-in-law's affairs, and about a feud he had been having with Stelzriede family.

Many of the local farmers knew that Boeltz had borrowed money from the Stelzriedes—hundreds of dollars over three years—and that it had been a source of arguments between them. The Stelzriedes had placed a chattel mortgage on Boeltz's property until the debt was repaid. (The Stelzriede's had a lien on two of Boeltz's mules and sixteen acres of his wheat.) It was said that Boeltz grew embarrassed by financial woes and became offended when the Stelzriedes asked him to pay his debt. Words were had and tempers flared. Both sides dug in. Carl, who drank too much and increasingly found himself in arguments with everyone, including his own son, Fritz, didn't back down easily.

The situation escalated until Boeltz refused to speak to the Stelzriedes. Then he forbade his wife from visiting them. For several months leading up to the murders, Margaret couldn't murmur a word to her sister, lest she draw the ire of her angry husband. To make matters worse, Carl made no secret of Boeltz's messy business affairs and told anyone he stumbled across about the unpaid loan.

Now the people who knew Boeltz were quick to hang him with unflattering descriptions. Based on their comments, the *St. Louis Daily Globe* reported that Boeltz "does not bear the cleanest character in the world among the Germans in the neighborhood," though they never gave a specific reason as to why.

The crowd watched Boeltz as he arrived.

"His limbs knocked together and his whole frame seemed to be agitated," the *Globe* reported. "Perspiration was perceptible, and these maneuvers, together with the rumors existing, placed Fred in an unenviable light."

Aside from his wife and children, Boeltz didn't have a single friend among the hundreds of frightened and angry people stamping across the Stelzriede lawn.

The *Daily Globe* continued: "His clothes were scrutinized, his boots were a subject of much comment, his every movement betokened something to the excited crowd, and not one among them believed him to be innocent. There seemed to be a terrible feeling aroused in the hearts of the German friends of the murdered family!"

"Do you think these men would hang the murderer if they were to catch him today?" a *Daily Globe* reporter shouted to one of the men leading Boeltz to the crime scene.

"Sir," the man responded, "he would never be hung!"

"What do you mean?" the reporter asked.

"I mean that hanging would not be sufficient punishment for the brute."

An unnamed law enforcement official jumped into the conversation.

"Well," he said, "my duty is to keep the peace, but if the murderer is ever caught, and these people desire to punish him in their own way, I will be absent on business."

The crowd clattered with that kind of talk. The burning desire for vengeance coursed through everyone's heads—even the people who didn't know the dead family.

"He should be torn to pieces," came a shout from the crowd, which started to gather around Boeltz.

"Tortured," another man yelled.

"There's the man there!" screamed a man with a thick German accent, pointing to Boeltz. "He did it! I'll bet my life upon it!"

The crowd's rage began to grow. The men and women had already judged Boeltz based on gossip.

Sheriff Hughes stood before the people and sought to calm them. He discussed his theory of the murders—that they happened fast, by one assailant, not for money—and answered some questions. Everyone wanted to know about the bloody tobacco leaves. Hughes had little additional information to offer about that, but he played to the crowd.

"The murderer was injured in some way, and he took some of the old man's [Stelzriede's] tobacco, and tried to stop the bleeding. The tobacco was found blood stained near the road about one mile from here, and in the direction of that man's house," Hughes said.

He pointed his finger straight at Fred Boeltz.

Hughes then questioned him about everything. The bloody tobacco leaves. His whereabouts the night before. The borrowed money. The family feud.

Boeltz appeared so nervous and scared that a "confused and ominous murmur" ran through the crowd. He was stripped of his clothing and searched, but he appeared to have no visible wounds.

Every piece of clothing was inspected for dried blood. But nothing could be found. His damp boots, however, appeared to have red streaks around the toes, as if blood had been scraped off. Still, it was impossible to tell if that's what it really was.

Were Boeltz's boots really wet from wading in water, or had he tried to clean them? The answer was unclear.

Hughes didn't care about the uncertainty. Having already made up his mind, and with Boeltz's answers making little difference, he ordered the man to be held pending results from the coroner's inquest. He expected Boeltz to be arrested after the jury came back with a finding.

Hughes felt the situation was under control. He didn't need to be present for the inquest, so he left to handle business in Belleville.

Schoolteacher and Justice of the Peace Isaiah Thomas, Constable William Bangert, and the *Daily Globe* reporters left the scene to search Boeltz's property, which was about three miles from the Stelzriede farm. Based on the circumstantial evidence, they expected to find something linking Boeltz to the crime. Namely, something with blood on it. Blood-stained clothes. Bloody weapons.

"The locality is neither beautiful nor picturesque, and it is not of that kind that fills the soul with poetic thoughts, but rather makes one feel for himself and guard himself when in the vicinity," the reporters remarked.

The search party arrived on the farm with great fanfare. Margaret, Anna's sister, was there. They told her they were given authority from the sheriff to search the premises. She didn't stop them. They searched everything: haystacks, corn cribs, chicken houses, onion beds, featherbeds, trunks, bureau drawers, attics, cellars. Everywhere anything could be hidden. For two hours the party tore apart the farm, dismantling everything looking for the slightest clue or the smallest drop of blood.

The effort was futile. They found nothing and gave up.

"We left the house as wise as when we entered it," a *Daily Globe* reporter remembered.

If Fred Boeltz murdered his in-laws, he smartly got rid of the evidence, they thought.

One item they did remove from the property was Boeltz's boots. Mud boots with soles studded with broad nails were taken to make footprint impressions. Investigators could compare them to prints left around the Stelzriede property.

They arrived back on the Stelzriede farm, where the crowd had swelled to over five hundred people. Excitement built for the inquest, as if the crowd was anticipating a grand performance. Coroner John Ryan had arrived at about two o'clock from East St. Louis. He was accompanied by East St. Louis Police Chief John Webster Renshaw and several of his officers, City Marshal Michael Walsh, and two physicians. The added police presence stoked the tension.

Coroner Ryan wasn't a pretty sight. He had a "gnome-like" face that appeared to lack eyebrows or eyelashes, which accentuated his buggy eyes. His diminutive body was stiff. He stood in stark contrast to the dashing Sheriff Hughes.

Ryan knew little about medical science. He had investigators for that, men who could measure head wounds, dig out bullets from flesh, cut open dead bodies. That work wasn't for Ryan. He just knew the procedures of holding an inquest, a formal inquiry before a jury to determine how someone died.

The medical examination was performed by Dr. Adolph Schlernitzauer, a physician who practiced in Millstadt.

Ryan got down to business right away and began the task of finding a six-person jury to judge the inquest. Their chief job would be to decide the cause and manner of death of the Stelzriede family. The proceeding could expand on information already obtained during the fledgling investigation.

Ryan, with Dr. Schlernitzauer by his side, examined the bodies inside and then looked over the areas surrounding the Stelzriede house. He and his investigators found blood traces in the yard, as if somebody had dragged a bloody ax across the ground. Footprints on the wet ground also were an important clue. The person suspected of the crime appeared to have worn shoes with nailed soles. The prints "undoubtedly showed nail prints," the investigators deduced.

Dr. Schlernitzauer's physical examination of the bodies led to testimony.

The inquest was done on the Stelzriedes' front lawn, before the large crowd. Fred C. Horn, of the nearby town of Flora, was named the foreman. Five other men were selected to join him.

No transcript survives of the proceeding. But by the laws of the time, Ryan would have begun the proceeding like this: "Gentleman of the jury, any witness and those present, I, John Ryan, duly elected and commissioned coroner of St. Clair County, State of Illinois, and empowered by Illinois Statutes Act of February 6, 1874, do hereby open an inquest into the manner and cause of death of Carl Stelzriede, Friedrich Stelzriede, Anna Stelzriede, Carl Stelzriede, the younger, and Anna Stelzriede, the younger. They were found dead yesterday, March 20, at or about five o'clock in the afternoon by Mr. Ben Schneider. This is not a civil or criminal trial procedure. It is an inquest into the manner and cause of death of the persons mentioned. However, the findings of this jury may have a bearing in a criminal trial should one be held."

The jury was sworn in. Silence fell over the crowd. This is what they were waiting for.

Ben Schneider was the first person to be questioned. He testified, according to the St. Louis-based *Anzeiger des Westens,* that "he just happened to stop by the Stelzriede farm in order to get some potato seedlings." He said everything appeared strangely quiet and when he opened the front door he discovered the bodies. Schneider said he ran away to inform the neighbors and get the justice of the peace, Isaiah Thomas.

Thomas appeared before the jury next and corroborated Schneider's story, saying that Schneider had alerted him of the discovery and that the bodies were found just as he had described. John Afken, the grubber and former employee, also was called as a witness. He testified that he was the first to tell Boeltz of the murders that morning. Of course, they had been found in a spirited conversation that day. Investigators were theorizing that Afken may have been an accomplice to Boeltz. After all, he was much larger and capable of producing a higher body count than Boeltz. But under rigid questioning, and knowing he was a possible suspect, Afken "kept wonderfully cool."

Even if Afken was guilty, he held up like a fine stage actor. Only occasionally did the blood "mantle his face."

The crowd was unbelieving. The *Daily Globe* reported that "taken altogether, he seems to be a man put up for murder or stratagem."

And who would have put him up for that? Ryan then called the witness everyone wanted see and hear: Fred Boeltz. Although Ryan's investigation consisted of determining the cause of death, he had some limited leeway going beyond those bounds in questioning.

Boeltz was small in stature and appeared "rather weakly built." He certainly didn't display the type of brutish muscle that could kill an entire family. He was thirty-five years old and had lived in the country for about six years.

"He has chin whiskers, but no mustache, and is not a powerful man by any means," a *Daily Globe* reporter wrote. "His features are rather on the delicate order, and he has a meek expression."

Boeltz was religious. The residents of Saxtown knew that. He taught Sunday school.

"It is said that he is a little crazy at times on the subject of religion, and it is argued by some that he might have committed the deed under the influences of religious fanaticism," the *Daily Globe* reported.

Boeltz was sworn in. He was immediately made to look at the bodies, the very thing he said he didn't want to do. Boeltz resisted, but he was eventually pushed through the front door of the Stelzriede house and forced to look at his dead in-laws. The jurors examined his face and body language. They didn't do him any favors.

At once, he turned his back to the bodies, although there were so many it was hard for him to position himself. When asked why he couldn't look at the dead bodies, he responded that when he was a little boy he had seen a friend who had drowned and he could never look at a dead body afterward. Under questioning, however, he admitted that he had seen other dead people, but clarified that he meant that he couldn't look at people who had suffered an "unnatural death."

Boeltz appeared agitated during the questioning. At one point it looked as though he would faint. "His voice was tremulous and his answers incoherent," the *Daily Globe* reported. He often answered with rambling sentences that found no end.

But his physical discomfort was somewhat of a red herring. The smell was so bad inside the house that the jury could enter only in the presence of the coroner's physicians, for fear that they themselves would faint.

Still, after having been pushed before the bodies, Boeltz wouldn't look at his brother in-law, Fritz, who lay in a pool of blood. So he was forced.

"He writhed in agony, sank into his chair like a woman, his eyes looked as though they would start from their sockets," the *Daily Globe* reported. "Such a picture has never been seen before in the West. This man had professed to be a Sunday school teacher, and, while nobody had accused him, or even hinted to him of being implicated in the murder, he shrank from the ghastly sight as if from a snake."

The investigators turned over Fritz's body in front of Boeltz. Exposed in front of him was his brother-in-law's crushed skull and thrashed body. The sight sickened the crowd. Men and women alike had a hard time handling the view. Boeltz was said to have taken it in "without a look of pain, a look of anger or a look of sorrow."

"Nothing but a vacant stare," the *Daily Globe* reported.

Boeltz was questioned about the tobacco, for which he had no answer. It was shown that the tobacco found along the roadway near Boeltz's farm came from the Stelzriede house.

While being questioned Boeltz showed "terrible fear." As time passed, however, he appeared to grow more comfortable. He became exceedingly guarded and cautious in his answers and "very artfully avoided incriminating himself."

One of the jurors, assuming the murderer had been injured because of the tobacco leaves, asked for an examination of Boeltz's body. That examination, just as the one the sheriff had conducted, showed no wounds.

The lack of wounds made what once appeared to be an easy arrest much less certain. The jury determined that Boeltz's extreme behavior was understandable and that there was no longer a reason to be suspicious.

Before a hushed crowd, as midnight approached, the jurors made public their findings: The three oldest persons died of hitting, stabbing, and cutting wounds. The two children died of blows to the head. All by unknown hands.

Boeltz was set free. The crowd reacted with shock. Public opinion had already judged him guilty, especially based on his conduct at the inquest. Did a murderer just get set loose? Would he attack another family?

"Many of the influenceable and rich citizens of the area had a meeting with Coroner Ryan discussing the necessary steps to be taken for finding the murderers," the *Anzeiger des Westens* reported. "They all agreed to hiring secret police to heavily guard the entire area. In Saxtown itself, in [Millstadt], at Centreville Station, in Belleville, private Secret Police were hired to follow the weak leads that were known. The citizens of St. Clair County are decided to shed light on the terrible deed and they are prepared to spend any money and use all their endeavor to bring the suspects to justice."

The crowd remained into the night, most afraid to be alone. They drank beer and ate deer meat and prepared for what to do next.

Coroner Ryan got in his carriage, left the rural chaos, and headed back to his home in East St. Louis. When he arrived he gave an interview with reporters from the *Anzeiger des Westens* and the *St. Louis Democrat* that offered stark disagreements with Sheriff Hughes's original investigative work and public assertions.

Ryan first stated that he had "seen many horrible things during his lifetime, but that he had never set his eyes on a crime scene so gruesome and terrible as he witnessed in the house of the Stelzriedes in Saxtown."

Ryan then began poking holes in Hughes's theory that one person committed the crime. Ryan said he was convinced that two people were involved.

The *Anzeiger des Westens* reported his theory thus: "One of the murderers had only a knife and the other one only needed an axe. It is not possible that only one person could change the murder weapons [knife and axe] so quickly committing five murders in such a short period of time. One person alone would not have had the time to set down the knife and then use the other weapon."

He also noted that Hughes was inaccurate when he said that money wasn't stolen. Witnesses testified that Fritz should have possessed at least one hundred dollars he had received from the mill. And that money was missing from the scene. Not to mention any possible gold fortune. No gold was found at the scene. Just an empty basket that had been seen hanging around Fritz's neck earlier in the week.

Ryan said that just because *some* money was left in the house, it didn't mean that the murders were not committed for plunder. Pocketbooks found in the victims' clothing only had seven dollars in them. Ryan said it would have been too dangerous for the murderers to take them for risk of getting bloody. Ryan cautioned that the "whole affair will take time to be brought to light."

As Saxtonites remained scared and fumbled for protection, the investigation was already in dispute.

CHAPTER 10

Saxtown

SHERIFF HUGHES WAS FURIOUS.

He had returned to Belleville from the sad, sad business at the Stelzriede farm expecting the coroner's jury to hold Fred Boeltz and send him to the St. Clair County jail. Instead, his suspect had been set free.

Hughes was at his house on Charles Street, likely asleep, shortly before midnight on Saturday when the inquest had ended, just over twenty-four hours after he had first arrived at the murder scene. Its result upended his dream of swift justice and gave him a sobering punch more powerful than the cold front that was jumping through Southern Illinois that Sunday.

The jury had decided of Boeltz that "besides the extreme behavior . . . at the beginning of the investigation, which was understandable because the dead body was that of his nearest relative, and it was hurting him badly, there was no reason to be suspicious of him anymore," the *Stern des Westens* wrote. They believed that Boeltz, while acting strangely at first, had absolved himself of guilt, mainly because he had no marks on his body, no sign that he had committed a wholesale murder.

The hard-minded sheriff plotted his next move as his theory floated through his head. He firmly believed that Boeltz was responsible for the murder of the Stelzriede family—and that he did it to end, once and for all, some nasty family feud. But was he the man who actually swung the ax? Was he the man who pounded the faces of two sleeping children, then dispensed of three adults with precision blows? Hughes gave way to the idea of accomplices—and theorized that farmhand John Afken could have been dispatched to kill, possibly for a cut of the money stashed inside the Stelzriede home.

Tension mounted between the county officials. Coroner Ryan had publicly questioned Hughes's one-killer theory and surmised that more than one person may have killed the family. Hughes, despite potential embarrassment, appeared to accept Ryan's finding, ordering his deputies to figure out who else may have been involved. They had plenty of possibilities to choose from, and it seemed like any plausible evidence would satisfy Hughes.

The lack of an arrest had kept the Saxtown farmers up all night. With nothing more frightening than the unknown, they spent the hours camped on the Stelzriede lawn in panicked fits of make-believe, eating German-style sausages and talking of whom the perpetrator might have been. All the while they knew that person could be right there among them.

They also had much work ahead of them on that night. By custom the neighbors were expected to make the coffins and bury the dead. The sound of falling timber crackled in the darkness and created an unnerving echo amid the whispering farmers' voices. Fear and anxiety grew as they talked into the night.

Their thoughts surely turned to the Benders, the spooky, nomadic German family that had made headlines the year before, in May of 1873, when a search of their vacant house and farm near Cherryvale, Kansas, had turned up nearly a dozen corpses.

The news from the western frontier state had rattled nearly everyone in the St. Louis area, one of the closest big cities. For several years leading up to the discovery, men had walked on Osage Mission Road in Labatte County, Kansas, and never returned. One of the first disappearances to gain notice was that of an old man and his granddaughter, who had headed down the road on his horse-drawn wagon toward Fort Scott, Kansas. Searches turned up nothing. Talk in nearby Cherryvale, where the man had lived, turned to others who had gone missing along that road, which was on the direct line of the Leavenworth, Lawrence, and Galveston Railroad.

Dr. William York had sought to solve the disappearances and headed from Fort Scott to Cherryvale. He too went missing, which caused a great stir. He was not only a doctor, but also the brother of Kansas state senator Alexander M. York.

Investigators traveled up and down the Osage Mission Road, questioning everyone who lived near the dusty path. They had little reason to suspect the Bender family, the four folks who lived in a small cabin that operated as a wayside inn for hungry travelers headed into the deeper unsettled lands. There was William Bender, who had a venerable appearance; his white-haired wife; a son who incessantly studied the Bible; and a beautiful, red-faced woman named Kate.

Kate Bender was about twenty-five years old and a spiritualist who advertised in local newspapers a professed power to "cure all sorts of diseases." Blindness. Fits. Deafness. Dumbness. She made potions from roots and herbs and claimed the fluids had "magic powers."

It turned out that her real power was death.

The Bender family had come to Kansas from Germany in 1871 and squatted on land that once belonged to the Osage Indians. After the Civil War the United States moved the Indians out to present-day Oklahoma and turned the land over to homesteaders.

"In a gloomy valley, so deep and somber that the house was invisible a hundred yards away, they built a frame shanty sixteen by twenty feet, about fourteen miles east of Independence, Kansas, and opened a rude inn," the *St. Louis Post-Dispatch* reported.

And that's when the disappearances began.

Men went missing here and there—but all curiously close to the ramshackle Bender cabin—until Dr. York's disappearance thrust the mystery onto handbills and posters throughout much of Kansas. The Benders apparently grew worried as investigators stopped by with increasing regularity to ask questions and show pictures of missing persons. They often suggested that wild Indians may have killed the men and women in the photographs.

In reality, most of them had been the Benders' guests.

By the time mounting evidence pointed toward their cabin, the Bender family packed up their belongings and left. A neighbor passed by and noticed that no smoke was coming from the Bender chimney, that the house appeared boarded up, and that a calf on the property had died of starvation. The neighbor suspected their flight meant they had something to do with the disappearances. He went to Cherryvale, where people remembered that old man Bender recently had sold some belongings. They flocked to the Bender farm.

Inside, every crack and crevice was analyzed. Things appeared normal until some beds were pushed aside to reveal an indentation in the floor attached to some hinges. It was a trapdoor.

The door was lifted up by some of the men, who then stared down into a dark pit. They gathered some lights and headed into the abyss, a well six feet deep and five feet wide. They found damp splotches on the ground. They touched the wet puddles with their hands and then held them up to the light.

"The ooze smeared itself over their palms and dribbled through their fingers," the *Weekly Kansas Chief* newspaper reported.

It was blood.

"Thick, foetid, clammy, sticking blood," the newspaper said. But the well revealed nothing else. Blood, but no bodies.

The search party left the house believing the Bender family had killed passersby and buried them somewhere on the property. They glanced at the garden, which bore the staples of any good German garden: tomatoes, beets, apples, cherries. Strange marks appeared in the soil. The men started to dig. Their shovels soon unearthed a corpse with a swollen face.

"My God, it is Dr. York!" someone among the crowd exclaimed.

It was indeed Dr. York. He had been struck on the back of his head and hit so hard that one eye was detached from its socket.

York's grave led to another grave. And then another. Bodies were found sprinkled throughout the Bender property. It appeared that all of their skulls had been broken with a sort of hammer and their throats cut, similarly to the Stelzriede bodies in Saxtown less than a year later. All but one. An eleven-year-old girl was found with her hands clenched and filled with dirt. She had been buried alive.

"The methods employed by the Benders were simple and brutal," the *St. Louis Post-Dispatch* wrote. "Any guest whose property excited their cupidity was seated at supper with his back close to a canvas partition, which divided the hut in two. His watchfulness was beguiled by the patriarchal old fruit farmer's artless confidences, his wife's bustling hospitality, the youth's piety and Kate's sinister attractiveness. But suddenly, as he ate, a sledge hammer, wielded by the athletic arms of the girl, would crash from behind the curtain upon the head of the traveler, felling him to the floor. Instantly father, mother and brother would be upon him, stripping him of every valuable. Then, as they held him over a slot made by removing a plank from the floor, Kate would cut his throat. The body was flung into the cellar through a trap door under a bed, to be buried on the first dark night."

The story made national headlines. The governor of Kansas even issued money for a sizable reward. Various clues were investigated, but, as the *St. Louis Post-Dispatch* noted, "the clues were usually furnished by men ambitious of winning the reward offered, and proved false."

A year later, those ambitious men were turning their eyes to Saxtown. And the Saxtown farmers were remembering the whole bloody Bender affair. The family had been spotted everywhere from northern Mexico and Canada to their homeland of Germany. And all throughout the United States: in Arizona, Michigan, Utah, Missouri, and quite frequently Illinois.

As men hacked and sawed to build the caskets for their Saxtown neighbors, they couldn't help but wonder if the Bender family had struck again.

The next morning, the *St. Louis Daily Globe* was quick to squash that fear.

"It was not a Bender affair, for the Benders had slaughtered their victims one by one, and the blood of the first was washed from their hands before they drew the blood of the second," the newspaper wrote.

While the question lingered, they wondered about motive. The Benders killed for plunder. The Stelzriedes appeared to have been killed for inheritance or because of a personal dispute. Or both.

August Chenot, a wealthy farmer from a nearby hamlet, recognizing the fright in his neighbors' eyes, raised money to hire private police to protect Saxtown residents and to help investigate the case. In 1874 police protection and detective work were not widespread. Rural parts were often left to fend for themselves because formal police officers were miles and miles away and lacked swift transportation.

Saxtown itself was open for investigation. The places. The people. The past. An examination of the small, tight-knit German farming community perhaps held a clue to the murder.

To understand Saxtown is to understand Germany. Most of its people came from the European nation between 1850 and 1870, a time when Germany was under great strife. During that period, after nearly a century of failed democracy movements and territorial wars, 1.7 million Germans immigrated to the United States amid growing fears of social discrimination and religious persecution.

Most Saxtonites came because of farming—and land.

Saxtown took its name from Lower Saxony, a place many of its inhabitants once had called home. Lower Saxony was part of Prussia, tucked in northwestern Germany. Most of its land belonged to noblemen. Acreage wasn't given away in Lower Saxony like it was in America to fill up the young nation's wide-open spaces.

Many of the lower rungs of Saxon life yearned for their own land so they could farm their own ground in near isolation, without government involvement.

Would a German kill for land? Possibly. How would someone steal the Stelzriedes' land? Through inheritance.

Farming was in a Saxtonite's blood. Dating back to the first century, the Roman historian Tacitus described some of the Saxon areas thusly: "The people of Germany do not live in towns. They cannot endure houses in close proximity to each other. Scattered and separated, they settle where attracted by a spring, a pasture, or a grove."

By the 1800s little had changed. The Germany known to Saxtown residents wasn't a land of "spires, turrets, and towers." It was a hard, desolate place.

A quiet, steady work habit was ingrained inside them. In 1845, an old-style crop failure hardened most of the Germans.

"Peasants could not pay their rents, mortgages and other debts, which led to increased levels of foreclosure and hurt rural crafts that depended on agricultural prosperity," wrote David Blackbourn in *The Long Nineteenth Century*. "Crop failure also doubled the price of basic foodstuffs like rye and potatoes. Parts of the rural population were reduced to eating grass, clover, and potato peelings."

"This place may have attractions for simple souls," an Illinois immigrant remembered of a farm town in northern Germany. "It is a little agricultural town without art, science, or literature; no poet's name is a household word here and, in the evenings, the cows are milked before the owner's door. The people wear wooden shoes, and it is to be regretted that even the servers at mass do the same . . . even the daughters of well-to-do citizens are dressed no better than servants. Not a romance is here to be found and, to a certain extent, fashion exists not; clothes are worn, regardless of style, until no longer fit for use."

And things were even simpler in the re-created German farm communities in America.

Maurice Klostermann, a Catholic priest who emigrated from Germany, wrote, "Illinois, indeed, is pretty well settled, but things are mostly in their initial stage of development and there are still regions which appear rugged and wild. The small towns are often very miserable and by far incomparable."

And that was Saxtown, where life was rough. Men were scarred from fights with wolves; women were haggard. Many citizens had hands with missing fingers and mouths with no teeth—and the really old ones, like Carl Stelzriede, wandered around mumbling in incoherent Low German, the language of the rural and uneducated. Saxtown was an outpost in the wilderness. They were far from the refined German harmonies of Bach, Mendelssohn, and Wagner.

Still, the Germans had a lot of pride. They looked down on Americans, mainly because they thought American agricultural skills were primitive at best. But also because the Germans felt somewhat unwelcome. Temperance movements throughout the country appeared targeted at the German immigrants' beer-swilling culture.

Boeltz had come from Oldenburg, a city of sloped roofs surrounded by an eighteenth-century castle. Boeltz had called the agrarian areas on the city's outskirts his home.

The Oldenburg air was filled with ideas of class warfare. Local author Wilhelm Raabe wrote stories featuring areas of Lower Saxony. Some of his writings were considered anti-Semitic, but his fiction was often read as the "rise (and fall) of little people." Children there, like most in Lower Saxony, were scared into doing good through the moralistic stories of Wilhelm Busch. His Max and Moritz illustrated stories showcased the mischievous antics of two boys who were eventually ground down into grain and fed to ducks.

Boeltz came to America in the 1860s, when Germany was uniting its kingdom and fighting three successful wars against Denmark, Austria, and France. While it's unclear why Boeltz immigrated, it's likely that he was either running from armed conflict or seeking land.

The value of land was buried deep inside him. Investigators assumed he lusted after the Stelzriedes' success, which was compounded by his own financial failures. The Stelzriedes had a lien on his land—which means they were a threat to the thing German immigrants valued most. Investigators, with Sheriff Hughes being a leading proponent, surmised that Boeltz had snapped as the feud grew.

One fact escaped the public debate: Afken also had emigrated from Oldenburg. Boeltz and Afken shared a local culture and may have known each other in the Old World. That connection would have bred the type of loyalty and trust that was prided among Germans.

As investigators studied the past of the Saxtonites, the bodies of the Stelzriede family were moved into the large wooden barn that stood near their house. They had to be prepared for burial.

The bodies were removed one by one. Investigators started to wonder who had died first and who last. As talk of a family feud grew, with inheritance of land being a major possible motive, it would be important to establish the death order. Under Illinois law Boeltz would inherit the property by default only if Anna, his wife's sister, had died last. If Carl or Fritz had died last, it would go to their next blood relative: Carl's estranged brother.

Although it appeared that the men had died last, time of death was impossible to prove scientifically. Circumstantial evidence indicated that Anna was still in bed with her children when she was killed, meaning she likely died first. She surely would have gotten out of bed to stop someone from killing her husband.

Regardless of those details, on the Sunday morning after the murders, Sheriff Hughes had had enough. He dispatched his son, Deputy Julius Hughes, to return to Saxtown to arrest Boeltz and Afken.

Hughes ordered them to be arrested as Saxtown mourned at the Stelzriede family funeral.

CHAPTER 11

The Funerals

THE BLUEBIRDS WERE GONE.

A sudden cold front had scared the gentle creatures from the skies over St. Clair County back into their winter nests over the river in Missouri. A sign of life had flown away amid the mourning.

"Start them out again, we'd like to have them around," the *St. Louis Daily Globe* pleaded.

But the bluebirds' low-pitched warbling was of no use to the Saxtown farmers, whose ears would hear only sad songs on Sunday, March 22, 1874—the day they would bury their slain neighbors.

The men had spent the previous night watching the coroner's inquest of the Stelzriede family, and then making wooden coffins to hold their bodies. They had to improvise. German custom dictated that a living farmer would pick out an oak tree to someday be used for his coffin. When death came a simple funeral process began. His family and neighbors would chop down the tree and cut the oak into boards for a coffin. His wife would put on her wedding dress. A pastor would read a short eulogy.

The Stelzriedes hadn't planned their funeral. They hadn't expected to die. By custom, the grief-stricken neighbors were charged with shoveling the mud from the ground and laying the family to rest.

Their tasks fit the gender stereotypes of the nineteenth century: Men built coffins; women cleaned corpses. They had worked deep through the night and into the morning. The women washed the bodies and prepared them for burial. It was important to get them into the ground fast. There was a lack of preservatives and cold storage. The bodies were already badly decayed. The task, as expected, made many of the workers sick. There was a lot to clean. Each body was flecked with dried blood and had numerous open wounds. The heads were swollen and black.

During the early Sabbath morning hours, the five bodies were wrapped in bedsheets and placed into the blanket-lined handmade coffins. Eventually, after some prayer, the men nailed them shut. The mutilated faces of the dead Stelzriede family would never be seen again.

The bodies were turned over to the Reverend Jacob Knauss. He was the man charged to comfort the fearful and preach the Stelzriedes into the afterlife in front of one of the biggest audiences of his ministerial career.

Knauss, a German immigrant from the Kingdom of Württemberg, had buried hundreds of people in the cemetery at Saxtown during his twenty-four years as the area's evangelical pastor. So many so that death was linked to his growing legacy.

In 1849 Knauss had faced a Saxtown community crippled by another cold-blooded killer: cholera.

It started in St. Louis that year. A big wave of German immigrants and gold prospectors got off of steamboats and thundered through the city "like a drunken man through a plate-glass front," the *St. Louis Post-Dispatch* remembered. They swelled the city's population to 75,000 and often came with a nasty disease. Cholera is an infection of the intestine spread through dirty water. It causes diarrhea and dehydration and often kills swiftly, within hours of infection.

The disease was common among the Germans and Irish because they lived in close quarters on unsanitary ships and in crowded immigrant ghettos. And they often drank water contaminated by human waste, although at that time, they didn't know water was the cause of the disease. (Some blamed rotting vegetables, while others blamed the summer heat because the disease reached its fury during warm months.)

In 1849, St. Louis was bursting with immigrants, but it had no sewer system. The city's wastewater infected the drinking water and went on a relentless killing spree. Dozens of people grew sick with fever and ejected a milky "rice-water stool" from their bodies.

"We saw large, strong-bodied men suddenly struck and expire in a few hours, and before we could remove one corpse, a second, a third, and a fourth were ready," said Sister Francis Xavier Love of the Sisters of Charity, speaking about her experience treating cholera victims. "Everyone who had health ran away from us; the washer-women went off, leaving the tubs full of wet clothes."

They ran and ran and ran. Anything to get away from the mysterious killer. More than 120 died of cholera in April 1849. The toll increased over the months that followed. By July about 2,200 had fallen to disease. About one in eleven souls living in St. Louis died. The frightened city was flummoxed. It banned vegetables, quit tolling church bells because the sound played on everyone's imaginations, burned tar to battle "foul air," and converted schools into hospitals.

Because the disease was particularly brutal within the German immigrant community, some "established residents" blamed sauerkraut. The worst death rates were in the slums on the north and south ends of present-day downtown, where bodies were buried in ditches. Merchant R. S. Elliott wrote that "real estate will sell but slowly, when no one was sure from day to day whether he would need more land than enough to bury him."

Wealthy residents fled to the country. But the disease also struck them. Pierre Chouteau Sr., a member of one of the city's French founding families, was killed as the epidemic reached its peak.

The disease made its way to St. Clair County that summer and sent everyone into a panic. People were afraid death was around the corner. Business ground to a halt. Hogs weren't slaughtered. Wheat wasn't planted. Stores were closed. No one walked the streets.

In Belleville immigrant Gustave Koerner remembered this scene: "Doctors were running around. Coffin-making was almost the only business which was carried on. To the cemetery downtown funeral trains were constantly moving. No one seemed to feel quite well. On the public square and other places, large piles of wood were lighted for the purpose of purifying the air. Thick smoke enwrapped the whole city. No one who has not witnessed a raging epidemic can have any idea how people feel in the midst of it. It was a new experience to us, and a terrible one."

Reverend Knauss had been Zion Evangelical Church's pastor for only three years when the epidemic hit the farms of Saxtown. He operated out of a small wooden cabin church and ministered to a flock yearning for God in the lonely wilderness. The congregation had been built by his predecessor, Reverend John Jacob Riess, who was considered the "Evangelical Pioneer in South Illinois." Riess had started preaching—his simple, flat sermons always in German—once a month in Saxtown in 1835. Early Saxtown settlers Johannes Freivogel, George Henckler, William Probst, and George Seibert Sr. later served as elders for his fledging church; services were often held on Freivogel's lawn.

Riess provided an example of early life in Saxtown. In 1836 St. Louis pastor Joseph Rieger visited the congregation and wrote, "Brother Riess was so happy to see me! He is living with his wife's folks in a one-room log cabin. His wife is a very pious person. Her parents came from Wiesbaden and have been in America only a year. They have seven children. We read and prayed together and then retired. They had fixed a bed for me on the floor. I marveled to find Brother Riess so content under such abominable living conditions. . . . We rode to church this morning in an ox-cart. About 100 people had gathered at the home of Farmer Freivogel. I preached on the final judgement."

The final judgment, the moment when the Bible says God judges the living and the dead, became a familiar topic for Knauss. The cholera epidemic meant he had to preach at more funerals than he had ever expected. Sick old ladies. Small infant babies. Devoted husbands. Knauss had to find comforting words for all of them—and he did. He proved himself "to be the real shepherd as he ministered to the afflicted and the sorrowing," according to a Zion church history. When death came the people of Saxtown turned to religion.

During his twenty-nine years as pastor of Zion, Knauss performed 878 funerals for a scattered and small rural population. His service was not continuous: Knauss left Saxtown in 1866 to preach in Indiana for about five years, until 1871, when Zion lured him back. Another pastor had resigned, and "the thoughts of many members turned to the former pastor, Rev. Jacob Knauss," who was revered as a spiritual leader. He returned to a warm welcome. The congregants always remembered his work during the cholera epidemic.

Knauss had spent much of his time at Freivogel Cemetery, a plot of land that Freivogel had donated to the church by Saxtown farmer Freivogel. There, Knauss had buried the cholera victims day after day under the hot summer sun. From July 16 to July 23 in 1849, five children of Daniel and Elisabetha Wagner were dropped into Freivogel's dirt. All of them—Jacob, Heinrich, Elisabetha, Friedrich, and George—died in rapid succession as the disease took hold. Such was the case for mother Magdalena Heitz, who died in September. Three days later, cholera took her three-year-old son.

Many of the dead were buried at Freivogel in unmarked graves.

The Stelzriedes had arrived in Saxtown before the cholera outbreak. Despite their penchant for bad luck in the old country, the disease spared them. They were among the panicked families of the area that boiled their clothes and didn't leave the house. Fears abounded that cholera was a contagious disease, even though it wasn't.

Knauss knew the Stelzriede family. He had baptized their children and seen their faces during Sunday services at the Zion church, which had relocated to Millstadt in 1850. Almost a quarter century later, instead of watching them fold their hands and pray, he was watching their wooden coffins slowly head toward three holes in the ground at Freivogel Cemetery.

A large crowd gathered for the afternoon ceremony. Friends and neighbors and curious onlookers packed the wooded land. Many came to hear the gossip and stoke suspicion. Rumors spread of an impending arrest or a crack in the case.

"A thousand eyes are turned upon every one to whom the least suspicion attaches," the *St. Louis Daily Globe* reported.

One thing that was missing at the funeral was a living Stelzriede. Carl's brother, who lived a few counties away, didn't attend. Nor did any of his children. Their absence didn't go unnoticed by the farmers of Saxtown—and the dozens of private detectives who were arriving from around Illinois and Missouri, lured by the prospect of a big reward and a tantalizing mystery.

An enormous crowd, one like Saxtown had never seen before, showed up to take part in the burial. The *Daily Globe* took note: "The fact that every person living for miles and miles around, except the kindred of the victims, were at the scene of the murder and at the funeral; that every town for twenty and thirty miles in every direction was represented by curious visitors, and that every available public official had flocked thither, was sufficient proof of the extraordinary interest which the appalling event had aroused."

People lined Saxtown Road as the coffins were placed on creaky wagons. They were taken from the Stelzriede farm a short distance down the road to Freivogel Cemetery. The body of Carl, the patriarch of the family, went first and led the procession. Then Fritz, then Anna, and then the two children together. "A long, never ending train of farm wagons followed the coffins to the cemetery," reported the *St. Louis Democrat*.

More than one thousand people watched in silence along the route and at the cemetery, where Reverend Knauss walked across unmarked graves of the dead he had previously buried. The procession arrived and pallbearers carried the coffins to the graves in the northwest section of the rectangular cemetery, surrounded by oak, maple, and sycamore trees.

Knauss gave what was described as a "very moving eulogy." His exact words went unrecorded.

One person who wasn't moved was Fred Boeltz, the in-law who stood at the cemetery with his wife and listened to Knauss's words and memories of the family he had known intimately. A religious man, but not a member of the Zion congregation, Boeltz was observed to "not have shed a tear." Nearby stood John Afken, the man who the day before had come into the glare of Sheriff James W. Hughes.

It was said that the large crowd recited the Lord's Prayer in unison. "Our Father, who art in heaven, hallowed be Thy name. Thy kingdom come . . ."

Deputy Sheriff Julius Hughes, sent by his father, arrived while the funeral was in progress. Out of respect for the dead, he was under strict orders to do nothing until it was over. But a commotion would be unavoidable. Hughes watched the funeral not like a mourner, but like an investigator.

The police presence was unmistakable, serving as a reminder of the unanswered questions.

"The absorbing question was, who did the deed?" asked a *St. Louis Daily Globe* reporter who attended the funeral. "What fiend in human shape could be so far fallen as to slay a sleeping mother with her infant reposing upon her bosom? The devil hearted monster who conceived and the merciless arm that executed were not those common to the ordinary murderer or those whose object was money. The completeness of it betokens that the capture of booty and a safe escape were not the objects of the perpetrators. The work was well done. This was no half-way butchery."

Knauss gave his closing remarks. The coffins were placed into the three graves. The old man in one. The married couple in another. And the children in another.

"After the very moving burial ceremony the earth covered the bodies," the *Stern des Westens* wrote.

Knauss gave the last rites.

And that was it. Deputy Hughes couldn't wait any longer. The zeal for an arrest was too great. Immediately after the last spiritual words were spoken, he arrested Boeltz and Afken. Upon arrest the two men appeared silent, unaffected. The St. Clair County deputies took them into custody and then to jail in Belleville.

"The evidence on which they were arrested was purely circumstantial, and was based on the fact that they had both had trouble with the deceased family," the *Belleville Advocate* wrote.

The Saxtonites appeared circumspect of the police work. Long after the graves were filled with earth, and after the arrests were made, hundreds of people stood around in groups and discussed over and over the question, "Who is the murderer?"

Everyone had an answer. Yes, some thought Afken and Boeltz could be culpable. But most were gravitating to other suspects. *What about the odd actions of the Schneider brothers, or George Killian?* they wondered. *And where was Carl's brother?*

The latter question was becoming one of great importance, especially among the private detectives. Word was spreading that Carl's brother would be the sole heir of the family's money and property.

"It has often been said that unprovoked murder cannot be long hid," wrote the *St. Louis Daily Globe.* "And, when it is contemplated what searching inquiry and what degree of determined investigation is being made by those more directly interested in the revolting murder of the Stelzriedes, a speedy detection of the real criminals will not create surprise."

That speedy detection was on Sheriff Hughes's mind. He waited for his prisoners' arrival at the Belleville jail on that Sunday evening. The hard-charging sheriff was hoping to elicit a confession—the one thing that he thought would bring peace to the people of Saxtown and solve the case.

CHAPTER 12

Sweating

FRED BOELTZ SAT IN HIS CRAMPED CELL AND REQUESTED A BIBLE.

The two-story county jail was built in 1849 at the corner of East Washington and Jackson Streets in Belleville. It housed up to twenty-four prisoners and was surrounded by a high brick wall to help keep them there. The building was a small improvement over the previous jail on Illinois Street, which was said to have been an "excellent example of a dungeon, for it had no ventilation, no windows, a few holes three or four inches wide in the ceiling, and the air in it was hardly fit for reptiles."

Yet such was the environment Sheriff Hughes wanted for Boeltz. A position where he felt vulnerable, scared, compelled to tell the truth. Boeltz got there at about six o'clock in the evening, after being arrested miles away at the Stelzriede funeral. The trip from arrest to jail was often one of the most difficult for law enforcement officers to handle. Outlaws found ways to escape from slow-moving wagons, or their criminal friends often came to their rescue by hijacking the procession.

Hughes was relieved that Boeltz was now behind his bars.

While Boeltz wanted scripture on this Sunday night, Hughes wanted a confession. The sheriff hoped to use the religious fervor in his favor.

"At times he seems crazy on religious questions," the *Waterloo Republic* wrote of Boeltz.

Boeltz was a member of the German Lutheran Church in nearby Flora, where he also taught Sunday school. The man who was accused of killing five people appeared to want nothing more than to teach and read the word of God.

"Boeltz is known as a religious enthusiast, and it would not be at all surprising that if really guilty he may yet make a confession," the *St. Louis Times* reported. "The officers and others who have watched his course since his arrest are of the opinion that if he did not commit the crime with which he stands charged, he knows all about it and if properly managed he may yet be induced to squeal."

Hughes and his deputies watched Boeltz at almost every hour, looking and listening for any moment that would exact the details of the Stelzriede murders.

Noted detective Allan Pinkerton reminded detectives in 1880 that a criminal's "crime haunts him continually, and the burden of concealment becomes at last too heavy to bear alone. It must find a voice; and whether it be to the empty air in fitful dreamings, or into the ears of a sympathetic friend—he must relieve himself of the terrible secret which is bearing him down. Then it is that the watchful detective may seize the criminal in his moment of weakness and by his sympathy, and from the confidence he has engendered, he will force from him the story of his crime."

News of the Saxtown murders had now spilled onto front pages across the nation. That Sunday's *New York Times* reported on the Stelzriede murders with a headline that said there was "no clue to the assassins." The article appeared alongside news about the death of Siamese twins, about an Arkansas judge shot to death by a lawyer upset over remarks made on the bench, and about the growing temperance movement in the United States.

"The women of Queens County having at last taken up the gauntlet, are fighting King Alcohol with a vim unsurpassed by their sisters in the West," the *Times* wrote.

The passion that those alcohol-hating women had, often fueled by religion, was exactly what Hughes wanted to appeal to in Boeltz.

"The officers and detectives are hard at work, however, in attempting to unravel the mystery, which so far, seems to baffle their efforts at finding out the perpetrators of the fiendish crime," the *St. Louis Times* wrote.

While people began to worry the case would go unsolved, Hughes began sweating his suspect.

Sweating for information was a term first used in the 1750s. It carried different meanings from person to person but largely meant that a suspect was put under intense questioning, hoping that it would cause the person to break and divulge important information. The word *sweating* was used because a suspect under duress often sweated. To enhance that salty process, closet-size interrogation areas were often warmed by fire or body heat. In later years, when electricity was in use, detectives would shine a bright, hot light on suspects. The aim was to get the suspect to answer to, admit to, or add to previous lies, and in the process make him so shaken that he had to confess.

In 1874 that was the best path toward solving a case. And possibly the only. Hughes knew that. It was staring back at him in the daily newspapers.

"From present indications it would seem that . . . the crime will remain a secret for all time to come unless the perpetrators should voluntarily choose to divulge it," the *St. Louis Times* wrote.

As time ticked by, Hughes had few tools at his disposal. He worked in an era before fingerprinting, blood testing—and even before standardized police training. Police used telegrams, not telephones. Rural areas, like in the Stelzriede case, often had to wait hours for police help. Important time for someone to get away or kill again.

It all came down to the confession. The importance of a confession had been showcased in 1827 in Putnam County, New York. Jesse Strang, a drifter, met Elsie Whipple at a bar. The two became lovers and eventually conspired to kill Whipple's husband, John, so they could elope. First they unsuccessfully tried to poison his tea. John Whipple grew suspicious and began carrying a loaded gun. Then they thought of hiring a hit man but couldn't come up with the money. Instead, they spread rumors that men were out to kill Whipple over business matters.

Strang stalked Whipple and shot him dead through a window, then fled to establish an alibi.

Strang drew the suspicion of investigators and was arrested. He was pummeled with questions from those hoping he would confess.

A grand juror told him: "Strang, mark my words, you will confess it before you go to the gallows."

After several weeks of the hard questioning behind bars, he broke down and confessed.

"Feeling conscious of my own guilt, and much reduced in bodily strength and mind . . . I felt as though my body would burst," Strang said.

Strang told a law enforcement official "that Mrs. Whipple was the foundation of the whole of it." And then told him where to find the murder weapon.

Of course, he was deeply affected by religion.

"I pray the God of all grace, in his abundant mercy, to admit my poor soul, and that it may not be doomed to everlasting torments; which I now most sincerely believe, will, and ought to be, the fate of the finally impenitent," Strang said.

"And I do most humbly confess that . . . until the time of my confession, I believed there was a God and Savior; yet that God had decreed and directed all things; and that he would not punish any of his creatures, (no matter what sins they may have committed here,) in the world of spirits."

Strang was convicted, largely on his confession, and sentenced to death. Elsie Whipple was acquitted, largely because she didn't confess and Strang couldn't testify against her at trial.

Strang's public hanging was botched. The fall didn't break his neck. He swung back and forth for half an hour before suffocating. Before his death, he wrote Elsie a poem, which read in part:

> Kneel then I pray to one who died,
> to save thy soul of passioned pride
> Repentance may in after years
> Redeem thy soul from sin;
> An ocean of a sinner's tears
> must wash thee pure again.
> Haste, guilty one, to that bright stream
> Lit up by heaven's redeeming gleam.

Hughes needed to exact that kind of passion in Boeltz. He expected the same type of remorseful confession. But the German didn't break.

Boeltz appeared nervous. His frail, twitching body didn't lend itself to believability. The *Belleville Advocate* said he "displayed considerable uneasiness" but cautioned that such an appearance could be caused "by a natural feeling in contemplating the position in which he is placed."

His denials remained steadfast.

A clergyman visited him in jail and brought along some religious tracts and papers. It didn't make Boeltz want to confess his sins—if he had any to confess. But it did start a rumor.

Newspapermen and excited Belleville residents gathered outside of the jail and watched people come and go. The lack of facts led the information-starved people to gossip and spread rumors.

"Rumors concerning the arrest of various parties, as perpetrators of the awful crime, have been circulated all day, but none of them were found to be true," the *St. Louis Democrat* wrote. "It was stated that a detective had been placed in the same cell with Boeltz on Sunday night, and that the latter had made a full confession of having committed the murder. This is altogether a mistake."

It was then erroneously reported that Boeltz's wife was arrested as an accomplice and lodged in the jail. She had simply visited her husband.

"All the rumors have no bearing and are solely the result of fantasies that people develop in cases like that," the *Stern des Westens* wrote.

Meanwhile, John Afken wasn't talking. Boeltz appeared to be the investigators' only hope.

Afken sat in a separate jail cell and was "mum as an oyster."

"If any facts are elicited in regard to the murder, they will not come from him," the *St. Louis Times* reported.

After days of questioning, both men had very little to say. Their friends were making "strenuous" efforts to secure their release. Hughes appeared to be at a dead end.

"Every little bit of news in connection with the murder is being received with great eagerness," the *Anzeiger des Westens* wrote. "Unfortunately everything is still in the dark concerning the horrible deed and even though there are many suspicions around, there is no proof for anything."

As in the case of the bride's murder a few years before, it seemed like Hughes would be unable to solve the crime. A murderer, yet again, would shuffle off into the darkness.

The idea of professional police coolly investigating crimes was still in its infancy. About seven years before, Belleville had gotten its first police department—and it largely consisted of night watchmen. St. Louis created its first formal police department in 1846. In 1869, five years before the Saxtown murders, the city created its first "Police School of Instruction."

Up to the Civil War era, the St. Clair County sheriff's duties had little to do with hard-boiled police work. One of the lawman's major jobs was to deal with runaway slaves. Belleville, in free Illinois, was on the road between slave states Virginia and Missouri.

"Any Negro who could not present the proper credentials of freedom to the county authorities was regarded by law as a run-away slave," wrote Alvin Louis Nebelsick in his *History of Belleville*. "He was arrested, held in the county jail, and the sheriff advertised his arrest. If the owner did not reclaim him within six weeks he was sold into slavery for a period of one year, at the end of which time legally, at least, he was entitled to his freedom unless the original owner appeared."

Hughes had about eight policemen—some from different parts of the area—working on the Stelzriede case. He had received assistance from East St. Louis and from the chief of detectives in St. Louis, Laurence Harrigan, who was about a month away from being named the big city's chief of police.

Harrigan, a former shoemaker who came to St. Louis from Ireland, was "feared by lawbreakers and admired by his associates for his intrepid bravery, his iron determination and his tireless activity."

And he had a mustache. That was important for credibility. Local legend had it that Belleville required its city marshal to have a mustache, in addition to being tall.

Saxtown was stuck in the frontier. The law was built around Constable William Bangert and Justice of the Peace Isaiah Thomas.

"The law was wherever he was, and sometimes the question was, where was he?" Nebelsick wrote of the frontier justice system.

On Monday, March 23, St. Clair County Judge F. H. Pieper was in his courtroom near Belleville's public square and appointed Frederick Eckert and Charles Kemper, neighbors of the murdered family, as administrators of the estate. Immediately after their appointment, they offered an additional reward of one thousand dollars.

The money fanned the flames. Private detectives couldn't stay away.

"Stimulated by the hope of gaining the reward offered and of getting a reputation, a number of the shrewdest detectives of this state and Missouri have actively labored in this vicinity all the week for some clue to the murder but are still unrewarded," the *Belleville Advocate* wrote.

And this was still a decade before the world fell in love with Sherlock Holmes, the Victorian private detective with a judicial logic created by Arthur Conan Doyle.

In the mid-nineteenth century, private detectives flourished among the wealthy, who used them to track down jewel thieves and frauds and hucksters. The detectives shadowed employees and investigated bank robberies. It was much easier than waiting for the small-staffed police departments.

But the detectives also flocked to the sensational crimes—quick to make a name for themselves and grab reward money.

The most famous firm was the Pinkerton agency created by Allan Pinkerton, a Civil War veteran who made a name for himself afterward solving train robberies and chasing Missouri outlaw Jesse James.

What tactics did a private detective use? What special qualities did one possess? Thomas Furlong, a St. Louis private detective operating in the 1870s, put it this way:

To my mind, a real detective should possess all the elements within his general make-up, which would be necessary to make him a success at any of the leading professions. He should possess the keen perceptive abilities of a trained or successful journalist, be able to read between the lines, as it were, or recognize the value of a clue, as the journalist does the value of a bit of news. He must be well posted on the law, especially that part pertaining to criminals. He must have the foresight and judgment of the successful merchant or tradesman. He must be sympathetic and just to the same degree as is the beloved pastor of a large congregation. And he must be an actor. One of the versatile kind of actors, who can play any kind of a part or assume any character without months of rehearsing. He should at all times act natural, even while assuming a character, for if he overdoes the part he assumes, it is more than likely to attract unusual attention to him, which a real detective should avoid at all times.

Remember another thing: All crimes, nine hundred and ninety-nine out of every thousand, have a motive. True, these motives are often veiled and are not discernable at a mere glance. You must be a good diagnostician to handle these veiled cases—to diagnose them, as it were, as a learned physician diagnoses his case when called to the bedside of a very sick patient—find the cause. When you have found the motive for a crime, the balance of the work is usually easy.

St. Louis hated private detectives so much so that they later sought to ban them.

"Of course there are exceptions to all rules, but the average private detective is first and foremost a blackmailer," a St. Louis police official told the *St. Louis Post-Dispatch*. "If it wasn't for blackmail they couldn't live. That makes the principle object to all of those who are in the business. In the next place they interfere with the regular police work. In a great many cases, when a merchant or anybody else has a theft or an embezzlement committed against him, he goes to a private detective and puts him to work on the case. If the work implies a trip to another city where the private detective is not personally known to the police, he can get no assistance whatever; the very fact that he is a private detective proves him to be, among people who do not know him, of, to say the least, doubtful moral character."

The official continued: "By the time we get the case, and it has become so tangled up, and the alarm has been given so thoroughly that we can do nothing."

As the Stelzriede case became tangled, private detectives arrived in Saxtown. One of them from St. Louis made a big splash. People around Belleville whispered that detective Louis Reinhardt had made a major arrest. One German newspaper tipped the story before checking the facts.

"Although we have news that would be of interest to all readers, we cannot, for obvious reasons, share the latest findings," wrote the *Stern des Westens* on Tuesday, March 24. "Tomorrow we hope to be able to inform you about the arrest of at least one of the murderers and the latest findings."

The newspaper electrified readers: "For two days now, a very well known detective of St. Louis has been at work and what he has discovered so far does not leave any doubt about his successful findings."

Later reports said Reinhardt had arrested a man near the crime scene whose "hands bore evidence of having been badly cut by knives, and that one of his fingers seemed to have been bitten almost off."

It was a fabrication.

While everyone was enthralled with lies, Sheriff Hughes was heading back to Saxtown to follow a lead. A clue here, a clue there. Nothing really fit together. Everything was offset by something else.

But Hughes was zeroing in on Afken.

The *St. Louis Dispatch* appeared to build a case against Afken and his "vicious and murderous countenance." It defied constitutional expectations and said Afken might have to "prove himself innocent," even though there was no evidence against him.

Now Hughes thought he had found that evidence in the form of Afken's boss. If he didn't have a confession, he needed a witness.

Henry Boeker, the farmer who employed Afken as a grubber, said that Afken was not at home on the night of the murders.

CHAPTER 13

Bloody Evidence

St. Louis detective Louis Reinhardt said he had found the murder weapons.

The Stelzriede family had their heads smashed and battered by swings of an ax, investigators surmised, partly because marks of a bloody, dragging ax were found on the Stelzriede front lawn. But their throats had also been slit and their bodies punctured with swift jabs. On a clear and cool Tuesday afternoon, four days after the discovery of the Stelzriede bodies, Reinhardt told the Belleville-based *Stern des Westens* that he had found two knives at the crime scene.

"The blood of the Stelzriedes covered the blades and the grips of the knives, which were most definitely sharpened before the murder," the German-language newspaper wrote. "Where the knives were found cannot yet be told, but the bloody blades are a lead which will make it impossible for the murderers to get away with this gruesome crime."

The dispatch shocked information-starved readers looking for a break in the case. Soon other newspapers added to the news.

"The *Stern des Westens* this evening electrified its readers with the announcement that the detectives who have been engaged for the past two days in working up the case, had met with some success, as they had found at the house where the tragedy took place two knives, blood-stained and gory—the one a large butcher knife, and the other a pocket knife," the *St. Louis Democrat* reported. "Both of them were as sharp as razors. They were found secreted in a stove."

The *Democrat* reported that it interviewed the editor of the *Stern des Westens*, who was so emphatic about his newspaper's accuracy that investigators even allowed him to personally handle the knives. The newspapers said former St. Clair County State's Attorney R. A. Halbert corroborated the story.

The pocketknife was foreign made and reportedly large with an iron handle.

"It is believed that one of the knives furnishes a sufficient clue to finally lead to the capture of the perpetrators of the bloody deed," the *Democrat* reported.

The newspaper reminded readers that the murderers were "thought to have been two in number" and declared that their identities would soon be known and they would be housed in the local jail.

The reports forced Sheriff Hughes to address the situation. He confirmed that during the early phase of the investigation, investigators had found two knives in a chest belonging to the elder Stelzriede. But then Hughes said that physicians had used the knives to cut the clothes off of the five victims and the knives "thus became stained with their blood." When finished, the knives were placed on the stove, he said.

Hughes maintained that the knives had been used by the Stelzriedes to butcher hogs the previous fall and had been stored for safe keeping. He didn't think they had any connection to the murders.

Incredulous newspapers reported that investigators privately insisted they were the knives that helped kill the Stelzriede family. Others said they were representative of an overzealous press seeking to feed anything to their readers.

"To such a pitch is public excitement and curiosity raised that the most improbable stories are told and eagerly devoured," the *Belleville Advocate* wrote.

Hughes, unconcerned with the knives, had sent his son and other deputies back to Saxtown to question John Afken's whereabouts on the night of the Saxtown murders. Farmer Henry Boeker had told investigators that Afken, who never went out at night, was away from his usual sleeping quarters on the night of the murders. Hughes hoped that information would turn up evidence against the farmhand and Boeltz.

"The houses of both men have been most thoroughly searched for some evidence to implicate them in the terrible tragedy but thus far every effort has proved fruitless," the *Belleville Advocate* wrote. "If nothing further develops to point to them as the possible criminals or accessories they will probably be released in a few days." Hughes was in danger of losing his men.

Afken had no outward fear of Hughes's investigation. He was said to remain in the St. Clair County jail displaying the "utmost unconcern."

Afken's sleeping quarters in Saxtown had been searched and produced no evidence. But because it appeared Afken wasn't home the night of the murders, some other location could have important clues, investigators surmised.

Under questioning Afken coldly admitted he hadn't slept at Boeker's house the night of the murders.

Afken said he had stayed at the farmhouse of a man named Jacob Becker, which was less than a mile from the Stelzriede home. Afken said he slept at the farmhouse in the same bed with a man about sixteen years old and returned the next morning to Boeker's farm, where he had been working. Afken said he remained there and did not hear of the Stelzriede murders until that evening, when he went to the murder scene.

Deputies arrived in Saxtown and found Becker. A light rain had sprinkled the roads, which helped keep the dust in check. Becker said that Afken had indeed stayed at his house the night of the murders and slept in a room on the front porch. Becker said Afken and a young man went to bed about half-past nine o'clock and remained there for the rest of the night.

The porch, however, was reported to be entirely "separated from the main house, so that a person sleeping in that room might have gone out without [the others] knowing anything about it."

Hughes's deputies searched Becker's property. They turned up a black oilcloth sack that Becker later identified as belonging to Afken. The *St. Louis Times* reported that "it was found ready packed as if for traveling, the top and sides bespattered with mud, and the bottom covered over with blood." It was confiscated and taken to Belleville as evidence.

Afken reportedly didn't have a "satisfactory reason" for the bag being found on Becker's property. Nor for why he didn't bring it with him when he returned to Boeker's farm on the day the bodies were discovered. Still, investigators reported that the bag's contents contained nothing suspicious other than the bloodstains.

While Hughes pondered the situation, it appeared public sentiment was beginning to absolve Boeltz.

"The theory of the murder is that some relative, hoping to heir the property, did the bloody deed, as the innocent children were slaughtered as well as the older members of the family," said a dispatch published the following day, Wednesday, March 25, in the *St. Louis Democrat*. "The opinion of quite a number of parties is that Boeltz, whose wife is the sister of the murdered Mrs. Stelzriede, did not commit the deed, as he would not be an heir to any of their property."

The *Democrat* also said that Boeltz didn't do it to free himself of money he owed the Stelzriede family, noting that bank notes showing the debts were at the murder scene. A wise criminal would have removed that information. (Although if Boeltz paid the so-called "half-witted" Afken to commit the crime, Afken may have stolen the money and not bothered to search and destroy records at the murder scene.)

The Stelzriedes' bank notes showed that Boeltz had taken out three loans from the family: the first for three hundred dollars in February of 1871, the second for one hundred sixteen dollars on the day before Christmas Eve of 1873, and the third for fifty-five dollars on February 3, 1874.

Acknowledging that the evidence against Boeltz had hit a dead end, Hughes decided that another theory must be entertained. Another thread in the mysterious yarn had to be examined. He looked at the Stelzriede family tree.

On a cold March day, Sheriff Hughes and Belleville city marshal Henry Bauer packed up and headed to Washington County. Hughes wanted to speak with Carl Stelzriede's brother.

CHAPTER 14

Next of Kin

With his brother's family dead and buried, Charles Stelzriede was under police watch.

In the days after the murders, Sheriff James W. Hughes had dispatched a man to spy on Charles, who lived on a farm near Richview, Illinois, about fifty-five miles from the Saxtown murder scene. A detective was given strict orders to analyze everything: his land, his animals, his children. Charles was the only surviving brother of Carl Stelzriede—and had fast become a suspect in the murder of his sibling's family. The suspicion was triggered when the fifty-seven-year-old Charles didn't attend his relatives' funeral. Investigators focused on a motive that the murderer or murderers wanted to cut off heirship within the five-person family. They presumed that could be the reason why someone would brutally kill everyone, including two young children.

"This unnatural exhibition of callousness aroused the indignation of everyone," the *St. Louis Daily Globe* reported.

On Tuesday, March 24, Hughes headed for Richview, in Jefferson County, to investigate the situation himself. He wondered: Was there bad blood within the Stelzriede family?

There was.

Charles had once lived in Saxtown near his brother and nephew. The newspapers, sometimes prone to exaggeration, reported that his former neighbors said he "was always considered as a man capable of doing desperate things."

Charles didn't always gravitate to open landscapes or dreary backwoods. His first home in the United States was the rising metropolis of New York City. He and his family had been hardened by the buzzing clatter of the nation's largest city as it hummed with activity in the years before the Civil War.

Arriving in the 1840s from the country village of Hille, Germany, shortly after his now murdered brother Carl, Charles brought along his wife, Liezette, who was from Hanover—the capital of Lower Saxony—and little else. The couple opted to stay in Manhattan, where they joined a third Stelzriede brother named F. W. The two men worked together and operated a corner grocery store under the name "F. W. and C. F. Stelzriede" at 649 Washington Street in the Greenwich Village neighborhood.

Charles found the city environment a complete departure from the bleak, desolate German village where he had been raised. Gaslight glowed on jaunty streets packed with immigrants speaking foreign dialects in the shadow of three-story Greek Revival townhouses. Their store, at the northeast intersection of Washington and Christopher Streets, was a block away from the Hudson River, not far from the Hoboken ferry. The area boomed with an exciting mix of respectability and impropriety. Merchants of all kinds set up shop. Shipbuilders and seamen walked by beer gardens and brothels. Dressmakers, blacksmiths, tailors, architects, doctors, and lawyers crossed paths on the neighborhood's grid of jagged streets. A nearby corner storefront was advertised as a "good place for grocery, liquors, restaurant, or lager beer."

At night, hucksters and scavengers loomed. Drunks staggered on the streets. Newspaper briefs documented the dozens of people arrested daily for public intoxication or indecency. One was a thirteen-year-old girl named Mary Riley, who admitted to slugging beers at a saloon and was committed for ten days. The *New York Times* made sure to print the saloon owner's name: Patrick Farrell.

It should be of no surprise that Edgar Allan Poe stalked the neighborhood's drinking houses and found inspiration in the darkness to write his famous poem "The Raven."

As the city pulsed beneath, the Stelzriedes lived above their shop and appeared to have avoided the debauchery. They focused on family. While in New York, Charles and his wife started having children. Henry was born in 1849. Martin in 1851. And William in 1854.

Although the Stelzriedes no longer had to endure the tough labor of farm life, they were now on streets stained from hand-to-hand bloodlettings. Epic brawls started over anything ranging from a half-smile to a schlock of red hair. This was the era of the gangs of New York, roving street fighters who battled over turf and power and religion.

"Bill the Butcher" lived just a block away on the same street. The handsome thirty-four-year-old butcher by trade, whose real name was William Poole, had a finely developed chest, a large mustache, and a chiseled face recognizable to everyone around. He took to his meat-cutting business with great zeal. He opened a business at Washington Market. But he had a dark side.

His house, which looked similar to most others on Christopher Street, including the Stelzriedes', was said to be "one of a neat row of small brick houses, respectable outside and comfortable within. The parlors are neatly carpeted, and the walls hung with various paintings and large prints."

Despite such outward respectability, the American-bred Bill the Butcher's hatred of the Irish forced violent turf wars in a city being remade by immigration. The Great Potato Famine, which began its starvation in 1845, had sent millions fleeing Ireland for New York. The Butcher headed a street gang opposed to immigrant groups, particularly the Irish Catholic. He beat up just about every Irishman he saw. Especially the "papists." (Not a problem for the Protestant Stelzriedes, but their Germanic background was a cause for concern during the anti-immigrant wave. They too were new to the country and often faced the scorn of those who had lived on American land long before.) The Butcher had written a poem that read:

No foreign hands can we allow to hold
the helm of State, or offices of gold

No base born serf, to trample on the ground,
Or holy principle, by which we're bound . . .
Here let them have the blessings of our law,
Let justice shield them, and let justice awe,
But let them not presume beyond to go,
And teach Americans what they should know;
Let not our country in their hands be given,
And thus betray the trust received from Heaven.

With that as his guiding spirit, the Butcher led a local group called the True American Party, part of a nativist movement known as the Know Nothings that stoked fear of the foreign-born. Former president Millard Fillmore, who struggled to find a political party after the Whigs disintegrated over slavery, was among its followers. (In 1856 Fillmore won the party's presidential nomination.)

A pamphlet for the Know Nothings warned that "hundreds of thousands of German Papists are preparing to come to the United States. So great is the desire of the Belgian population to emigrate to America that a Belgian paper says: 'The authorities are determined to ship all her poorest class here.'"

Many American-born Protestants didn't want Europe's scraps—Irish, German, whatever. They considered them all to be trash, just like the tobacco juice and bad cabbage that littered the streets.

Still, the Butcher appeared the most enraged by the Irish. He spent his time collecting votes for his party, which often led to barroom brawls with Irish opponents, particularly those supporting the city's growing political machine known as Tammany Hall, which sought to maximize Irish votes at the ballot box. He never engaged in a formal prizefight but was known as a "rough and tumbler," ready to throw down—biting, brawling, gouging—at any moment.

In February 1855 the Butcher ran into John Morrissey at Stanwix Hall, a bar on lower Broadway. The Butcher had been feuding with the young Irish-born prizefighter and Tammany operative.

"You're an Irish son of a bitch!" the Butcher shouted.

"You're a black-muzzled American son of a bitch!" Morrissey responded.

Morrissey pointed a pistol at the Butcher and pulled the trigger twice. Click. Click. The gun didn't fire. The two left the bar. The Butcher returned later and ran into some of Morrissey's cohorts. One of them threw off his cloak, grabbed a revolver, and fired it but accidentally shot himself. He fired another shot and hit the Butcher in the leg. As the Butcher stumbled and swayed, another man in the gang shot the Butcher in the heart. The men fled.

The Butcher, unwilling to go down without a fight, grabbed a carving knife and chased after them, only to collapse at the barroom's door. He was taken to his home on Christopher Street, where he survived for fourteen days, going in and out of consciousness. A few moments before he died, he declared, "I think I am a goner. If I die, I die a true American; and what grieves me most is thinking I've been murdered by a set of Irish."

The Stelzriedes couldn't have missed the Butcher's massive funeral; 155 carriages and six thousand mourners jammed the street of their home and business. "Windows, iron railings, branches of trees, the roofs of houses, and every available standing place, were brought in requisition," the *New York Times* wrote.

The funeral procession began at the Butcher's home, a few doors down from the Stelzriedes, and headed to the Green-Wood Cemetery in Brooklyn. Four horses pulled the Butcher's American flag–draped coffin. On both sides of the horse-drawn hearse appeared the words "I die a true American."

The Times labeled it the "Stanwix Hall Tragedy."

It remains unclear how the Stelzriedes felt about the event that stirred the immigration debate. Did they resent the Butcher? Or did they just learn to live with him by ignoring him? Charles packed up his family in the days surrounding the incident in 1855 and headed halfway across the country to Illinois. The written record doesn't state whether they left because of violence, ethnic persecution, money, or a disagreement with Charles's brother and business partner.

Regardless, F.W. remained in Manhattan with his wife, Rachel. The grocery store he once operated with his brother became a liquor store and distillery. A sure bet for a German from the old country. The business was a modest success.

Charles settled into the Illinois frontier and plowed the soil on a seventy-two-acre farm in Saxtown next to his older brother, Carl. The farm, which sprouted wheat as its main crop, was valued at fourteen hundred dollars. It had a small number of livestock—a pig, some oxen. No horses.

With three growing boys and two young daughters, Charles made extra money as a broom maker. Germans liked to keep things clean. Life was simpler and certainly a major change from the family's dangerous years along the Hudson River; now their days were characterized by backbreaking labor on a farm.

In late 1862 news arrived from New York: F. W. Stelzriede had died. The third brother and his wife had no children—nor a last will and testament.

The two surviving Stelzriede brothers, both farming ground tucked into the Saxtown countryside, fought over the estate. F.W.'s money and property were put into the hands of a court-appointed administrator named William B. Howenstine. Because F.W. had a distillery, he had a lot of bad debts. It took two years for Howenstine to collect on them, but many of the debtors "could not be found or heard of at all." Howenstine said that those who could be tracked down "were utterly irresponsible."

By the time things were settled, Charles had moved from Saxtown to a farm posted on the western edge Jefferson County, near the Washington County line. The place was a good journey away from Saxtown, deep in the heart of Southern Illinois, but it had enough of the same rural customs for him to feel at home. Social life was devoted to corn-husking bees, pie suppers at the local one-room school, and games of checkers. In the fall there were "apple cuttings," where many of the younger kids gathered to peel and cook apples to make apple butter. The parties often devolved into playful food fights in which the kids threw apple peelings and cores at one another, a Stelzriede ancestor

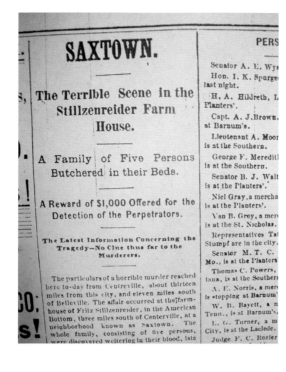

St. Louis Dispatch headline on March 21, 1874, announcing the discovery of the Stelzriede bodies on a farm in Saxtown, Illinois
ST. LOUIS DISPATCH

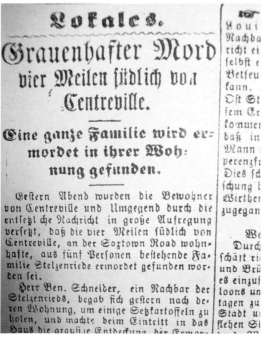

Headline from Belleville, Illinois, German-language newspaper the *Stern des Westens* on March 21, 1874. In English, headline means "Gruesome Murder."
STERN DES WESTENS

Suspect John Afken's writ of habeas corpus in 1874. Afken was released on bail of $3,000.

Grand jury document on April 28, 1874, refusing a bill of indictment against suspects John Afken and Fred Boeltz

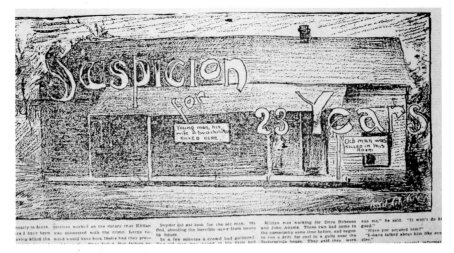

St. Louis Post-Dispatch illustration of the Stelzriede house in 1897. The drawing shows captions for where the bodies were found in the small house, which was demolished in 1954. *ST. LOUIS POST-DISPATCH*

Naturalization papers of suspect Fred Boeltz, who became a US citizen in 1877
NATIONAL ARCHIVES

Undated photo of James W. Hughes, a Democratic politician who served as St. Clair County (Ill.) sheriff from 1870 to 1874 and was the chief investigator of the Saxtown case LABOR & INDUSTRY MUSEUM, BELLEVILLE, ILLINOIS

Telegram from Sheriff James W. Hughes to Illinois Governor John Beveridge asking for state resources to help hunt for the Stelzreides' murderers ILLINOIS STATE ARCHIVES, SPRINGFIELD, ILLINOIS

St. Louis Post-Dispatch drawing of suspect George Killian, in 1897, who was arrested on suspicion of murdering the Stelzriede family eight years after their bodies were found ST. LOUIS POST-DISPATCH

The barn built by the Stelzriede family before their deaths in 1874, as viewed today. It is the only surviving structure on the property in Saxtown from the time of the murders.

Interior view of the Stelzriede barn as seen today

Sunlight streams through the second story of the Stelzriede barn, as seen today.

The house built in 1954 on the site of the original Stelzriede house. Several people who have lived there have complained about the presence of ghosts.

Grave marker, written in German, of Maria Christina Stelzriede, the matriarch of the Stelzriede family. She died more than eight years before the rest of her family was murdered.

Freivogel Cemetery in Saxtown area near Millstadt, Illinois. The Stelzriede bodies were buried here in unmarked graves.

Members of the Zion Evangelical Church dressed up like the Stelzriede family in 2010. The church celebrated its 175th anniversary with a cemetery walk at Freivogel Cemetery. ZION EVANGELICAL CHURCH, MILLSTADT, ILLINOIS

Monument to the Stelzriede family at Walnut Hill Cemetery in Belleville, Illinois, erected several years after the murders. Saxtown residents refused to allow the Stelzriede bodies to be moved. They remain buried eight miles away.

Close up of German writing on Stelzriede monument. In English it reads "the murdered family."

remembered. Some of the Stelzriedes who immigrated to Illinois were said to be too religious to "tolerate dancing," although it remains unclear if Charles permitted it.

By 1874 the area was crisscrossed with railroad tracks. The Illinois Central Railroad and the St. Louis Southeastern Railroad intersected in Richview—giving the Stelzriedes better access to the larger world around them, including St. Louis. But Saxtown was still far removed from a rail line. Farm goods couldn't reach a broader market unless they were thrown onto a horse-drawn wagon and pulled long distances.

The exact reason why Charles moved away from Saxtown and his brother is unknown. Some surmised it was because of bitter feelings over his brother's estate, which was unfolding alongside the US Civil War. Between the two surviving brothers, Carl had reportedly received the larger share of F.W.'s money, by about fifteen hundred dollars. That infuriated Charles, who felt slighted.

"It is said that this excited the jealous anger, and that there had been a quarrel between them about it, and [Charles] has expressed himself bitterly toward his brother," the *St. Louis Daily Globe* reported. "They have not visited each other for some time."

Another paper said Charles had vowed to seek revenge.

Could that revenge have come in the form of murder? Investigators learned that Charles's sons apparently had been in the St. Clair County area in the days surrounding the murders.

"Suspicion rested upon a couple of nephews, who it is stated have frequently endeavored to get the family to assist them with money, but were always refused," the *St. Louis Dispatch* reported.

Henry, Charles's oldest child, had been spotted in the St. Clair County area on Thursday, the last time his relatives were seen alive. Although he didn't attend their funeral, he was seen the day after near Fred Boeltz's farm.

"It was found out that he had a large cut on his hand and this made him even more suspicious, as it was reported earlier that one of the murderers had to be wounded," the *Anzeiger Westens* reported.

~~

Sheriff Hughes arrived in Jefferson and Washington Counties four days after the murders ready to make an arrest. He couldn't ignore the bitter family dispute and the wounded son. Rumors spread that one of his detectives had already arrested two of Charles's sons and taken them to St. Clair County. Such was communication during the unfurling investigation. In reality, all three of the sons—Henry, Martin, and William—had been arrested but quickly released.

Henry appeared to be an upstanding young man. He had just gotten married earlier in the month and was a railroad employee in Washington County. After his brief arrest he voluntarily went to St. Clair County, intent on looking at the murder scene and paying his respects. But he was dissuaded from doing so when he arrived in the area because, as the *St. Louis Democrat* said, "he might get into trouble there, so many stories are afloat as to who the perpetrators are."

Hughes interviewed acquaintances of the Stelzriede family and unexpectedly found a swift defense. They indicated that the elder Stelzriede didn't attend the funeral of his brother and nephew because he hadn't learned of the murders in time—and he was sick. One of the interviewees, L. H. Higgins of Richview, had just shipped off a letter in defense of Charles Stelzriede to Joseph McCullagh, the editor of the *St. Louis Daily Globe*. It read:

> *In your account of the Stelzriede tragedy, in the daily of the 23d, you state that there was a strong feeling against [Charles] Stelzriede, brother and uncle of the murdered. Also, that one of his boys was seen in the neighborhood a few days before the tragedy. I wish to say a word or two in reference to the family of [Charles], in relations to their standing in this place. The old man has lived near this place about ten years, and now lives about three miles east of here, in Jefferson County. Henry and William live in this place. Martin lives in Nashville, and is section boss on the St. Louis and Southeastern Railroad. This makes three sons, instead of two nearly grown. I have*

been personally acquainted with them for five years past, and I cannot, neither do I, believe that they are in any way connected with, or knew anything about the murder of their relatives until last night or this morning, and this is the feeling of this entire community. They are considered quiet, peaceable, inoffensive men, by all who know them here, and no one believes that they could conceive of such a hellish act, much less execute it.

Henry has affidavits of citizens of this place that they saw him every day from March 12 to March 21, 1874, inclusive.

William has affidavits to his being here Friday and Saturday, and I saw men this evening who will make affidavit as to his being here Wednesday and Thursday.

The old man has been sick three or four weeks, I am informed by the attending physician. Martin is at Nashville, Illinois, and of course no one here can say where he was during that week, but he can, undoubtedly, prove by the men under him, as to his whereabouts, if he was attending to his business.

There was a detective here today, and he arrested Henry and William, but on the strength of the affidavits gotten up for them by some of our most respectable citizens, he released them again. I have no doubt but what he thought he had good grounds for arresting them. I do not write this article to find fault with what is said in the article of the 23d, nor in order to shield them from suspicion and punishment, if there is any ground for it, for I certainly think no punishment too severe to be meted out to the perpetrators of such an awful deed, but merely to show what the feeling is here in reference to both the old man and his boys; and I hope you will give this the same publicity in your paper that you have the article referred to of the 23d.

A group of more than two dozen Richview residents signed an affidavit on March 24 stating:

We, the undersigned, citizens of Richview . . . hereby certify that we have been well acquainted with [Charles] Stelzriede and his three sons, Henry, Martin, and William, for the past five years; that they are peaceable, inoffensive men, and that we do not believe that Henry or William were absent from this county from March 15 to March 21, 1874, both days inclusive, and we do not believe any of them are in any way connected with or know anything about the late Stelzriede murder in St. Clair County, Illinois.

It was neighboring county against neighboring county. The St. Clair folks swore to seeing two of Charles's sons in their county in the days surrounding the murders. Washington and Jefferson County folks said that couldn't be true.

Information such as that offered in the affidavit gave Sheriff Hughes pause. It betrayed the growing sense that the family had murdered their kin. Hughes acknowledged that the surviving Stelzriede clan had a motive, that Charles was jealous of his brother, and that money was often the root of crimes, especially among the land-lusting Germans. Charles didn't get what he wanted from F.W., but now he would get it through his murdered brother, the thinking went. Being the nearest living heir, Charles stood to inherit everything—at least ten thousand dollars in land and cash (valued at about two hundred thousand in today's dollars)—unless someone could prove that Anna Stelzriede had died last, which under Illinois law would change the order of succession to Fred and Margaret Boeltz.

"But such an event is not at all probable, in view of the impenetrable mystery surrounding the awful crime, and even if the real parties should fortunately be discovered, it would be almost next to impossible for a court to ascertain the exact order in which the deaths occurred, with that degree of certainty, at least, so as to enable it to change the order of succession as fixed by the statutes," the *St. Louis Times* reported.

That proof would come only in the form of a confession. If the murderer recounted who he killed and when. It appeared unlikely that the last to die would have been Anna, since she was still in bed when an ax fell on her body. Carl, the oldest, appeared to have known about the ensuing carnage. His body was found with a jacket in his hand. Perhaps he had attempted to flee.

The sons' alibis meant Hughes had little to go on and little chance of discovering the order of succession in Richview, Illinois. He headed back to St. Clair County.

The next day, on Wednesday, a sick and ailing Charles Stelzriede arrived at the jail in Belleville to provide his own alibi. The city was preparing for a theatric performance of the comedy *It Never Rains but It Pours*. Others got on a railcar and headed to Ben De Bar's Theatre in St. Louis to see Edwin Booth, the brother of the man who shot Lincoln, play Shakespeare's Hamlet.

Charles was accompanied by his lawyer, Thomas Quick of Richview; his wife; and his eldest son, Henry, who had stayed the night in the area and met up with his parents that day.

The neighbors had said that Charles was sick, but they couldn't say that they knew where he was when the murders were committed. He provided a note from his doctor.

Charles looked old and "appeared to be in feeble health," it was observed.

"He had a certificate from his physician showing his whereabouts on the evening of the murder, though that seemed unnecessary, since his physical appearance indicated that he was entirely incapable of the effort involved in the commission of the crime; and in fact, he has been sick for nearly a year," the *St. Louis Times* reported.

Then something odd happened. Charles visited both Fred Boeltz and John Afken, who were still behind bars. A nexus between all three parties appeared to exist. Stelzriede had known Boeltz and had previously employed Afken. All three had been suspected of having some connection to the crime—and now were allowed to commiserate.

"Boeltz recognized the party immediately, but they seemed to be unacquainted with Afken," an observer reported.

The lack of recognition was surprising. The two knew each other. Why would they suddenly act like strangers?

Regardless, authorities had allowed all three suspects to be in the presence of one another. Charles spent considerable time with the two men, peppering Afken in particular with questions about his whereabouts on the morning of the murders. Afken reiterated his story about having slept at the Becker house and returned to the Boeker farm in the morning.

Charles later went to the courthouse and confused anyone who thought he had any knowledge of his relatives' killings. He offered an additional one-thousand-dollar reward for information leading to the arrest and conviction of the murderers.

The case appeared to be at a dead end. But one possibility tugged at the sheriff's mind: One of the sons, Martin, had yet to establish an alibi.

Martin was the twenty-three-year-old middle child and a section boss on the St. Louis and Southeastern Railroad, which was chartered in 1869 and built out from East St. Louis. In 1874 it ran southeast to Evansville, Indiana. Martin oversaw a stretch of track that ran from Ashley, Illinois, to Nashville, Illinois, in Washington County.

Sheriff Hughes remembered that a railroad conductor had spotted someone suspicious on the Cairo Short Line route in St. Clair County the morning of the murders. Who would know the railroad routes better than a section boss? Who would know how to get in and out of somewhere fast?

Martin Stelzriede did. So did his brother Henry.

CHAPTER 15

Cursed

Life on the Saxtown farms plowed ahead.

Farmers started planting, hunting, fishing—preparing their land for future life. They had no choice. Several days had passed. On the first day of April, a bright sun shone cheerfully above the Saxtown skies. Eleven days had passed since the Stelzriede bodies had been found. The farmers wondered if they'd ever know who had killed their neighbors—or if they'd have to live in fear for the rest of their lives. The weather, at least, finally appeared to be breaking in Saxtown's favor.

In St. Louis men and women devoured news reports about the unfolding sensation in Saxtown, but the improved weather gave them a respite to think about the approaching Easter season. The fashionable St. Louis women switched to a simpler, elegant style that was dominating the day on the East Coast. Their bodies were clothed. They wore refined silks in soft, pleasant colors, chose spring bonnets with unique brims, and preferred shorter skirts to "demi-trains." Owing to their religious views, the Saxtown women wore rag skirts that nearly swept the dirty ground. They didn't care. Everyone was still in a daze as they resumed daily chores.

No matter how clear the sky or warm the sun, the green grass and brown dirt seemed pale. Mystery shrouded everything.

The Stelzriede house presented a "peculiarly sad and desolate appearance," but the land surrounding the house was in an "excellent state of cultivation." Neighbor Fred Eckert Sr., who was an administrator of the estate, took it upon himself to keep up the farm. He looked over the healthy wheat field west of the house and fed the livestock in the front yard. It appeared to breathe life into the death house.

"The place literally seems alive with chickens," someone observed.

Inside the house Eckert and neighbors had washed and scrubbed the floors, although bloodstains still showed. Everything else remained just like it had been left. The big bed stood where it always had in the front room. Anna's nightcap, flecked with clots of blood, still hung from the bedpost. The walls remained marked with blood spatter that just wouldn't go away without a coat of paint.

Eckert was a thrifty and successful farmer. His farm was almost three times the value of the Stelzriede land and stock. He was the perfect care-taker for the property. Maybe he would do it some good.

Eckert lived in Saxtown with his wife and ten children—most of them boys.

The Eckert men were tough. When a pack of five full-grown moun-tain wolves threatened Saxtown by killing sheep and poultry in the pitch dark or broad of day, one of Eckert's sons, Jacob, went on the hunt. Authorities had offered a ten-dollar bounty for every wolf skin.

The wolves appeared and disappeared without anyone finding them. Then, one day while perched in the Saxtown woods, Jacob spotted one. Alone. He got up as close as he could and got a good look. He grabbed his gun and fired at the wolf. The violent animal jumped into the air and howled into the big sky.

It didn't die.

The wolf lunged onto Jacob, who was strong and smart enough to keep its teeth away from his neck. Jacob jammed his hand down the wolf's throat and then struck its head with the butt of his gun. The stunned wolf fell back. He fired and shot the animal through the head. The fight was over.

Jacob dragged the wolf hide to the authorities and was given the ten dollars "without question."

The Eckert family was large enough, strong enough, and tough enough to watch over the Stelzriede house and farm.

While they kept the farm in good condition, Sheriff James Hughes visited and revisited the murder scene, struggling to find clues as to the murderer. His theory and examination of railroad routes had failed to pin the murders on the sons of Charles Stelzriede. Oddly, no one seemed to be bothered by his failure. One newspaper even praised his hard work.

"Sheriff Hughes and his deputies are entitled to much credit for the able and indefatigable manner in which they have labored to throw some light on the terrible affair," the *Belleville Advocate* opined. "Skilled detectives, schooled in the secrets of crime, are bending all their energies to the task of unraveling the mystery and we hope that for the sake of humanity they will be able to bring the murderers to a swift and speedy justice."

The article used the word *murderers*. Plural. Despite the praise, it was Hughes who first swore that the murders were committed by one man. After public comments from Coroner John Ryan, he adopted the theory of a conspiracy, which led to the arrest of Fred Boeltz and John Afken, who remained his prisoners. And then several others.

While Hughes shifted strategies to focus his investigation on a conspiracy, he failed to question several groups of men who appeared to act strangely when the bodies were first discovered. Particularly the Schneider brothers and the Killian brothers, one of whom fainted near the murder scene as the details of the crime unfolded.

The same article that praised Hughes seemed to suggest he didn't have a chance at catching the killers.

"Several murders have been committed in St. Clair County within three years and the perpetrators have all escaped," the article noted. "It is such recollections as this that excite a population to deeds of frenzy when a murderer is caught, and the same recollection makes us fear that the Saxtown murder will pass into history with the additional word 'Mystery' pinned to the name."

That was heavy stuff for Hughes to swallow. His reputation was on the line. Murderers and outlaws kept slipping through his hands—and it had to stop. Perhaps that's why he fumbled to make arrests.

Hughes's actual schooling in "the secrets of crime" was limited. He was a politician who played a lawman. One of his chief duties was not to solve crimes, but to collect taxes. He studied neither the theory of crime nor the psychology behind it. As was the case for most of his deputies. They lacked most of the tools used in modern investigations, and the mental study of deduction to go along with it. The great age of Victorian detectives with smoking pipes and magnifying glasses hadn't yet begun.

In fact, it would still be two years before Alexander Graham Bell said the words "Mr. Watson, come here. I want to see you" into his newly patented telephone—a device that ushered in modern life.

Hughes didn't have a telephone, but he had footwear impressions. The sheriff was able to make casts of the shoe prints left behind at the scene of the crime. Investigators looked at them over and over, hoping they could match them to the Stelzriede murderer.

Without any luck the case languished into Easter Sunday, April 6. The previous warm weather was a flimflam. "Gloomy, cloudy, and depressing" weather moved into the area and made outside travel nearly impossible.

On Tuesday, April 8, Hughes threw his investigation back into activity and ordered his son Julius to make two more arrests. Fred Eckert Jr. and Jacob Petrie were the young sons of respected farmers, but both were said to have "dissolute character."

Hughes failed to immediately explain exactly why he arrested the two men. Julius declared that he and his father had "well founded suspicions that they are in some way connected with the tragedy."

Hughes later revealed his evidence: the stamping of their feet.

"Both men reside within a half mile of the Stelzriede farm, and about a quarter of a mile from each other," one newspaper disclosed. "The footprints which were supposed to have been made by the murderers correspond exactly with the feet of these men."

The men appeared before Judge William Snyder at his Belleville courtroom on the Saturday after they were arrested. Snyder, who had been a soldier in the Mexican War, was a better politician than he was a lawyer, some said. He hated legal technicalities and often brushed them aside for what he called a "square deal."

It appeared that Hughes had little evidence to convince Snyder to keep them behind bars. How could anyone prove which footprints belonged to the murderer? The Stelzriede farm had been trampled by so many friends and neighbors in the frenzy after the crime. Police arrived hours after the mob. Footprints, including those of the Eckert men, who were the Stelzriedes' closest neighbors, were everywhere.

A large number of Saxtown and Millstadt residents attended the proceedings in support of Eckert Jr. and Petrie. Snyder was sick and unable to hear the arguments. Because there was no evidence, both the state and the defense attorneys agreed that the young men should be let go. Eckert Jr. was released on a seven-thousand-dollar bond that was secured by his father.

New pressure was put on Hughes to show his evidence against Boeltz and Afken, who remained in jail. He didn't have much. It was all circumstantial.

On April 23 Afken petitioned for a writ of habeas corpus, which required authorities to produce him before a court and justify his detention.

Afken's attorney wrote that he had been detained "without an authority of law, for a supposed criminal matter." He showed that Afken had demanded Hughes to produce a warrant for his commitment—and that Hughes had failed to do so. (There's no evidence that Hughes ever obtained a warrant to arrest Boeltz or Afken.)

The two men, who had been jailed for more than a month on suspicion of murdering the Stelzriede family, appeared before Snyder two days later to learn whether they could be granted bail. Boeltz was reportedly "visibly affected" when he was told that he might get released. Boeltz and Afken were granted bail of three thousand dollars each, which was agreed to by the state's attorney.

Friends gathered around Boeltz and congratulated him. He appeared "completely overcome" with emotion. Three days later Boeltz and Afken reappeared at the brick courthouse at Belleville's public square.

On April 28 a grand jury heard the matter. The foreman was Jefferson Rainey, one of the oldest settlers of St. Clair County, born just two years after Illinois became a state. The jury refused to indict Boeltz or Afken. They ordered Hughes to release them for lack of evidence.

Hughes, unable to keep any suspect jailed, returned to his theory that one of Charles Stelzriede's sons might have committed the murder. In

May St. Louis detective Louis Reinhardt was sent to Washington County to arrest Henry Stelzriede.

Henry hired R. A. Halbert, one of the best known lawyers in Belleville, to defend him. Halbert was the former state's attorney who had erroneously corroborated information about knives found at the Stelzriede murder scene.

Detectives were unable to match him to the description given by Conductor Fleischert, who said he might have seen the killer aboard his train the morning of the murders. Henry was quickly released.

The incident prompted his father, Charles, to rescind the additional one-thousand-dollar reward he had offered in the case, saying it "had stimulated the detectives to an unusual degree, so much so that they arrest innocent persons on the barest suspicion."

One of those detectives was schoolteacher and Justice of the Peace Isaiah Thomas. He became obsessed with the case to the point that he could talk about nothing else. Saxtown residents listened to his theories. Fingers pointed in every direction. They could only suspect each other.

As St. Clair County residents began celebrating the change of seasons with ice cream and strawberry festivals, and as St. Louis prepared to inaugurate the Eads Bridge spanning the Mississippi, Saxtown remained haunted by the murders from a few months before.

Local residents repeated the phrase "murder will out" over and over in hushed conversations. The killer will eventually be caught, they hoped.

Days after Hughes lost his prisoners, he was nearly killed by a wild horse.

"The painful news [is] that Sheriff James W. Hughes, of Belleville, met with a serious accident," the *St. Louis Dispatch* reported. "Mr. Hughes was out riding in a buggy behind one of his fast horses which shied and threw him out. The horse ran off and finally fell, receiving such injuries that he will not recover. The buggy was a total wreck. Mr. Hughes, though severely injured, is not fatally hurt."

At about the same hour, his wife fell down a stairway at their Belleville home and broke her leg.

Some started to whisper that the case was cursed. The superstitious-minded Germans, who had brought with them from the old country fears of witches and spells, couldn't help but wonder if some evil force was at work.

The day after Hughes's accident, Constable William Bangert, the Millstadt man with police jurisdiction over Saxtown, was thrown from a buggy on East Main Street in Belleville by a pair of runaway horses.

Bangert broke his leg.

CHAPTER 16

Deathbed Confessions

"THERE IS NO REFUGE FROM CONFESSION BUT SUICIDE; AND SUICIDE is confession."

The words of Massachusetts statesman Daniel Webster were repeated in the Saxtown case. Days passed. Months passed. Years passed. Someone would confess, the investigators thought. And closure would come along with it, they hoped.

That's why the sleuths wanted to sleep underneath every dying Saxtown man's bed. Some of them went as far as to sneak underneath floorboards, thinking a suspect would talk in his sleep as he slipped into death and reveal his complicity in the Saxtown case. Or so said a developing legend.

Two years passed without much news to summon attention to the cold case. James W. Hughes was no longer the sheriff of St. Clair County. He left office at the end of 1874, but the Saxtown case stayed with him as the most publicized crime of his tenure.

His exit didn't deter investigators. Private detectives seemed to lurk around every corner. They repeatedly questioned everyone. Some took up residence in Saxtown; some went undercover and attempted to goad suspects into revealing details about the crime. The environment created a tableau of distrust.

In the interim the effects of the economic depression worsened, with increased unemployment and bankruptcies throughout the nation. Immigrants flocked to the St. Clair County Farm Board, where meals were served to paupers and transients. Some men spent years in unemployment trying to crack the Saxtown case, hoping to one day collect a reward.

The economy wasn't the only national worry. In Washington, DC, Indian Inspector E. C. Watkins warned of "wild and hostile bands of Sioux Indians in Dakota and Montana." A year later, in 1876, General George Armstrong Custer was killed in the Battle of the Little Bighorn after commanding a small group of men to attack a four-thousand-person force led by Sitting Bull.

That year, the four o'clock afternoon edition of the *St. Louis Dispatch* issued a headline that returned the Saxtown case to the forefront for information-starved readers: MURDER WILL OUT—A CLUE AT LAST TO THE STELZRIEDE MURDER.

The Dispatch reported that Christian Orp, a detective employed to find the Stelzriede murderers, had "at last struck the right scent, and is now preparing to state authoritatively who committed the deed and under what circumstances it was prompted."

Orp had moved two miles north of the murder scene. That brought him some notoriety among the people gossiping about the case and searching for the killer. In May of 1876 a letter arrived addressed to Orp from a man named Henry Gretting, who had reportedly once worked as a farmhand and laborer in the Saxtown vicinity. They letter was said to have given a "full account of the dark deed." But Gretting, staying in Memphis, Tennessee, apparently cautioned that he would kill himself before the letter was delivered to Orp.

"The writer says he did the bloody work for pay, but has been haunted with the specter ghosts of the murdered parties ever since the night of the butchery," the *Dispatch* reported. The paper added that a man fitting Gretting's description had been found drowned in Memphis.

Gretting didn't mention who allegedly hired him to kill the Stelzriedes. The absence of specifics cast doubt over the whole claim. Was he the man spotted leaving the area on the train? (Or was that perhaps one of the Stelzriede nephews?) It was impossible to know. But the revelation, true or not, offered a reminder that the Saxtown case remained an unsolved mystery.

Deathbed confessions were common in the late nineteenth century, particularly in high-profile, sensational cases. The wives of suspected criminals closely watched their husbands, and prevented others from visiting when their husbands were dying to avoid any embarrassing disclosures. Religious people put a premium on the confession of sins before death.

The confessions were fueled by newspapers, which made a sport of reporting details of sensational crimes. Even if they were old.

The infamous Bender clan vanished into Kansas history in 1873, but years later, respected Chicago businessman George Evans Downer laid on his deathbed, called for his lawyer, and said he was part of a vigilante posse that had killed the murderous Bender family. Downer had lived in Independence, Kansas, when people had started going missing near the Bender Inn. Downer said he had formed a four-person "vigilance committee" and tracked the Benders as they escaped justice.

All of the family members but Kate, the supposed mastermind, were killed during a standoff. Kate, who was wounded, was tied up. Downer said she told him she enjoyed killing because she "liked to see the blood come." One of the vigilantes shot Kate dead after she reportedly grabbed and fired a pistol.

"We buried them while the moon hid its face, and destroyed all trace of their property," Downer said. "We swore a vow of silence, and next day spread the report that the Benders had escaped by train. This is the true story of the extermination of the murderous family."

The story couldn't be verified. The area where they were reportedly buried had been planted over with corn—and plowed over for decades. The Bender bodies never turned up.

The Bender situation represents the complexity of what was going on in Saxtown. As more time passed, deathbed confessions were nearly impossible to confirm. But they were irresistible to the press. They stirred emotions among anyone who wanted justice, or to hear a good tale.

The letter to Orp in 1876 rekindled the Saxtown case. The next year, in November of 1877, Sheriff Herman G. Weber investigated a farmhand in Trenton, Illinois, who in a delirious fever muttered in German "something about a murder" without giving a location.

Weber, who continued searching for anyone fitting the description of the suspect seen by railroad conductor Fleischert, rushed to interview the farmhand—and to get a good look at him.

The man, known just by his last name, Dickmann, had shot himself in the head with a rifle. Few other details could be gleaned, other than that prior to his illness he had been in a "morose disposition. " During his illness, others around him said, he raved continually about some unspecified crime. His rambling speech made the details hard to decipher.

The *St. Louis Dispatch* reported that "in a measure, he corresponded to the description given by Conductor Fleischert, but was a much sparer man, which possibly resulted from sickness and that haunting shadow of a crime."

The specifics of his appearance weren't given. He had been shot in the head, which surely made it more difficult to compare to Fleischert's description.

The *Dispatch* appeared skeptical of the story with this passage: "Certain is it that the suns of [four] summers have shone upon the five graves in the little country churchyard near Millstadt, where rest the remains of the Stelzriede family, and no clearly defined clue has ever been reached as to the perpetrator of the most bloody murder that stains the annals of Illinois."

Meanwhile, former Saxtown resident Charles Killian lay in East St. Louis, dying from a gunshot wound. While in the woods he had shot himself in the head in an apparent suicide attempt. He was found and taken for treatment.

His brother George Killian, a farmhand who had acted suspiciously at the Stelzriede murder scene years before, rushed to his side and was said to have forbade a Catholic priest from ministering to his dying brother. Perhaps to conceal the secrets of the Stelzriede murders.

CHAPTER 17

The Feuds

Six long years had passed, and Isaiah Thomas couldn't let it go.

Harvest after harvest. Biting winter after biting winter. As the wind blew across the fields of corn and wheat, the Saxtown schoolteacher remained obsessed with the Stelzriede murders. He spent his days at a chalkboard teaching children how to read and write, add and subtract. He spent his nights talking. Talking about the five deaths that forever changed his tiny corner of the world.

The names of Charles, Fritz, Anna, and the children were constantly on his tongue. As were the names of the people who he thought murdered them.

Thomas turned the case into legend while he taught his students, who were so young they had no memory of the sensation that had unfolded in their once-peaceful outpost. Rural schoolteachers like Thomas taught all of the classes and all of the age groups. They were paid very little, and required to do everything from fetching the firewood in the mornings to sweeping the floors and setting the mousetraps when the days were done. They also had to be responsible for their pupils' lives.

Not everyone bothered to use the schooling, though. Legally, rural children didn't have to attend school. Many of the farm boys stayed at home to help in the fields and cut the wheat. Families—at least the ones that still bothered to plow the soil—had little money to pay for hired help. They certainly didn't have the money for farm machinery, which had started coming into use.

Thomas had a profession based on learning, which made him stand out from his neighbors. He was surrounded by men who worked hard with their calloused hands, not their minds. Carpenters, wagonmakers, stonemasons, coal diggers. During the 1870s, as the effects of an economic depression worsened and sent agricultural prices plummeting, many of Saxtown's folks struggled and gave up farming. Ben Schneider, who had discovered the Stelzriedes' bodies, picked up and moved from a Saxtown farm to nearby Millstadt. He traded a wheat farm for a small backyard garden with tomato plants.

It was in this environment that Thomas saw the world change, and he was charged to explain it to the children. The Civil War that seemed so long ago. The scientists who were embracing Charles Darwin's theory of evolution. In 1876 Rutherford B. Hayes, a Republican lawyer from Thomas's home state of Ohio, was elected president after losing the popular vote.

But there was still some simple joy. That same year, Thomas and his wife, Hannah, welcomed a baby girl. They named her Minnie.

Thomas could only hope that his growing family wouldn't face the same fate as the Stelzriedes. Despite the new baby, Thomas appeared to focus on his side job as a justice of the peace—and he was dead serious about it. He naturally turned to the Stelzriede murders. By 1876 news was trickling out about tall tales and deathbed confessions. That year, Christian Orp, the private detective who had moved to Saxtown, claimed that a former Saxtown laborer had written him a letter in which he confessed to the murders and then killed himself in Memphis, Tennessee.

The news stoked an incredulous Thomas. He didn't believe Orp's story, but he felt the truth would eventually be told. Thomas tried to make sure of that. He threw himself into the case—questioning suspects, talking to detectives, keeping the mystery alive. Never mind that the case had been investigated. Never mind that so much time had passed. Never mind that seven people had previously been arrested but never indicted for the murders. It seemed unlikely, if not impossible, that new information could be gleaned to put someone to justice.

"It looked as though the crime would pass into history as an unsolved mystery, so well had the perpetrators concealed their tracks, and so in all probability it would if it had not been for the untiring energy of Isaiah W. Thomas, a resident of the vicinity, who maintained all along that the murderers were to be found in the immediate neighborhood," the *Belleville Advocate* wrote.

Thomas was brave. He dared to push the case forward while believing that a killer who had slaughtered an entire family was walking with him on the dirt paths of Saxtown. Perhaps the killer was following him? Listening to him? Most people whispered about the case in private but were too afraid to show that they were trying to avenge the killings, lest they rouse a murderer's anger.

Not Thomas. He put all of his spare time into the case and wasn't shy about it. In doing so he made "enemies of quite a number who, from remarks they let drop, had incurred his suspicions."

Saxtonites couldn't forget the name of the last person to make enemies: Carl Stelzriede. And they remembered what had happened to him.

Thomas suspected three men: George Killian, George Schneider, and George Fritzinger. Killian was a farmhand and laborer. Both Schneider and Fritzinger had been butchers, two men skilled at cutting flesh.

Killian and Schneider had left Saxtown shortly after the murders but remained in the general area. Thomas had heard about the death of Killian's brother, Charles, in East St. Louis, and found it suspicious. He started to believe that Charles Killian hadn't committed suicide at all. Rather, like many others, Thomas thought Killian had been killed by the same people who murdered the Stelzriede family.

Burned into Thomas's memory was the way George Killian and Schneider acted the day the bodies were found. The fainting. The heated conversations. The odd remark that Killian made before viewing the bodies, indicating that he already knew what they looked like. Also in his mind was the fact that George Fritzinger had sold the Stelzriede family their dog, Monk, which was found penned up in a back room of the house, although it normally roamed the farmstead. Thomas believed the killer knew the family and knew the dog. Monk was distrustful of strangers; only a friendly face could have made it past the dog without awaking the family.

Thomas began telling other people of his suspicions. First confidants, then anyone who would listen. He kept chattering about it until nearly everyone knew his story.

By 1881 George Schneider had had enough. He denied that he had anything to do with the Stelzriede murders and sought to silence Thomas. In May of that year, a lawsuit hit Thomas with a thud. Schneider had gone to Belleville and sued Thomas in St. Clair County court for defamation.

"For whereas [Schneider] is, and from his youth has been, of good fame and reputation among his neighbors, and is, and ever has been free from the crime of murder, and was never convicted or suspected to be guilty of that crime; nevertheless, [Thomas], not being ignorant of the premises, but fraudulently, maliciously and wickedly [is] continuing to injure, blacken and defame the plaintiff in his good fame and reputation, and to injure him in his trade," wrote Belleville lawyer John Breese Hay, a powerful Republican politician hired to represent Schneider.

Hay, who had served two terms in the US House of Representatives until losing reelection in 1872, continued by saying that Thomas, in the presence of "good citizens of this state, and in conversations with the same, with a loud voice, [did] speak, utter, publish, and proclaim the following false, scandalous and malicious words of and concerning [Schneider]: '[George Schneider] murdered the Stelzriede family'; '[George Schneider] is a murderer'; '[George Schneider] had a hand in the Stelzriede murder'; 'George Killian killed the Stelzriedes, George Schneider cut their throats'; 'George Schneider and George Killian and George Fritzinger are the murderers of Stelzriede.'"

But Hay didn't stop there. He went one step further, alleging that Thomas not only had the gall to accuse his client of murder in English—but he also said it in German. Perhaps that was worse, Hay said, because that was the language Saxtonites best understood. The language they had learned in the cradle.

"[Schneider] has been, and is greatly injured in his said good name, fame, and brought into public scandal," Hay wrote, asking a judge for relief.

Thomas appeared unfazed by the lawsuit. He fought back with his own filing, saying that Schneider was well acquainted with the Stelzriede family and that he lived a short distance from them near his brother, Ben, who had found the hacked bodies. Thomas alleged that tracks in the field in front of the Stelzriede house led to George Schneider's house—and that the tracks showed two people running.

Thomas threw his neighbors into the spectacle. He revealed confidences and named names. No conversation was kept in private. Nothing was off-limits.

Thomas said that Mary Karl, the wife of local saloon owner Joseph Karl, overheard a conversation between George Schneider and a man named John Reichling in which they talked of the murders. Karl reported overhearing them say that if they had told what they know "we would have been hung long ago."

He also alleged that Schneider told Peter Strauss, the local undertaker, that he "knew how the murder of the Stelzriede family was done."

None of the people Thomas mentioned would agree to testify on his behalf. Thomas had to ask for subpoenas.

The lawsuits shook Saxtown. People grew worried and frightened. They didn't want to get involved, afraid of what might happen to them if they did. Some changed their stories; some said nothing at all. The situation bred extreme distrust among the farmers of Saxtown. Several of the witnesses Thomas intended to call in his defense claimed they couldn't appear because they were sick. One witness had died.

Thomas settled in and kept fighting the legal battle, hoping it would bring about more information in the case. Perhaps the St. Clair County sheriff would take interest? Or perhaps former sheriff James W. Hughes would offer counsel?

On October 17, 1881, as the Saxtown murder case roared back into public view, Hughes walked through the large limestone columns of the St. Clair County Courthouse in Belleville, the place where he had tried in vain to close the case. Instead, year after year, grand juries were impaneled to look into the case without ever making an indictment.

Hughes was handling a minor legal matter on that Monday—something far less thrilling than an unsolved murder.

The cherry-colored brick courthouse had been built in 1861. It embraced a neoclassical style with a tip of its cap to a Roman temple in Nîmes, France, and a similar look to the Thomas Jefferson–designed Virginia State Capitol.

Hughes, who was alone, left a circuit courtroom on the second floor. He walked underneath the lofty ceilings and descended the cantilevered cast-iron stairs.

His body was found later on the stone basement floor.

Hughes had split open the left side of his head. He was unconscious, but alive, when his body was found. Soon, others rushed to the ex-sheriff's aid as he clung to life. He was taken to his home on South Charles Street, where he was given medical attention. Dr. Washington West trepanned Hughes's skull, which involved drilling a hole in the head to relieve pressure. It did no good. The crack was too big, the blood loss too great.

Hughes died about two hours after he was found.

"He was a great politician, of the Democratic school, and wielded considerable influence," memorialized the *St. Louis Globe,* mentioning little of his law enforcement career.

There were no witnesses. The assumption was that as Hughes descended the staircase, he lost his balance and plunged over a railing and down twenty-five feet to the slab stone floor below.

The news was a blow to Saxtown. While an ineffective investigator, Hughes knew more about the Stelzriede murder case than anyone else alive—other than the murderers. And now he was dead.

US Congressman William R. Morrison attended his funeral. He was buried at the Walnut Hill Cemetery in Belleville, where a monument had been erected to the Stelzriede family.

Soon, amid the jostle of rampant speculation, rumors spread that Hughes hadn't simply fallen, as originally reported. Hughes was only fifty-five years old and known for his impressive physical condition. He didn't seem like someone who could lose his balance and fall over a railing.

Some believed that Hughes had been pushed.

CHAPTER 18

The Case Reopens

"Is the mystery about to be solved?"

The *Belleville Daily Advocate* posed the question in 1882, eight years after the crime.

A stiff March wind blew through St. Clair County under a clear and cold sky, a complementary chill to the thoughts of anyone considering the impending anniversary of the Saxtown murders. Talk, as it had been during all the previous years, was that the case was on the verge of being closed. A new scintillating clue was always just around the corner. But it was always just talk.

The world changed as the Saxtown murder investigation pressed on.

It had taken more than five hours for Saxtown residents to report the murder of the Stelzriedes to Sheriff James Hughes in 1874. By the spring of 1882, such a task was becoming much shorter. Telephone lines were beginning to crisscross cities and change American life.

Messengers on horseback were becoming obsolete.

In St. Louis the Bell Telephone Company was in a legal battle over whether it could place telephone poles on Sixth Street between the busy Olive and Locust Streets. In Belleville, St. Clair County's former sheriff Herman Weber, who had inherited Hughes's office, helped procure telephone depots across the city to connect factories and hotels and railroad depots. They would make reporting crimes much easier. But telephones were still largely business oriented and not in many homes—and far from Saxtown.

"Before the year 1876, the practical uses of the telephone were altogether unknown," the *St. Louis Post-Dispatch* wrote. "The world at large would have scoffed at the idea of hearing words spoken 100 or even fifty miles away. Today the telephone has come to be regarded as an almost necessary part of office furniture. Its use is universal. The ordinary business man says 'Hello' a hundred times oftener every day than he says his prayers."

Telephones were just a precursor to the next new thing: electric lighting. Inventor Thomas Edison created a new incandescent lightbulb in the late 1870s. But before it was put to widespread use, he had to assure everyone that it was safe.

"I beg to say that the system of electric lighting of the Edison Electric Light Company is absolutely free from any possible danger from fire, even in connection with the most inflammable material, and that it is the intention of the Edison Company, before actually furnishing light to the public, to invite your board to give a most critical test of the absolute safety," Edison told the New York Board of Fire Underwriters in an 1881 letter.

Edison's experiments with electricity captivated everyone, and his ideas were soon transferred to criminal justice. By the end of the decade, he testified before a New York state committee seeking to find a "humane method" of execution. Edison said 1,000 volts would "surely kill a man." The electric chair was born.

Despite these innovations (some of which could have been tools to help solve the case if invented a decade before), the people of St. Clair County remained transfixed with the Saxtown murder case. The twists and turns had morphed the hunt for the killers into an action-adventure novel, with detectives going undercover, drunks allegedly implicating themselves, and dying men allegedly confessing to the crime.

While the case hemmed and hawed, the city of Belleville had transformed itself from a quiet village into a smoky manufacturing center where workers built stoves, brewed beer, and put together sewing machines. "It is only a matter of months for Belleville to become the Pittsburgh of the West," the *St. Louis Post-Dispatch* remarked in 1882.

The city was also the epicenter of the reemergence of the long-cold Saxtown investigation.

While Isaiah Thomas found himself in a courtroom fighting slander lawsuits in early 1882, his theory that three men—George Killian, George Schneider, and George Fritzinger—had killed the Stelzriede family caught the attention of R. D. W. Holder, the St. Clair County state's attorney. Holder felt it was time for him to act. The legal squabble had kicked up so much spit and controversy that it was impossible for him to ignore. The nonstop feuding in Saxtown over the murders meant something had to be done to clear everyone's mind.

Holder was a smart and ambitious Democratic politician looking to make a splash. He was fresh out of law school when the Stelzriede murders had spilled onto the pages of newspapers across the country; now, almost eight years later, he was in his second year as the county's top prosecutor. He knew that putting someone to justice in the case would cement his reputation as one of Southern Illinois's finest lawyers.

Holder, a bachelor at thirty-five years old, had grown up in Jefferson County, Illinois, where he learned to fend for himself. His father died in the Mexican-American War, just four months after he was born. The death meant Holder had to scrap during his early life and help support himself. No one was there to do it for him.

Years of hard farm labor helped to send the studious Holder to McKendree College in Lebanon, Illinois, and then to the University of Michigan's law department in 1874. He went to Belleville after graduation and set up a law practice, where he impressed nearly everyone he met. For years he had focused on complicated legal cases and, of course, politics. But now he was trying to solve the Saxtown mystery. To crack the complicated case that had eluded his predecessors.

On Monday, March 6, 1882, the area had just gotten a dose of sensationalism. Days before, Queen Victoria had escaped an assassination attempt in London.

"As the Queen was entering her carriage this evening, a man in the station yard deliberately fired a pistol at her," a special bulletin read, assuring everyone that the long-reigning queen wasn't injured but bragging about her brushes with death. It continued: "Previous to the attempt on her life today the Queen has been three times shot at. Once struck in the face, once threatened with a loaded and once with an unloaded pistol."

But authorities in St. Clair County had something more shocking in store. That day, Isaiah Thomas walked across the stone floors of the county courthouse in Belleville where former sheriff James Hughes had fallen to his death and defended himself against the three men suing him, the latest being George Fritzinger. The stakes were high. Fritzinger was asking for a hefty ten thousand dollars, alleging Thomas had destroyed his reputation.

Thomas said he did not slander them. The schoolteacher and justice of the peace maintained that circumstantial evidence pointed in their direction. Thomas said George Killian, for example, told multiple people in "unguarded moments" that he "knew all about the murder." And in other moments much, much more.

Based on Thomas's insistence, Holder also began to suspect the three men. He believed Killian was the key suspect—the person who knew the gory details and was a possible accessory, but not the actual murderer. Killian had a reputation of liking to drink but being unable to hold his liquor. So Holder figured that Killian, if sweated by authorities, would be willing to tell the Saxtown secrets and roll on the other suspects. A few days in custody without alcohol would be as good as getting him drunk.

Holder needed an indictment, a means "to frighten Killian, and get him to tell the story," the *St. Louis Daily Globe-Democrat* observed. One week later another paper noted that "Killian undoubtedly possesses valuable knowledge, but whether or not he will divulge it remains to be seen."

Holder figured, according to the newspapers, that a grand jury would be "more to frighten Killian, and get him to tell the story, more than anything else."

That Monday, the three suspects were in a stuffy Belleville courtroom watching the civil legal proceeding unfold against Thomas. They hoped to send a message that would end the constant speculation that they were murderers. They partly got what they wanted. After a brief trial Fritzinger won his slander case against Thomas and was awarded by a jury two hundred dollars (not exactly the ten thousand he was looking for, but a victory nonetheless).

Thomas was unfazed by the verdict. He approached reporters afterward and started to tell a scandalous story about Fritzinger but was stopped by his attorney. Before being cut off, Thomas indicated there was a witness willing to come forward and detail the murder conspiracy, but the unnamed person "was in mortal fear that the murderer of the Stelzriedes will murder him for telling what he has told."

Fritzinger's victory didn't last long. New worries were ahead. In the same courthouse another set of jurors was considering testimony that had the potential to vindicate Thomas and upend the case.

The publicity surrounding the lawsuits just amplified the alleged slander.

State's Attorney Holder had impaneled a grand jury. For days jurors had sifted through evidence and heard sworn testimony. Their presence was hardly a secret. Numerous reluctant witnesses, with subpoenas in hand, were questioned—many of whom had refused to testify for Thomas, saying they either were in bad health or didn't want to get involved. Every grand jury for eight years had been charged to hear evidence in the murder case, but had failed to indict a single soul. Holder wanted that to change. He wanted the jurors to take action. And he got his wish.

The grand jury indicted Killian as an accessory "after the fact" in the Stelzriede murders. The news coursed through the courthouse and soon spilled onto the streets normally packed with dressmakers, upholsterers, and undertakers. The town quickly was awash in chatter and commotion about new events in an old case.

"The veil of mystery which has so long enveloped the murder of this German farmer family is about to be lifted and the crime traced to the demon or demons who enacted it," the *St. Louis Republican* newspaper wrote.

When Sheriff Frederick Ropiequet got news of the indictment, he quietly walked up to Killian and took him into custody. Killian appeared prepared. He slipped a sheriff's bailiff five dollars to remain with him in his hotel that night in Belleville before going to jail. That gave him time to avoid questioning and have his lawyer convince a judge to reduce his bail amount from two thousand dollars to five hundred, which he strangely had available and was able to furnish.

Interestingly, Killian was represented by Charles P. Knispel, a Belleville lawyer who had been the state's prosecuting attorney from 1872 to 1876; the Stelzriede case was still fresh at the end of his term. Knispel had been unable to indict any of the men arrested by Sheriff James W. Hughes for the Stelzriede murders. Now he was defending a man who had been indicted for them.

The news of Killian's arrest electrified the telephone exchanges, which sent it into the world beyond. The newspapers couldn't let it alone.

"Light soon to be thrown on the butchery of five persons in St. Clair County eight years ago," the *Chicago Daily Tribune* reported, preparing Illinois as if what was about to come was high theater.

A story soon spread that Killian had taken a portion of the money stolen from the Stelzriedes in exchange for keeping the matter a secret.

"The grand jury believe, as stated by one of their number, that they have taken the step which will revenge the murder of that quiet, industrious and honest German family of Saxtown," the *St. Louis Republican* declared.

Perhaps the three suspects did it to themselves. Their lawsuit against Thomas touched a nerve and became so public that the authorities couldn't ignore the details.

"From yesterday's indictment, the county may thank [Isaiah Thomas] that the perpetrators of the foulest crime committed in any county will be brought to justice," the *St. Louis Times* said.

Killian, Fritzinger, and Schneider appeared to have few friends.

According to testimony before the grand jury, a man named D. A. Robinson had come to Saxtown and opened a coal bank. He had several comrades, including George and Charles Killian, George Schneider, and George Fritzinger, who spent their days "prospecting" the black rock and their nights drinking whiskey together in a rickety cabin they shared near the Stelzriede farm.

In a gully near the Stelzriede home, the men said they were "prospecting" for coal.

"Why they should prospect the farmers could not understand, as everybody knew there was coal in the ground," the *St. Louis Post-Dispatch* wrote. "In places it cropped out."

The Killians and Fritzinger left Saxtown two or three days *after* the murders. Robinson completely disappeared two days *before* the murders. Charles Killian went to East St. Louis, where he later committed suicide (or was murdered, depending on who told the story). George Killian, George Fritzinger, and George Schneider all rattled about before eventually winding up in nearby Millstadt, where they were soon ensnared in Thomas's suspicion.

Fritzinger had the misfortune of living near Thomas.

"When they had all departed the stories which linked their names with the Stelzriede tragedy were told," the *St. Louis Daily Globe-Democrat* reported.

Thomas himself testified before the grand jury that George Killian had said to him, "I know that George Schneider was one of the men who assisted in the murder of the Stelzriedes. He got the most money too. I know who the other murderers are, but I won't tell."

L. J. Wagner and undertaker Peter Strauss corroborated Thomas's claim, both saying that Killian told them that he knew who had murdered the Stelzriede family but that he wouldn't give them away. (Both Wagner and Strauss had been entangled in the civil lawsuits involving the slander allegation.)

Other witnesses testified that one night Killian quarreled with Schneider over the division of money. During a heated exchange he shouted that Schneider was a murderer. They said that Killian had said that he awoke the morning after the murders and saw Schneider asleep near a basin full of bloody water—and wearing a pair of bloody boots. (A bloody trail and bloodstained tobacco leaves found near the murder scene had indicated the murderer may have been injured.) The inference being that Killian inquired about the presence of blood, learned that the Stelzriedes had been killed, and then demanded a cut of the stolen loot to keep quiet.

Perhaps the most personal, sensational claim was testimony from several people that Killian's mother knew various details of the murders and was known to spill the secrets on occasion. She allegedly said that George Fritzinger had done the work.

"George used the knife," Killian's mother reportedly told others. "It took a butcher to use a knife like it was used that night. George is a butcher."

But State's Attorney Holder remained stone-faced and tight-lipped about what hard evidence he had on Killian.

"There's pretty strong evidence that connects Killian with the crime," Holder told reporters. "But this is all that I can say at present to you."

It appeared he focused on what all of the others before him had: the bloody footprint trail.

"The trail from the Stelzriedes' led through the fields to a pond, where it was lost," the *St. Louis Daily Globe-Democrat* reported. "Near the pond a vest with blood spots upon it was found. This vest witnesses alleged was the property of Killian."

Killian later admitted the vest was his, but explained that he had thrown it there while working on the coal in the "hollow back of the Stelzriede house."

"Plaster casts of the boot-prints were taken, and one of these casts shows that a man making the prints wore No. 5 boots that were run down at the heels. Killian is a trifle bandy-legged and runs his boots down at the heels, and a shoemaker named Petrie, who did Killian's shoemaking, testified that the print of the foot on the ground leading to and from the scene of the murder must have been made by Killian or some one wearing his boots," the *St. Louis Daily Globe-Democrat* reported. "Another of the footprints was made by a man wearing an eleven boot, and witnesses claimed that this looked like [George] Schneider's."

Ben Schneider, who had discovered the bodies, testified that he didn't know if his brother wore big or small shoes.

Then came stories about the chain of events after Ben found the bodies.

It was said that George Schneider walked to the crime scene with others after the discovery and fainted as the Stelzriede house appeared in the distance. George Killian, who was with him, walked into the Stelzriede house, looked at the covered bodies, and reportedly said of Anna,

"Let me see how bad her head is hammered out of shape and if that eye is sticking out yet."

"Upon the day that the murders were discovered, Killian, in entering the house where the five ghastly butchered corpses lay, cold and stiff in their clotted blood, and gazing upon the revolting spectacle, by his manner of acting and appearance attracted the attention of a few who were close observers of all that was going on," State's Attorney Holder said.

The witnesses of those comments—farmer Fred Eckert Sr., whose own son was once accused of the murders, and laborer Nick Baum, who boarded with the accused men—testified that they asked Killian how he knew this unless he had previously seen the body. Killian said very little and walked out of the house. He left with George Schneider. When they had gotten about two hundred yards from the Stelzriede property, Schneider fainted a second time. He was so weak that they had to stop for a while at the farmhouse of neighbor John Schellhouse.

Testimony soon turned to Monk, the Stelzriedes' dog that was found alive at the scene but shut in a back room. The murderer was able to kill five people, including a baby, but apparently refrained from killing a dog.

"Those finding [Monk] argued that those committing the murder had known the dog, for he had been running at large the night before and must have entered the house at the heels of the murders," the *St. Louis Daily Globe-Democrat* reported. "Then they argued the murderers had locked the beast up after finishing their bloody work, to prevent him from following them."

Fritzinger had sold the dog to the Stelzriedes.

When Killian faced reporters, he told them, "I know no more about the murders of the Stelzriedes than you do."

Asked if he ever had said that he knew who killed the Stelzriede family, Killian replied, "I don't remember that I ever did say I knew who they were, but you know a man will say a good deal when he is drunk."

Killian declared that he had enemies in Saxtown who were trying to ruin him.

His story after the murders was long and winding. Killian, a laborer who would do anything for pay, initially went to Du Quoin in Perry

County, Illinois. Talk of the murders there, while a good distance away, was rampant because Carl Stelzriede's brother, Charles, lived in a neighboring county.

People in the area grew impressed with the gossip Killian appeared to have about the crime. But it appeared as if he knew too much. News of his knowledge spread back to St. Clair County. A group of people there sent a private detective to Perry County to see if Killian had any worthwhile information or was connected to the horror.

The operation was done undercover.

The detective became a laborer on the same farm where Killian was working. Over time he befriended the suspected killer. The two laughed and talked and drank. Eventually, Killian started having him over to his house for dinner in the evenings and on Sundays. Killian would drink to excess and often talk about the Stelzriede murders, his red face getting redder with each intoxicating sip. The undercover detective, soaking it all in, witnessed that when Killian drank too much, he hit and punched his wife.

The detective could do little to help, considering his real motive was to entrap Killian and claim thousands of dollars in reward money. But he knew that was his opportunity. The wives always have details. And an abused wife might be willing to share even more if it meant her husband might be locked up.

The detective befriended the wife. He reportedly consoled her after the beatings, sympathized with her awful situation, and listened to her problems.

Killian frequently got drunk and browbeat his wife and called her names. He threatened that he was going to desert her. The tearful wife confided in the detective that that would never happen because she knew too much, saying she could make trouble for her husband. If she wanted.

She said that she could tell authorities about something he had done in St. Clair County.

The detective eventually left the area and told his story to the *St. Louis Republican*. He said that he had learned much about the Stelzriede murder from Killian—and that "Killian is one of the Stelzriedes' murderers." He also said it was a conspiracy that involved four people.

"Yes sir, they have got one of the Stelzriede murderers this time, and you can bet on it," the detective told a reporter. "George Killian helped to do that job, and you can say so."

Killian's battered wife, however, never came forward to implicate him in the crime.

Killian, out on bail, soon returned to Belleville with his lawyer, Knispel, to quash the indictment, which they said was based on no evidence but hearsay. Dozens of Saxtown residents who had viewed the Stelzriede bodies after they were found arrived in Belleville to watch.

"The desire of punishing the offenders is as strong today as on the morning after the tragedy," the *St. Louis Post-Dispatch* observed.

No matter how much time had passed, St. Clair County wanted to avenge the Stelzriede deaths.

The courthouse crowd didn't get what they wanted. Judge William H. Snyder, who had through his years on the bench seen a handful of Saxtown suspects come and go, announced informally that he would quash the indictment, freeing Killian from the suspicion that hung over his head.

But Killian would spend the rest of his life defending himself.

CHAPTER 19

Hounded by Suspicion

"I HAVE BEEN HOUNDED NEARLY TO DEATH."

George Killian was haunted by suspicion. He couldn't shake the rumors. The petty whispers that, at best, he had covered up a brutal murder and—at worst—helped commit it.

"For twenty-three years I have been under suspicion of having killed the Stelzriede family," Killian said in 1897, more than twenty years after the murders. "I did not kill them. I don't know who did. But they keep on accusing me and giving me no peace. I will sue them and make them shut up."

No matter. He had sued before, and it never vanquished the suspicion.

Many of his old accusers had died off. But younger ones heard the local lore and spread it around. Killian walked among people who thought that he was cold enough, diabolical enough to raise an ax above an infant's head and crush its skull.

There was no real legal recourse for Killian. No lawsuit that would restore his name or stop the speculation. The residents of St. Clair County had decided that he knew something about the five-person murder. They wouldn't let him forget it, even if a judge had already set him free. No slander suit would quiet the Saxtown farmers' flapping lips.

Killian had sued Isaiah Thomas shortly after a judge quashed his indictment. He said Thomas went after him just to collect the large reward money offered in the case, like all of the private detectives, including the undercover detective who befriended his ex-wife.

"Killian claimed that Thomas offered him $1,000 if he would swear that George Fritzinger did the deed, and tried to tempt Mrs. Killian with a like amount to swear away the life of her husband," the *St. Louis Post-Dispatch* reported.

He was awarded nominal monetary damages—but it didn't restore his reputation.

Now, more than a decade later, in 1897, Killian looked back on the past twenty-three years "fighting for his good name, defying his accusers and protesting his innocence of the terrible charge they make by word of mouth and shrugging of shoulders."

William Hermann, who had taken over as village constable from William Bangert, was just about the only law enforcement agent left who was still investigating the case. He zeroed in on Killian. He watched his movements. Listened to his conversations. And talked about him.

"Bill Hermann and Peter Wagner are talking about me all the time," Killian told a reporter, indicating that he was going to sue them for saying he had something to do with the Stelzriede murders.

"Let him sue me," Hermann said. "It won't do him any good."

"Have you accused him?" Hermann was asked.

"I have talked about him like everybody else," Hermann said.

"Have you any special information as which to base a suspicion?"

"No," Hermann said. "I know nothing more than everybody else knows. I have not talked about the case for the last seven or eight months. I can't understand why Killian should want to get at me."

Almost a quarter century after the Stelzriedes were murdered, the men and women of Saxtown still feuded.

Killian, a drunk, spent his days laboring in fields and nights drinking in barrooms, plotting revenge. In Millstadt, where he lived a few miles from Saxtown, the conversation always turned to the Stelzriedes. No matter what. Nothing else seemed as interesting as the fading memory of the murders. And Killian was living flesh to blame. The German farmers sipped their beers and looked at him square to see if he was lying.

Killian was now forty years old and still fighting accusations of something that had happened when he was a young man. He had long ago divorced the wife he had beaten and threatened to leave.

"He is five feet six inches high, squarely, stockily built and strong as an ox," the *St. Louis Post-Dispatch* said.

Strength wasn't a positive attribute. It was a code that roused suspicion. The Stelzriede murderer, everyone knew, had to possess brute strength.

"In his younger days he was ready to fight any man on any provocation," the *Post-Dispatch* said. "His manner is frank, but his eyes of ashen gray, shifting constantly. His movements and speech are rapid. He laughs much like one who has been under a severe nervous strain for a long time. He laughs long over trifles and there is no mirth in his laugh."

Killian had been judged guilty in the barrooms and firesides and butcher shops. His uneasy laugh was a sign that he knew everyone was afraid of him—even though they outwardly acted as though they liked him.

That's not to say that the other men previously accused of the crime got away easy. The suspicion remained. But Killian's shifty demeanor put the spotlight on himself.

In the years and decades after the Stelzriede murders, Killian maintained that he was asleep the night the Stelzriedes died. Who did he say could verify his alibi? None other than George Schneider, the butcher and coal miner also implicated in the case. "I can prove by George Schneider that I slept at his house that night and did not leave it," Killian said.

After all, in drunken conversations, he had said that he woke up that morning and saw Schneider asleep next to a basin full of blood-colored water, and that Schneider gave him a cut of the Stelzriede loot. That alone indicated that Schneider, his witness, wasn't at home the night of the murders.

Killian drank and drank. His story twisted and turned.

One night in 1899, at a tavern, a Saxtown resident named Fred Muskopf accused Killian of murdering the Stelzriede family.

Killian couldn't take it anymore. The slander couldn't be solved with lawsuits or shouts of innocence.

The two men fought. And then Muskopf brandished a knife.

Killian was badly beaten. His once-sturdy frame could no longer win a fight. He endured several "dangerous knife wounds."

Killian remained steadfast. While drunk and bleeding he declared that "in the future he will tolerate no further aspersions and will resort to desperate measures to protect himself from vile slurs and insinuations."

Haunted and hounded until the end.

The violent streak worsened. Eight years later, he had an altercation with a woman named Louisa Boehm. He allegedly tried to beat her to death with a pair of shoes.

Killian was charged with attempted murder.

CHAPTER 20

Land of the Free

WHEN THE SLEUTHS CAME TO SHADOW THE SAXTOWN SUSPECTS, FRED Boeltz planned his escape.

It was the one hundredth anniversary of the Declaration of Independence. Men wore powdered wigs and remembered their forefathers. Children heard the now age-old stories of Franklin, Jefferson, Washington. The city of Philadelphia hosted a grand Centennial Exhibition.

The Fourth of July in 1876 was celebrated with much brio in cities and towns across the nation. In St. Clair County the locals became introspective, having prepared a historical sketch of their accomplishments. They talked of overcoming warlike tribes of Indians; the building of bridges and roads; the hammering of railways; the construction of schools, breweries, and factories.

"Who shall limit man's invention, or resist the combination of his power, when he drives tunnels under the rivers and through mountains, and chains the lightning, encircling the globe with a cable, and sending messages and receiving answers within a few seconds," the document concluded. "We unveil no statue chiseled in marble, or granite, or made of bronze, to commemorate their noble deeds and exalted virtues, but we bring the tribute of grateful hearts in which their memories are enshrined. And here under the brilliant rays of the summer sun, on this joyful day of our national birth, let us pledge each to the other, for ourselves our children and children's children, to transmit these blessings unimpaired to future generations. That will cause the next Centennial to be even more glorious than this."

And they talked of German immigration to St. Clair County.

"Immigration from the Germanic States set in with a flood tide, attracted by the superior quality and cheapness of our lands, the abundant harvests, and favorable location for home markets and foreign commerce. This stream of emigrants continued for several consecutive years, adding to our numbers wealth, intelligence, and enterprise, embracing many families of culture and refinement . . ."

That year, Fred Boeltz and his wife successfully petitioned a St. Clair County probate court for a share of the Stelzriede estate. They got some cash but not the farmland, the one thing many Germans valued more than money.

So Boeltz began setting the course for his exit.

As the nation swathed its buildings in bunting and sang patriotic songs to celebrate its grand anniversary, Boeltz initiated the process of becoming an American citizen.

A year later, on October, 6, 1877, he walked across the stone floor of the St. Clair County Courthouse in Belleville. He stood before a county clerk, swore on a Bible, and renounced any remaining loyalty he had to his native Oldenburg, Germany. He was an American now.

Boeltz was made a citizen of the United States of America under the same roof where three years prior he had been accused of murder.

A few years passed. Boeltz and his wife had another baby. And they prepared for another move. Another new life on another frontier.

They disappeared from Saxtown in 1886 after Isaiah Thomas pulled St. Clair County authorities back into the Stelzriede case. Boeltz, along with his wife and eight children—Katherina, John, Gustav, Emma, Amelia, Fred Jr., Henry, and Tillie—were never seen in St. Clair County or Illinois again.

His name was rarely mentioned again in connection with the murders, despite his being judged guilty by Sheriff James W. Hughes and in the minds of many of his neighbors in the days after the Stelzriede bodies were discovered. Suspect George Killian took the spotlight in the years after the crime. Boeltz faded away. His reported lack of concern for his in-laws, his inability to "shed a tear," his nervous body language at the murder scene, his feud with the Stelzriedes, his relationship with grubber John Afken, his wet boots—all seemed forgotten.

With his debts to the Stelzriedes erased, Boeltz headed to Nebraska. The land of the Oregon Trail, the Mormon Trail, the Pony Express—and cheap dirt.

Boeltz was land hungry. He was born with that lust. In his early years in Germany opportunities were limited and land ownership was available only to a chosen few.

His new citizenship gave him options.

After years of failure and financial problems in St. Clair County, he found his coveted ground in Merrick County, Nebraska, a sparsely populated area north of the Platte River. The county seat was Central City. It previously had been called Lone Tree. Residents who promoted the change said the name Lone Tree "gives the impression that the area is so desolate that it can afford support to only one solitary tree, and that the inhabitants are a wild, rough, uncouth, and uncivilized people."

Boeltz had managed to find a new home even more isolated than Saxtown. A place where he could forget his past. The accusations. The more than a month spent behind bars for a crime he may or may not have committed.

A few miles northwest of there, the Homestead Act gave Boeltz free ground—if he would just live on the desolate stretch for a few years. Now the Boeltzes were pioneers.

Boeltz and his strapping boys went to work. They built a sprawling farm in Midland Township near Archer, Nebraska, a sad cobble of homes and grain elevators along a Burlington and Missouri River Railroad depot. They had some money for construction. They hammered together a one-and-a-half-story frame house, a fourteen-by-thirty-two-foot horse barn, a twelve-by-forty-foot stable for more horses and machinery, a twelve-by-sixteen-foot corn crib, a twelve-by-forty-two-foot granary, a sixteen-by-twenty-four-foot buggy shed, a twelve-by-twenty-four-foot cow barn, an eighteen-by-twenty-four-foot shed, a fourteen-by-twenty-eight-foot kitchen, and an eight-by-ten-foot windmill.

They raised cattle and grew corn.

Life was tough out there. Filled with the pitfalls of farm life. Their hands cracked and bled while husking corn. Their minds raced while waiting for rain. But they were free. Free from the feudal chains of Germany. Free from the suspicions of Saxtown.

Boeltz built a better life for himself in the sun-dappled cornfields of Nebraska. He said the land was "prairie and bluff land most valuable for grazing." In 1893 the property was valued at three thousand dollars.

Curiously, Boeltz had made a slight alteration on his road to Nebraska. He started signing his last name with an *s*. It was now "Boelts."

It was a minor change but a noticeable one. Almost all of his previous documents, before he began the process of moving to Nebraska, used the name Boeltz. Including the chattel mortgage held by the Stelzriedes that tied up his property and made him so mad.

By 1899 Boeltz had amassed 480 acres in Nebraska. Free and clear from chattels and mortgages, the chains once held over his head by his in-laws.

Through the years, the land was parceled out and taken over by his sons, John, Gustav, Henry, and Fred Jr. Son Gustav and daughter Tillie became schoolteachers. By 1917 the Boeltz family land had expanded and expanded—eventually straddling the Chicago, Burlington, and Quincy Railroad line.

Frederick Boeltz died a month after his wife on October 16, 1902, and left behind hundreds of acres of land. He was buried at the Archer Evangelical Community Cemetery—in a marked grave etched with the last name B-O-E-L-T-S.

CHAPTER 21

Gone, but Not Forgotten

JULIUS R. HUGHES WAS AT WORK WHEN THE FURTIVE CLOUDS APPEARED in the distance.

More than two decades had passed since the former St. Clair County sheriff's deputy spent his days and nights in Saxtown searching for the Stelzriedes' killer. The excitement was behind him.

On May 27, 1896, almost fifteen years had elapsed since his father, James W. Hughes, died at the St. Clair County Courthouse from a mysterious fall over a staircase railing. In the years after, the younger Hughes had traded his badge to become a surveyor, and then a clerk for the East St. Louis & Carondelet Rail Way. He had failed to achieve his father's notoriety. He had grabbed attention while assisting his father's failed investigation of the Saxtown murders—and then nothing after.

Until that warm and sticky Wednesday afternoon.

While Hughes was near the jumble of railroad tracks in East St. Louis, a scary-looking mass developed west above St. Louis shortly after the noon hour.

Across the river the still air was filled with talk of three things: weather, politics, and silver. The Republican Party was divided over using silver as currency over the gold standard. An epic showdown was just weeks away, when the party's national convention was set to convene in St. Louis.

But politics and monetary policy would soon become trivial.

At four o'clock in the afternoon the warning signs were clear. The western sky was a giant wall of low clouds, the heat was oppressive, and the wind was still.

Thermometers hit eighty-six degrees. High humidity left everyone sweaty.

Then lightning strikes slashed from the sky. The winds started to rage. Three funnel clouds sprung from the clouds and decimated St. Louis—then leapt across the Mississippi River to East St. Louis.

"So destructive was the storm, and so irresistible, that some of the stanchest business blocks went down before it," the *New York Times* wrote of the devastation in St. Louis. "Iron beams were torn from their fastenings and carried blocks away, as if they were feathers. Roofs braced and held to their positions by every device known to the best builders of the day were torn off as if held only by threads. Telegraph poles fell in long rows, not coming down one by one, but in groups of a dozen or more at a time."

In East St. Louis the storm rocked the crowded rail yards, throwing cars and twisting metal tracks. Fifteen clerks were killed at one depot alone. In total, 118 people were killed in East St. Louis. As rain fell and thunder clapped in the hours after the storm, relatives pushed through the crackle of live electrical wires to find their loved ones. They competed with "ghouls" picking the pockets of the dead and injured.

The more honest searchers "would run from one temporary morgue to another, and in some instances push aside dead bodies in order to attempt to identify their relatives, and, when found, the cries would melt a heart of stone," said one newspaper account. "A mother would behold the distorted features of an only son, while at another place some other member would find a missing father, brother or daughter."

Among the dead was Julius Hughes.

The devastating tornado headed east and sliced through Southern Illinois, hitting the farms of Richview and Irvington, where Sheriff James Hughes had gone more than twenty years before to arrest various relatives of the Stelzriede family. Thirteen people there were killed.

Julius's death was symbolic. The Saxtown farmers took it as one more sign that anyone who investigated the case would somehow be doomed. They remembered the strange death of Julius's father. An ominous curse appeared to be at play.

Coroner John J. Ryan, who had commanded the Stelzriede inquest, had become ill in the months following the murders. The health problems dogged Ryan, already an old man, in the years following the murders—so much so that he once was erroneously reported to have died.

Isaiah W. Thomas, the man who had become obsessed with the case and fought civil lawsuits while trying to solve it, developed a long-term illness shortly after his persistence led to the indictment of George Killian. His wife, Hannah, died later that year. Thomas died five years later, in 1887, at the St. Clair County Poor Farm and Hospital.

The deaths of Julius Hughes and Thomas, important links to the investigation, didn't guarantee that the case would go cold forever. The actions of someone else made sure of that.

Two years before Julius was killed in the tornado, it was discovered that the St. Clair County grand jury investigative papers looking into the Stelzriede case had been stolen.

"There is no official record of the crime," the *St. Louis Post-Dispatch* lamented in 1897. "One who undertakes now to inquire into the case cannot draw the line between fact and baseless tradition. What was a mystery twenty-three years ago is now a hundred-fold a mystery."

Those in Saxtown and Millstadt remained obsessed with the mystery and pointing fingers. Such was their nature. Even the death of Mary Peter, the beautiful bride, continued to fuel unrest. Ten years after that crime, area resident George Wagner had a warrant issued for another man's arrest, saying the man had gossiped and accused him of having killed Peter. The case was dropped.

Legend reigned in the hills and hollows of Saxtown. At the dawn of the twentieth century, the men and women who had carried the Stelzriede family from their small farmhouse to their unmarked graves were almost all dead. And any futile hopes of bringing the killer to justice were dashed. Reality set in.

George Fritzinger killed himself in 1883, a year after he had won a judgment against Thomas for publicly accusing him of having committed the Saxtown murders. George Schneider, his alleged accomplice, died in

1907 at age sixty-six. He was buried in the Freivogel Cemetery, where the Stelzriedes had been laid to rest thirty-three years before.

The Stelzriede relatives in Washington and Jefferson Counties—Charles Stelzriede and sons—were shunned by Saxtonites. The nine-foot sandstone monument they had purchased at the Walnut Hill Cemetery in Belleville had to go unused. The Saxtown farmers had prevented the sexton from moving the bodies there, and the Zion Evangelical Church, which operated the Freivogel Cemetery, adopted an order prohibiting any removal.

Despite appearing to be feeble and near death in the days and months after his brother and family were killed in Saxtown, Charles lived for many more years on his farm near Richview. As the closest blood relative, he inherited most of their estate. Some of that money went to the monument, which by 1897 had gone "neglected."

"The monument tells us well of the tardiness of justice," it was observed.

St. Louis Globe Managing Editor Joseph McCullagh found other stories to fuel his broadsheet, from politics to murder. At the end of 1896, he had grown sick and old. On December 31 his body was found on the ground beneath his second-story window. His doctor said that there was "little doubt that McCullagh took his own life" and jumped out of his window. Friends disputed that account.

He was remembered and memorialized throughout the country. The *St. Louis Chronicle* said McCullagh was "the greatest editor in the West. He was one of the select to which Horace Greeley, Murat Halstead and Charles Dana belong." His journalistic style helped tell the story of the Saxtown murders and the ensuing events in a way that newspapers had not done with crime just a few years before.

Ben Schneider and his wife, Kate, stayed in Millstadt.

The town was much different than when he had first arrived from Saxtown—and much different than when the news of the Stelzriedes' death was shouted from tavern to tavern. Millstadt now had a bank, a lumberyard, a lighting plant, ten saloons, and easy transportation.

It was no longer cut off from the rest of the world. Paved streets made travel easier—even in the springtime wetness. Cars now shared the roads with horses.

"Millstadt is kind of a paradox," the *St. Louis Post-Dispatch* observed. "It appears to sleep as tranquilly as an English hamlet, and yet it has, in its degree, the finished appearance of a modern city."

Ben was a janitor at the Millstadt Public School "until old age and disability caused his retirement." He couldn't forget what he had witnessed when he tipped open the Stelzriedes' front door, setting off the Saxtown mystery. Schoolchildren knew what he had witnessed. They often asked him about it, and his stories contributed to the growing lore.

In 1924, on the fiftieth anniversary of the murders, Schneider still had to read the headlines: BAFFLING MURDER OF FIVE HALF CENTURY AGO STILL A MYSTERY.

"Suspicion also centered on left handed men, as the clubbing and cutting was done by one who held the club and knife in his left hand," the *Millstadt Enterprise* reported.

Even fifty years later, Ben, never implicated in the case, couldn't escape the town's whispers. After all, he was left-handed.

He died in 1927 at age eighty-one. His news obituary made no mention of the Saxtown murders. Kate died a few years later at age ninety.

Reverend Jacob Knauss, the evangelical minister who had helped the fearful Saxtonites find God in their violent world, lived almost seven years past 1874, and through much of the suspense and suspicion. The man remembered for his compassion died on March 10, 1881, while battling pneumonia. He had contracted it while preaching a funeral.

The Eckert family maintained their acreage near the site of the murders until natural causes killed them off. Locals always strongly suspected them of having some role in the killings; that suspicion continues even today. The Stelzriede house was sold at auction and purchased by an estate administrator. Since then, the property has known only three owners over a century-plus span, with the current owner being Randy Eckert—a descendant of the Eckert family.

Peter Muskopf bought the property in the 1880s.

"The Stelzriedes had money," he declared. "That's why they got murdered. We have no money, and so we are safe."

Muskopf wasn't dirt poor. But he was close. After all, he raised a family in a small, rectangular house where the blood of five people had stained the floors.

His view was the one adopted by nearly every soul living in Saxtown: The Stelzriedes had died because of their money—or rumors that they had it. The lesson: Never talk about money, even if you have it. And take it to the bank.

Most wondered why Muskopf wanted to live in the house.

"The house still stands on the lonely country road," the *St. Louis Post-Dispatch* observed years after the crime. "It has been enlarged and a porch built on the front. Under the carpet in the 'best' room there are dark stains made by the life blood of the Stelzriedes. On the woodwork are the dents made by misdirected blows of a murderous hammer."

In 1897, Muskopf, who had lived in the house for twelve years, talked to a reporter about the Stelzriede case and the rumors that swirled about. His neighbors were talking about him. They weren't casting aspersions that he had committed the crime. They were saying that he was living in a haunted house.

"No," Muskopf said. "We don't mind living in the house. And as for ghosts, if there are such things, we have never seen any of them around here."

Muskopf grew old in the house. He lived there well into his eighties—even after his son, Charles, and grandson, Percy, took over the property.

Percy played in the yard where the murderers had once walked, and on the wood floors where the Stelzriede children had left their toys the night before they were killed. The house was a constant reminder of what had happened.

Percy said a curious old man would walk by on the dusty country road in front of the house. An old man who appeared to know too much.

"He come every day past our yard," Percy later told the *Belleville News-Democrat*. "I won't mention no names, because his family is still in town. . . . I was eight or nine. I'd be on the porch or playing in the yard. He'd stop and start talking about the murders."

True to form, Percy sought to protect the name of the person. No need to ruffle any feathers. Saxtonites had been scared into not talking too loudly or saying too much. Fear of retribution had been ingrained in them.

The old man seemed to have a split personality to Percy. He would ramble, then switch to coherent words that painted "clear pictures of the crime."

"He told us Stelzriede had a big club sitting by the door," Percy said, indicating that the Stelzriedes were unable to fight back with a weapon. "But it didn't get moved during the murder. It was just sitting there like he never got to it."

Percy said the man knew for sure that the family had received money from Germany, and he believed that the man "may have been the murderer."

"It was in a basket," Percy said, referencing the willow basket Fritz Stelzriede was seen holding at the auction before he was murdered. "There was a big log hanging in that big room where they were murdered. It was ten inches square. . . .

"That old fella that used to come by told us: 'That's where the basket was hanging that the money was in.' When they found the bodies, the basket was still hanging, but the money was gone."

He continued: "They all had their throats cut. They was hit with a hatchet on their heads. That must have been a bloody mess. To kill five of them in that room. It was about eighteen foot square where it took place."

Percy slept in that room. His family sold the property to Jessie and Leslie Jines in 1945. Percy died in 1999.

No one was ever prosecuted for the Saxtown murders.

Almost from the beginning, the Stelzriede case became a synonym for failed investigations. A reference and guidepost for future unsolved tragedies. It was common for newspapers to reference the Saxtown murders when it appeared that a killer was escaping justice.

When police were investigating the murder of Lizzie Schmidt, a seven-year-old girl found raped and suffocated in O'Fallon, Illinois, the *St. Louis Globe Democrat* wrote: "It is to be hoped that this affair will not be allowed to remain a mystery, like the Stelzriede murder, but that the guilty will be hunted down and punished as he deserves."

Decade after decade, the St. Louis area slowly forgot about the Saxtown murders. Their nightmares were replaced by new horrors. But Saxtonites remained afraid. As late as the 1940s, locals feared that the Stelzriedes' killer would strike again.

"Stories about [the murders] circulated and were kept alive for years," the *Millstadt Enterprise* wrote in 1954.

The murders had a significant impact on the people of Saxtown. They often declined to discuss the incident with outsiders, giving preference to cruel whispers among themselves. Residents were afraid to flaunt money for fear of attack. They worried that they, too, would be murdered.

In 1921 sixty-six-year-old farmer Leonard Kolter was found dead in a stall of his barn with his hands and feet bound and a gunny sack over his head. Kolter, who lived alone on his farm north of Belleville, had been bludgeoned to death. His house was ransacked.

Kolter was a bachelor. His death set off a family feud over his estate.

Fingerprints were taken. Two unidentified men had been spotted leaving the scene. Rumors had persisted before his death that Kolter had buried money on his farm.

The case went unsolved.

The newspapers immediately drew comparisons to the Stelzriede case. But it represented how much the case had faded from everyone's minds—except those living around Saxtown. The *St. Louis Post-Dispatch*, when reporting on the crime, got the Stelzriede family's name wrong.

CHAPTER 22

Ghosts

LESLIE JINES WANTED TO TURN THE STELZRIEDE HOUSE TO DUST.

In the 1950s, he was tired of hearing about the Saxtown murders. Tired of the gawking passersby. Tired of the ghost stories. Tired of telling people where he lived and getting the same response over and over: "Oh yes, I know. The place where the Stelzriede murder was committed." Ghost stories had long been part of public discussion.

"That the unfettered spirits of the dead can wing their way back to earth, and make their intangible presence known to mortal vision, is an accomplishment which large portions of human kind will eagerly admit," the *St. Louis Daily Globe* noted. "In the days of chivalry every castle had its ghost, and every night the weird form flitted on the draw bridge or held orgies with its fellows in the crested tower."

As investigators sought the Stelzriedes' murderer in the days after the bodies were found, news stories were dedicated to the supposed ghost of a beautiful St. Louis woman who had hanged herself on a bedpost on St. Patrick's Day because she had been ravaged by a disease.

"Though the world at large does not admit it, yet frequent instances are recorded where the etherial [*sic*] part of man springs back to its native earth and holds dread communion with its old associates," the *Globe* reported. "Many have felt the clammy spell of the grave and been shocked by the apparition of departed friends."

Saxtonites were certain that their departed friends, or perhaps the killers of those friends, were still present in Jines's house.

Jines and his wife, Jessie, had bought the house and farm in 1945 from the Muskopf family. They had moved to the country from East St. Louis, where Jines worked for the M & O Motor Company.

By 1954 the house had seen better days—if it had ever had any good ones. The Jineses had the house—made of heavy, squared logs—demolished to make way for a brand-new house over the same foundation. The tear-down generated a small crowd and some fresh headlines. But Jines thought that would do it. End the talk. The speculation. The haunting stories. Close the "book on the Stelzriede murder mystery" eighty years after it began.

It didn't.

Talk of ghosts continued. The Jines's new house, a small, boxlike structure, was a spartan 1950s-style block meant for shelter and nothing more. But the house appeared to adopt the same myths and legends of the original structure. People were convinced some force was at work amid the quiet woods and fields of Saxtown.

The Jineses kept in place the old Stelzriede barn—the wooden structure that was central to the German-American family's farmstead. It was also the place that housed the Stelzriede bodies before they were put onto the back of wagons and taken to Freivogel Cemetery for burial.

Leslie Jines died in 1963. His wife continued to live in the house until she died in 1985.

Randy Eckert, then a young man in his thirties with a Midwestern accent and a pronounced mustache, took over the property. Eckert is a relative of the Eckert family that lived next door to the Stelzriedes in the nineteenth century. He stayed in the Jines house for about a week before something unexplainable happened.

Eckert and his wife were awakened by what sounded like a door closing and then by a dog barking. They looked outside and searched the small house and its surroundings. Nothing was there. But their own dog was posted silently at the foot of the bed—shivering, shaking. Scared to death.

Did the Eckerts have a brush with the long-dead Stelzriede family? Was their dog Monk still howling at an unknown killer?

Eckert didn't know. But he said the sounds recurred through the years. Particularly around the anniversary of the murders.

His story got out and was repeated in newspaper articles and barroom gossip. Eckert took the experience in stride—unafraid to give interviews and always hospitable to the curious onlookers who drove by the house looking for a brush with the paranormal.

He built a big house near the property at the end of a tree-shaded lane. He began renting out the smaller place that the Jineses had constructed on the old Stelzriede homesite.

Chris Nauman rented the house in the 1990s and reported his own fright-filled experience.

"It was six o'clock in the morning, and there was a loud knock at the door," Nauman said. "At the same time my girlfriend heard someone walking up the steps in our basement."

Nauman got out of bed. Checked the front door, and then the stairs. No one was there. The property appeared empty.

Nauman scratched his head and moved on.

The next day, Nauman told Eckert about what had happened. He asked him if the anniversary of the murders was coming up.

Eckert responded with a wry sense of irony.

"No, it was yesterday," he said.

"A cold shiver ran up my spine," Nauman remembered.

Through the years, tenants have come and gone—always aware of the historic murder. Some have heard things. Dogs barking. Doors closing. Hands knocking.

The place has become a magnet for old people on Sunday drives and teenagers looking for a good scare. Eckert says he often finds young people in his driveway, looking for the house of the murders. He always directs them to the right spot.

The murder case has enthralled those interested in the paranormal.

"Those of us native to this region know that the face of familiar landscapes has a way of changing as day turns to night," wrote Suzanne Hutcherson in a magazine article on the Saxtown murders. "At night, the boundaries between past and present can seem less distinct. The unexpected—and unimaginable—can take us by surprise.

"Such things still abide on Saxtown Road. Anna Stelzriede still sings lullabies and cradles her children. Monk still cries in the darkness. And whatever beckons entry at the threshold of the former Stelzriede homestead continues to seek its absolution for a crime that, now, only God can bestow."

In the 1980s psychics and spiritual mediums surrounded the property to look for gold said to have been hidden and buried by the Stelzriedes. None was ever found.

In recent years Eckert has allowed so-called "ghost hunters" onto the property.

The men set up video and audio equipment in the house seeking to track the voices of dead humans. A far cry from the primitive technology that helped the Stelzriede murders go unsolved.

Eckert said the equipment has picked up faint voices.

But Eckert noted that they were speaking English.

"Wouldn't they be talking in German?" he asked.

One paranormal researcher grew so afraid of the home that he said he'd never return.

"He said bad luck started happening to him; he broke his leg and some other things after he left here," Eckert said.

Perhaps it was the same malediction that appeared to strike Sheriff James Hughes, his son, and so many others as they investigated the case.

The Saxtown curse appeared to be at work more than a century later.

CHAPTER 23

Whodunit

TWO HUNDRED MEN AND WOMEN WALKED THROUGH THE CREAKY IRON gate of Saxtown's Freivogel Cemetery. In front of them stood the Stelzriede family.

Their hands moved, their bodies swayed. Carl was gray and rotund. Fritz was dressed in black; his wife, Anna, cradled a baby in her arms.

It was the year 2010.

The vanished world of dead bodies and German utterances was before the onlookers. It wasn't a ghost sighting or a scientific miracle. It was a "cemetery walk" held on an overcast Saturday to celebrate the 175th anniversary of the Zion Evangelical Church in Millstadt. The same church that had buried the Stelzriedes.

Folks dressed like figures from the past. They were the physical form of the bones buried somewhere beneath their feet. More than a century after their religious brethren had banded together to stop their bodies from being moved to another town, the Stelzriede family was once again the star attraction. The crowd jostled to get a view.

"I was decapitated and lost three fingers," said Terry Buecher, who played Fritz.

He talked of the depression, the struggles, the inherited gold—which was never found or proven to have ever existed.

"I was proud when our hard times were over," he said. "We had suffered as farmers for a long time. We had a lot of drought conditions and things weren't good. [The inheritance] was a sign that our troubles were over."

There was one actor missing: someone to play the murderer. There couldn't have been. After 136 years the Saxtown killer remained faceless.

There is no way to know for sure who he was. The secret will remain buried deep in the ground just like the Stelzriedes in their unmarked graves.

"And, who knows, a grave in that same cemetery may hold the secret of the Saxtown murders," wrote Wilson Baltz, a dentist who fictionalized the case in 1974 for the weekly *Millstadt Enterprise.* "Forever."

The newspaper issued a disclaimer, saying, "Some names remain the same; others have been changed to protect the privacy of living relatives."

That is the nature of a small town.

Remonstrance from many of Saxtown's older folks was to not put anything in writing, to not point the finger in any direction. To not name names. Especially because so many men had been accused and arrested on the flimsiest of evidence.

The lore of the Saxtown murders has become a generational affair. Passed down over time, spanning President Ulysses S. Grant to an era of presidents not yet known.

"The story gets bigger than life the older it gets," Mark Westhoff once said. "God only knows what really happened there."

Westhoff is the former director of the St. Clair County Historical Society. A native of Millstadt, he has heard the stories of the Saxtown murders for as long as he can remember. In the 1980s they became the basis for a lecture series titled "Legends, Folklore, and Tales of St. Clair County."

In his baritone voice Westhoff recounted the mythos of the case. That a private detective slept under the floor of a suspect's bedroom in hopes of hearing him talk in his sleep. That a wife of a suspect took unusual lengths to keep everyone away from her husband's deathbed for fear he would confess.

But the one thing the audience wanted to know was who did it. Who escaped the hangman's hand? Who got away with murder?

"You could make a case to blame everybody," Westhoff once said. "I could make a case to blame [several of the neighbors]. I could even make a case to blame the guy who found the bodies."

Ben Schneider was left-handed, after all. And Schneider's brother acted strangely when the bodies were found, fainting as others went into the Stelzriede house to examine the crime scene.

Randy Eckert, who now owns the old Stelzriede farm, has long-dead relatives who lived in Saxtown when the murders occurred.

"My grandpa would never say who he suspected," Eckert said.

One of the Eckerts was arrested for the murders but was released for lack of evidence.

Some in the community swear that the Eckerts had something to do with the murders—but they cite no evidence. The motive couldn't have been money. The Eckert family had more land and money than the Stelzriedes.

Maybe it was a love triangle.

Local lore is that an Eckert woman was one of the folks who forbade outsiders from approaching her husband on his deathbed.

"That's probably true about that person," Westhoff said. But he added, "I think it was just family members overreacting."

Those are the types of legends that have unfurled in the Saxtown backcountry.

Octogenarian John Luckherdt, who grew up down the road from the Stelzriede farm, told the *Belleville News-Democrat* in 1988 that he thought two brothers had committed the crime. But he wouldn't say which ones. Several brothers were implicated, including the Stelzriede relatives in Washington and Jefferson Counties, Ben and George Schneider, and George and Charles Killian.

He didn't shy away from adding to the lore.

"The men who done it were supposed to have gotten the sheriff drunk when he come to investigate," Luckherdt said. Sheriff James Hughes did stop in front of a Millstadt saloon before continuing on to Saxtown to begin his investigation. (There isn't any written documentation that he went inside and tipped a glass.)

"But it happened years ago and people want to forget about it," Luckherdt said. "You can't prove nothing. It all happened such a long time ago."

Luckherdt, however, was quick to absolve one suspect. It was the man who caught Sheriff Hughes's attention early in the investigation: John Afken, the farmhand and grubber.

"John Afken, he done some work at my grandfather's farm," Luckherdt said. "He done some grubbing or something. . . . He might have had blood on his clothes they thought. So they come out to our farm to see if he'd burned them there. They didn't find nothing. They looked for his buttons, too. They didn't think it was him. Now, I don't know nothing about him. But my father didn't think he did it."

Westhoff thinks he did.

"I know a little bit more about him than you'll find written," Westhoff said.

Westhoff said Afken was a "half-wit." He thinks Afken worked in concert with Stelzriede brother-in-law Fred Boeltz, who was deeply in debt to the family and in constant disputes over repayment.

The one thing Germans prided was land—and Boeltz's was shackled by a lien to the Stelzriedes.

"I think he was the one that [paid Afken to do it], thinking that in reality if they all died he would become the prime inheritor," Westhoff said.

Westhoff said Afken could "swing an ax from either arm."

"Any grubber can do that," he said. "You don't have to necessarily be left-handed. You had to learn how to do that or you couldn't really grub out stumps. You had to be able to swing from any direction."

He added: "A grubber probably would have done some pretty nasty work."

Afken was at the nexus of the main suspects who would inherit money—hence the necessity of killing the entire family. He had worked for the elder Stelzriede's brother, Charles. And he knew Boeltz. In fact, census records show the two had emigrated from the same town in Germany: Oldenburg in Lower Saxony.

Boeltz's boots were found wet the day after the murders. He had been out the night before. He refused to go to the scene to identify his relatives. He couldn't look at the bodies during the coroner's inquest and didn't shed a tear at his in-laws' funeral.

And he was spotted having a deep discussion with Afken shortly after the bodies were discovered.

Afken was one of the first people to arrive at the crime scene. He said nothing but listened to everyone.

As days passed he remained calm and collected, never breaking down to investigators—despite their attempts to "sweat" him.

After investigators and private detectives turned their eyes to other suspects, Boeltz sued for a share of the inheritance and eventually packed up and left. Where he went, nobody knew. Until now that information was missing from the written record and unwritten folklore.

Research for this book traced him to Nebraska, where he built a farm with his large family. It was free from debt.

His name went from Boeltz, which appeared on official documents, to Boelts.

"I always thought there was a name change there," Westhoff said.

Afken spent the rest of his life working on the struggling farms of Saxtown.

Westhoff said that Afken would come into Millstadt from time to time. The daughter of a barber that worked near the center of town disclosed many years later that her father had noticed something odd about Afken.

He used to come into the shop, where the local men got their haircuts, carrying with him a shiny watch. A watch that, Westhoff said, some thought belonged to Carl Stelzriede.

One other tale fell through the cracks of history.

Westhoff said that Ben Schneider claimed to have seen a hank of red hair in the hand of Carl when he found the bodies. That indicated that Carl may have pulled out his attacker's hair as he fought for his life.

The clue was never publicly documented during the days when investigators searched for the killer. Westhoff said, if true, it would have made Sheriff Hughes's job much easier. He could have avoided the years of twists and turns before he fell to his death.

"He could have just asked everyone to remove their hats," Westhoff said.

The fair and freckled Afken had red hair.

Epilogue: Mystery

I scribbled in my reporter's notebook amid the well-manicured lawns and winding streets of Columbia, Illinois.

Standing around me were weeping neighbors and stone-faced investigators. Before me was a tidy two-story home wrapped in yellow crime scene tape.

That day in May of 2009 a young mother and her two children were found strangled in their beds. Investigators mounted a tough investigation. They took blood samples, reviewed surveillance and security camera footage, snapped hundreds of photos, analyzed handwriting, examined cell phone records, traced computer IP addresses, built an elaborate mockup of the crime scene that looked like a dollhouse, dusted for fingerprints, explored the victims' wound patterns, and employed a forensic doctor to determine the time of death.

The evidence led to the bodyguard of televangelist Joyce Meyer—Christopher Coleman, the husband and father of the murdered family. No other suspects were identified.

Dozens of reporters and photographers descended on the courthouse for his trial. I served as a consultant for CBS News's *48 Hours.* The case included shocking details of sex and money and jealousy. Coleman was subsequently convicted and sentenced to life in prison for killing his family by ligature strangulation. Testimony said it took him five minutes per victim. Five minutes to stare into the eyes of his wife. Five minutes to watch the breath of his children become labored—and then nonexistent.

Nearly everyone I came across said the same: "You should write a book."

My response was always an emphatic "no." The case didn't have enough mystery.

Several years later the gravediggers came and dug up the Coleman family and moved their bodies from a cemetery in Southern Illinois to a cemetery in Chicago. Relatives didn't want the victims buried next to their killer.

It reminded me that the five-person Stelzriede family wasn't moved because they were murdered by an unknown assailant. To this day their bodies could be rotting alongside their killer.

Someone got away with murder because the tools and science used by today's investigators didn't exist in 1874. The Stelzriedes were killed in the days of the horse and buggy, before the collection and use of fingerprinting, before the patenting of the telephone, before electric lighting, before forensic DNA—even before the fiction of Sherlock Holmes.

No tools existed to examine the evidence. There was no way to preserve or test blood evidence. If transported back in time, today's forensic scientists would have been able to test the blood on the tobacco leaves found near the Stelzriede house and possibly match them to a suspect.

Although photography existed in 1874, it wasn't widely used in criminal investigations. And it wasn't used in Saxtown. Even if it had been, it might have been no help to history, because the main investigative case file was stolen.

It took hours for authorities to arrive at the Saxtown crime scene. And when they did it had already been trampled by a fearful mob. Sheriff James W. Hughes, in a quest to quickly clear the case, made arrests based on the flimsiest of evidence. Then he announced large rewards for anyone with information that would lead to a conviction. That announcement spurred private detectives, starving from a devastating economic depression, to descend on Saxtown. They complicated the case with competing theories in unbridled attempts to make the newspapers—which made accusations and often printed their claims verbatim.

Hughes's focus on large rewards enhanced the spreading of lies and legends. The main "science" used in the Saxtown investigation was conspiracy theories and conjecture.

But that is part of what makes the historical case interesting. The lack of technology and science helped transform the Saxtown murders into an unsolved puzzle. Of which we have so few.

It took me ten years, off and on, to put together the pieces of the Sax-town story. I drove to far-flung libraries and government offices seeking even the most basic documents that might shine some light on who these people were—which in turn might add to the mystery's canon.

For years the one man to escape my grasp was Fred Boeltz. Mark Westhoff, a historian who knows the case better than anyone alive, had told me he could find no record of Boeltz after he won a share of the Stelzriede inheritance.

Neither could I.

I searched computer databases, looked at yellowed documents, walked through old, overgrown cemeteries. Nothing.

Then one day I tinkered with plugging different spellings of his last name into a genealogical database. Finally, I found one that looked close. It was spelled "Boelts." At first I was disappointed. The birth information and name of his wife were off. But then I saw the names and ages of three of his sons. Gustave, Fred, Henry. They matched.

I tracked down United States Homestead documents to help confirm my suspicion that Frederick Boeltz had slipped from Saxtown lore because of a slight change of spelling and a move to central Nebraska.

It was true.

"Boelts" had included naturalization documents with his Homestead application. They showed he was from St. Clair County, Illinois. Saxtown.

Well over one hundred years later, the story still convulses into history. It twists and turns and runs like the Mississippi just to the west.

The mystery remains. Always.

ACKNOWLEDGMENTS

Newspapers are the "first draft of history."

The grand jury papers of the Stelzriede murder case were stolen sometime in the 1890s. In doing research, I was largely at the whim of newspaper accounts to breathe life into my investigation. I was lucky. Many of them, particularly the *St. Louis Daily Globe* of 1874 and the *St. Louis Post-Dispatch* in the latter part of the nineteenth century, were excellent sources.

The lack of official documents hamstrung my efforts for many years. The *Globe* filled much of the void and brought the case alive with vivid descriptions of the crime scene, from the clock on the wall to children's toys on the floor.

As a journalist I know the challenges of reporting on the twists and turns of a high-profile criminal case. I am forever grateful for the work of those that came before me.

Many of the original news accounts were in German-language newspapers. I remember being so excited when I found them on microfilm at the Abraham Lincoln Presidential Library in Springfield, Illinois. And then my subsequent disappointment when reality smacked me on the head; I couldn't read a word of German.

I spent hours staring at highly stylized German fonts while searching for keywords that I could recognize on the foreign language microfilm rolls. I'm indebted to Annerose Romer and Christine Romer, who translated the material for me.

I was able, however, to piece together the story of many of the people involved in this case through public documents stored on forgotten microfilm rolls scattered in government offices across the country.

My ten-year journey, which culminated in this book, was aided by record storehouses and databases in New York City; Springfield, Illinois;

St. Clair County, Illinois; Washington County, Illinois; Merrick County, Nebraska; St. Louis, Missouri; and St. Louis County.

Technology greatly aided this project. The years I spent writing this book were marked by an expansion of genealogical computer research. My examination of the Stelzriede case wasn't limited to the facts of the crime. It was about who the people were and how they lived. Ancestry .com and FamilySearch.org contributed to my understanding of the people who lived more than a century ago.

Brendan Kelly, the St. Clair County state's attorney, helped direct the county circuit clerk's office to locate civil court records that previously were thought to have been lost to fire. Lu Ann Henry, Rebecca McCollum, and my aunt, Sandy Glauber, all of that office, were extremely helpful.

I am thankful for the help of the Belleville Labor & Industry Museum, the St. Clair County Genealogical Society, the Belleville Public Library, the St. Louis Public Library, the St. Louis County Library, the Abraham Lincoln Presidential Library, the New York Genealogical and Biographical Society, and the New-York Historical Society.

I am grateful for the knowledge and work of Wilson M. Baltz, who in 1974 wrote a short, fictionalized narrative of the murders. I interviewed him on several occasions before he died in 2007. He was kind, courteous, and helpful.

Donald L. Slinkard, a record keeper for the Zion Evangelical Church in Millstadt, Illinois, helped share research of the Freivogel Cemetery in St. Clair County. He died in 2006.

Thanks to Mark Westhoff, a historian who had an uncanny knowledge of the legends and lore of the Saxtown case, and whose fascinating storytelling grabbed my interest and enabled this project.

I must say a word about the descendants of the Stelzriede family. They are now scattered across the country, though still tied to the patriarchs who immigrated to the United States from Hille, Germany, in the nineteenth century. Ron Nelson, a descendant, has done extensive genealogical research on the family, which is available online.

Many thanks to Kelso G. Barnett, who helped me research some of the facts of the Stelzriede case and read drafts. As well as thanks to friends Michael P. Davidson, Robb McFadden, and Phil Palisoul, who provided insight.

I must also say a word of thanks to my colleagues, past and present, at the *Post-Dispatch:* Tim Bross and Jamie Riley, who took a chance on me many years ago; Patrick Gauen, my former editor, who has made me a better reporter; Harry Levins, who has made me a better writer; and Christopher Ave, Matthew Hathaway, Mike Meiners, Tim O'Neil, Steve Giegerich, and Deborah Peterson, who all offered input and support.

A number of complications slowed my writing process—including a traumatic eye injury. Keith Wallman, my editor, was incredibly patient and made this a better book. I also owe a great debt to my literary agent Matthew Carnicelli, who believed in this project and made it a reality.

Ten years is a long time. I first set out to write a news article about the Saxtown murders in 2003. That turned into a decade of research, off and on, and then writing. There were times I thought this project would never see ink on paper.

I owe special thanks to my brother, Dan Pistor, my grandmother, Betty Dieckmann, and my parents, Anthony and Linda Pistor. My father was so interested in this project that he helped me research it in the early days. A family friend, Dennis "Doc" Marlen, also helped and went with him to various libraries to seek documents I had requested.

Doc died in 2004. My father died two years later.

My only regret is that they will never get to read this book. This is in memory of them.

The murder of the Stelzriede family was a horrific crime that shocked the nation—and then was forgotten. I am proud to have chronicled and preserved the events that unfolded all of those years ago. For all times.

Nicholas J. C. Pistor
St. Louis, Missouri
November 8, 2013

Sources

This is a true story based on hundreds of newspaper articles, government documents, church records, personal stories, and genealogical data.

Some information contradicted other information that was reported at the time. I tried to weigh all of the research and boil it down to what made the most sense.

The town of Millstadt was actually called Centreville in 1874. Millstadt was the name of the post office and soon after became the name of the town. I've consistently used the name Millstadt to make it less confusing for the reader. Also, many of the newspapers used as sources have either folded or had their names changed throughout the span of the Saxtown story. I've used the name of the paper at the time it was written.

Preface

ix. *the desks of inattentive students.:* I briefly had Cleary as a teacher. I later changed to another class. Cleary retired in 2003 and died years later in 2010.

ix. *deference to one of the priests.):* *St. Louis Post-Dispatch,* April 17, 1988.

ix. *a best-selling book and movie.":* Ibid.

x. *to have written to Blatty.:* Ibid.

x. *no doubts about it now.":* Ibid.

xi. THE STILLZENREIDER FARM HOUSE.: *St. Louis Dispatch,* March 21, 1874.

Prologue

xiii. *to make their stand.:* *St. Louis Post-Dispatch,* October 24, 1902.

xiii. *took to avenge it.:* My descriptions of the German farmers are based on the time period, the amount of time that had passed since the

Stelzriedes were murdered, and newspaper articles about the removal of the bodies.

xiii. *protect the bodies from him.:* St. Louis Post-Dispatch, November 9, 1902.

xiii. AM DER ERMORDETE FAMILIE.": *St. Louis Post-Dispatch,* October 24, 1902.

xiv. *buzzed with a frightening sequence.:* St. Louis Post-Dispatch, October 3, 1897.

xiv. *it was reported.:* Ibid.

xiv. *"midnight callers" slammed an ax down on Fritz's head.:* Ibid.

xiv. *the* St. Louis Post-Dispatch *reported.:* Ibid.

xiv. *his neck and finished him.:* Ibid.

xiv. *try to raise the bodies.:* St. Louis Post-Dispatch, October 24, 1902.

xv. *homes bereft and hearts broken.":* St. Louis Post-Dispatch, October 24, 1897.

xv. *avoid graveyards at night.":* Ibid.

xv. *It's all in their imaginations.":* Ibid.

xv. *are handled a second time.":* Ibid.

xv. *had returned after internment.":* Ibid.

xvi. *nine-foot-tall monument.:* St. Louis Post-Dispatch, November 9, 1902.

xvi. *use force to prevent it.:* St. Louis Post-Dispatch, October 24, 1902.

xvi. *remove the corpses.:* Ibid.

xvi. *remains in Walnut Hill Cemetery.:* St. Louis Post-Dispatch, November 9, 1902.

xvi. *say so do their ghosts.:* Oral discussions of ghosts date back to just after the murders. Written talk of ghosts dates to the 1890s and continues today.

Chapter 1: Escaping Tragedy

1. *farmer evading God's cold vengeance.:* Although Carl Stelzriede's birth information isn't documented, he was christened in the Evangelical

church on July 18, 1809, to parents Johann Cord. Stelzriede and Marie Louise Grandemann in Rahden, Germany. I used that to estimate his age at sixty-five at the time of the murders. FamilySearch.org listing for Carl Franz Henrich [*sic*] Stelzriede in "Germany Births and Baptisms, 1558–1898" index. "Deutschland, Geburten und Taufen 1558–1898," index, *FamilySearch*, Carl Franz Henrich Stelzriede, July 18, 1809.

1. *work with his hands.*: Albert Faust, *The German Element in the United States, Volume 2* (Boston and New York: Houghton Mifflin, 1909), p. 30.

1. *Stelzriede (pronounced stilts-ZEN-reeder) was no different.*: Pronunciation of name comes from interviews with locals and from a Stelzriede ancestral website dedicated to the descendants of Johann Friedrich Wilhelm Stelzriede, www.stelzriede.net/Spellings.htm. Also, the first newspaper accounts of the crime spelled the last name phonetically—the way they heard the German neighbors pronounce the name: "Stillzenreider," *St. Louis Dispatch*, March 21, 1874.

1. *elegy frozen in his mind.*: *St. Louis Daily Globe*, March 22, 1874. Reporters who witnessed the bodies at the murder scene said this of Carl Stelzriede: "The old man's hair was jet black."

1. *dead for eight years.*: Carl Stelzriede married Maria Christina Horstmann on May 4, 1833, in Hille, Germany. FamilySearch.org listing for Carl Franz Heinrich Stelzriede and Christine Horstmann in "Germany Marriages, 1558–1929" index. She died on June 10, 1866, according to her tombstone inscription at Freivogel Cemetery, St. Clair County, Illinois.

1. *up farming his sixty acres.*: Description comes from *St. Louis Republican*, March 22, 1874. The sixty-acre figure comes from St. Clair County, Illinois, property records as well as Township South 1, Range 9 West map, Historic Map Works, accessed August 27, 2013, www.historicmapworks.com/Map/US/1257238/Township+1+South++Range+9+West++Centerville++Roach+Town/St.+Clair+County+1874/Illinois/.

2. *had ended with a hangover.: The New York Times,* August 24, 1878.

2. *the* New York Times *wrote.: The New York Times,* November 3, 1907.

2. *streets and into unemployment.: The New York Times,* October 14, 2008.

2. *as relief rolls exploded.: Chronicle of Higher Education,* October 17, 2008.

2. *cash and gold from Germany.:* The story of a legacy fortune of cash and gold was reported in various ways by many newspapers at the time and later. The gold particularly became more talked about years after the Stelzriedes were killed.

2. *by nobility and kings.:* Most of Carl Stelzriede's early life events occurred in Hille, Germany, according to Stelzriede family genealogy and church records.

2. *with him," one wrote.: St. Louis Republican,* March 22, 1874.

2. *hand of an incendiary.:* Ibid.

3. *"less imposing domicile.":* Ibid.

3. *of their household belongings.:* Ibid.

3. *made it to adulthood.:* Friedrich Christian Stelzriede was christened on May 19, 1834, and died on December 24, 1838. Christian Friedrich Stelzriede was christened on October 20, 1839, and died on December 9, 1840. Christian Heinrich Stelzriede was christened on November 7, 1841, and died on November 8, 1841. Carl Friedrich August Stelzriede was born on March 27, 1837, and lived into adulthood.

3. *light, then came darkness.":* Book of Job, 30:26, New International Version.

3. *ships and swimming coffins.": New York Journal of Commerce,* 1853.

3. *found about a German cottage.": St. Louis Republican,* March 22, 1874.

3. *took about two months.:* Michael Brinkman, *Quincy, Illinois Immigrants from Munsterland* (Westminster, Maryland: Heritage Book, 2010), 30.

4. *Mark Twain once wrote.:* Mark Twain, *Life on the Mississippi* (New York: Grosset & Dunlap, 1917), 432.

4. *wrote of the city.:* Ibid., 191.

4. *whole sections of the population.:* Chiefly the cholera epidemic of 1849.

4. *taken down any day.":* Gustave Koerner, *Memoirs of Gustave Koerner, Volume I* (Cedar Rapids, Ia.: The Torch Press, 1909), 290.

5. *it forever," Koerner remembered.:* Ibid., 296.

5. *would be their home.:* My description of the pronunciation of *Sax-town* is based on oral history of the area and interviews with locals.

5. *in their labyrinthian cities.":* Joseph A. Dacus and James William Buel, *A Tour of St. Louis* (St. Louis: Western Publishing Company, 1878), 24.

5. *would have been too kind.:* St. Louis Daily Globe, March 22, 1874.

5. *through a nearby area.:* Charles Dickens, *American Notes* (London: Chapman and Hall, 1850), 125.

5. *and marked the route.:* St. Louis Daily Globe, March 22, 1874.

6. *Adolph Schlernitzauer, a doctor.:* Millstadt Enterprise, 1976 special supplement.

6. *in all its character.":* Description from Wilson Baltz. *Millstadt Enterprise,* March 13, 1974.

6. *the house as insulation.:* Millstadt Enterprise, August 19, 1954.

7. *ones Charles Dickens bemoaned).:* US Federal Census Non-Population Schedules, Agriculture, Census Year: 1870; Census Place: Township 1 S Range 9 W, Saint Clair, Illinois.

7. *than the native population.:* Faust, *German Element,* 29.

7. *Maria died in 1866.:* Maria Christina Steltzriede died on June 10, 1866, according to the tombstone inscription at Freivogel Cemetery in St. Clair County, Illinois.

7. *only during harvest time.:* Faust, *German Element,* 30.

8. *good prices at the market.:* St. Louis Republican, March 22, 1874.

8. *of God's inevitable retribution.:* St. Louis Daily Globe, March 23, 1874.

8. *over a relative's inheritance.:* Ibid.

8. *who farmed nearby ground.:* Ibid.

8. *often frustrated with slow payments.:* St. Clair County, Illinois, Chattel Mortgage Record, Illinois State Archives; *St. Louis Daily Times,* March 22, 1874.

8. *eight-month-old daughter.:* Several news reports discussed the baby having been sick. Whooping cough reportedly prevailed throughout Saxtown at the time.

9. *rich soil, and quiet houses.:* St. Louis Post-Dispatch, October 3, 1897.

9. *hanging from his neck.:* The local lore has been preserved in the oral tradition. "Saxtown Murders," Robert Buecher, last modified May 27, 2010, www.genealogy.com/users/h/a/s/Jim-Hastings-MO/FILE/0048page.html.

9. *kept stashed at home.:* Anzeiger des Westens, March 23, 1874, translation by Annerose Romer.

9. *at his farm house.:* Ibid.

9. *until the following Monday.:* Missouri Republican, March 7, 1882.

10. *one hundred thirty dollars.:* Stern des Westens, March 21, 1874.

10. *nestled against her bosom.:* Description based on how the bodies were found, coming from a variety of newspaper accounts, all of which described it this way.

10. *that would never come.:* Description of household items comes from crime scene reporting, particularly *St. Louis Daily Globe,* March 22, 1874.

Chapter 2: Death House

11. *knocked out by a thunderstorm.:* St. Louis Daily Globe, March 21, 1874, weather report showed humidity at fifty-six percent and temperatures reaching near sixty degrees.

11. *snow and heavy rains.:* St. Louis Dispatch, March 20, 1874, river report.

11. *joints of young and old.:* St. Louis Daily Globe, March 21, 1874.

11. *newspapers would later agree.:* Almost every newspaper, aside from a select few, placed the discovery at about five o'clock in the afternoon.

12. *before St. Patrick's Day.:* Millstadt Enterprise, February 20, 1974.

12. *Strong. Hunched back.:* My description of Ben Schneider comes from Wilson Baltz, who knew him in his older years. *Millstadt Enterprise,* February 20, 1974.

12. *by life on the farm.:* Millstadt Enterprise, June 24, 1927.

12. *back by Adolf Hitler.:* Ibid.

13. *occupied with his wife, Kate.:* Illinois Statewide Marriage Index, Illinois State Archives.

13. *from the house's chimney.:* St. Louis Post-Dispatch, October 3, 1897.

13. *yelled from the road.:* St. Louis Daily Globe, March 22, 1874.

14. *like spent gun shells.:* Ibid.

14. *murder of Abraham Lincoln.:* Author interview with Wilson Baltz.

14. *a gang of negroes.":* St. Louis Dispatch, March 21, 1874.

Chapter 3: Help!

17. *knew their daily habits.:* St. Louis Daily Globe-Democrat, March 8, 1882.

17. *of George Schneider's mining buddies.:* Ibid.

18. *wrote* Harper's Weekly.: St. Louis Post-Dispatch, January 24, 1874.

18. *for their winter's whisky.":* St. Louis Daily Globe-Democrat, March 8, 1882.

18. *he was a butcher.:* Ibid.

18. *to be among them.:* News accounts of the time were filled with stories about the difficulty wet weather made for travel, especially in rural areas. The *St. Louis Dispatch,* March 21, 1874, noted that "the roads are in almost impassible condition, and as the news spread like wild-fire, it seems almost impossible for the murderers to get away with any rapidity."

18. *affirmed one written account.:* Ibid.

18. *wrote from New Orleans.:* Letter from Henry G. Crowell. Louis Alfred Wiltz, *The Great Mississippi Flood of 1874* (New Orleans: Picayune Steam and Job Print, 1874), 7.

19. *above the river bluffs.:* Albert Faust, *The German Element in the United States, Volume 2* (Boston and New York: Houghton Mifflin, 1909), 35.

19. *had been wiped out.:* St. Louis Democrat, March 22, 1874.

19. *the Stelzriedes, was told.:* Ibid.

19. *at George Schneider's house.:* St. Louis Daily Globe, March 8, 1882.

19. *to explain what happened.:* Belleville Advocate, May 27, 1874.

20. *some evil force at work?:* Ibid.

20. *much older and wiser.:* Age comes from 1870 US Census.

20. *long coat and top hat.:* My description of Isaiah Thomas comes from Wilson Baltz. *Millstadt Enterprise,* February 27, 1974.

20. *acres in Saxtown in 1869.:* State of Illinois, Illinois, Public Land Purchase Records, 1800–1990.

20. *local justice of the peace.:* Millstadt Directory from 1874.

20. *Thomas of his discovery.:* Anzeiger des Westens, March 23, 1874.

21. *Stelzriedes were all dead.:* Ibid.

21. *face to revive him.:* St. Louis Daily Globe, March 8, 1882.

21. *It was now tainted.:* Some accounts said the crime scene was left as is, but clearly other details showed that things were moved.

21. *and red in the face.:* St. Louis Republican, March 8, 1882.

21. *Stelzriede house at dusk.:* St. Louis Daily Globe-Democrat, March 8, 1882.

21. *eye is sticking out yet.":* Ibid.

Chapter 4: The Bride

23. *The place smelled awful.:* St. Louis Daily Globe, March 22, 1874.

23. *summon law enforcement help.:* Stern des Westens, March 21, 1874, translation by Annerose Romer.

23. *killed by an unknown passerby.:* St. Louis Democrat, March 22, 1874.

23. *killing and robbing his benefactors.":* Ibid.

23. *in St. Clair County.:* Mary Peter's beauty was referenced in many news articles, including *St. Louis Daily Times,* April 25, 1871.

24. *woman came with a dowry.:* My description of German marital customs is based on a variety of literature, but mainly Michael Brinkman, *Quincy, Illinois Immigrants from Munsterland* (Westminster, Maryland: Heritage Book, 2010), 189.

24. *old country preferred to wed.:* Illinois Statewide Marriage Index, Illinois State Archives.

24. *wooden platform in the yard.:* This was a typical marriage ceremony for German-Catholics in Quincy, Illinois, which was similar to the customs used in St. Clair County, Illinois. Brinkman, *Illinois Immigrants,* 191.

24. *wedding gift from Mary's father.:* Missouri Democrat, March 24, 1871.

24. *meat on butchering day.:* The description of roles for women on a farm is based on Brinkman, *Illinois Immigrants,* 172.

24. *independent of their husbands.":* Missouri Democrat, April 22, 1971.

24. *from his father-in-law.:* Newspapers offered conflicting accounts over which relative Mr. Peter was traveling to. It appears his father-in-law was the most likely destination. *Missouri Republican,* April 24, 1871.

25. *wife to the front door.:* Ibid.

25. *someone had just left.:* Missouri Democrat, April 25, 1871.

25. *side of her neck.:* Ibid.

25. *of her husband's arrival.:* Ibid.

25. St. Clair County, Ill.: *St. Louis Daily Times,* April 25, 1871.

26. *occurred on Saturday afternoon . . . ":* Missouri Democrat, April 24, 1871.

26. *but no one really knew.:* Ibid.

26. *approximately thirty years old.:* Missouri Republican, April 24, 1871.

26. *torn at the toe.:* Ibid.

26. *returned to his business.:* Ibid.

26. *afternoon of the murder.:* Some schoolchildren saw the suspect. *Missouri Democrat,* April 24, 1871.

27. *was hacked and bruised.:* Missouri Republican, April 24, 1871.

27. *Her front teeth knocked out.:* Missouri Democrat, April 24, 1871.

27. *against the hot stove.:* St. Louis Daily Times, April 25, 1871.

27. *and steel-mixed pantaloons.:* Missouri Republican, April 24, 1871.

27. *next to Mary's body.:* Missouri Democrat, April 25, 1871.

27. *she hadn't been raped.:* Missouri Democrat, April 24, 1871.

27. *initials of the dead woman.:* Missouri Republican, April 24, 1871.

27. *of the murder spread.:* Missouri Democrat, April 26, 1871.

28. *joined in the pursuit.:* Missouri Democrat, April 25, 1871.

28. *"intense anxiety to catch the brute.":* Missouri Democrat, April 25, 1871.

28. *bottle of strong whiskey.:* Belleville Zeitung, April 2, 1874.

28. *a long, muscular frame.:* Stern des Westens, March 23, 1874.

28. *"strong as a giant.":* St. Louis Daily Globe, March 23, 1874.

28. *"fierce and straight.":* Ibid.

28. *"on first sight [it] would condemn him as a criminal.":* St. Louis Dispatch, March 23, 1874.

29. *on the Pacific coast.:* "U.S.A. Executions 1607–1976," Death Penalty USA, http://deathpenaltyusa.org/usa1/date/1874.htm.

29. *distance of six feet.":* Robert K. Elder, *Last Words of the Executed* (Chicago: University of Chicago Press, 2010), 53.

29. *evil spirit came over me.":* The New York Times, May 20, 1873.

29. *the cell without leg irons.:* The New York Times, May 2, 1874.

30. *didn't treat him well.:* US Federal Census, St. Clair County, 1870.

30. *facial expression of a Methodist.:* Belleville Advocate, March 27, 1874, reported that Afken was a member of the German Methodist church in Belleville.

30. *with and worked for them.:* St. Louis Daily Globe, March 23, 1874.

30. *an "unrest of mind.":* Ibid.

31. *boarded him at his house.:* St. Louis Times, March 27, 1874.

31. *ax from any direction.:* Author interview with Mark Westhoff, former director of the St. Clair County Historical Society. Westhoff said that grubbers had to be able to swing an ax from every different direction to be effective at removing tree stumps.

Chapter 5: Sheriff Hughes

33. *leave them home alone.:* My description of the frenzy comes from a variety of reports.

33. *Then one hundred.:* St. Louis Democrat, March 22, 1874.

33. *the news that evening.:* Stern des Westens, March 21, 1874.

34. *Millstadt's general legal headquarters.:* Millstadt Enterprise, August 19, 1954.

34. *immigrant from Nassau, Germany.:* US Census records.

34. *Germans loved Brenfleck's place.:* Valentine Brenfleck's was the most

famous place in town, and was later the subject of a play by the Liederkranz Club of St. Louis. *Millstadt Enterprise,* July 1, 1948.

34. *of pinochle and kloepper.: Millstadt Enterprise,* March 6, 1974.

34. *hill along the way.: St. Louis Daily Globe,* March 22, 1874.

35. *deep in mud and slime.":* Charles Dickens, *American Notes* (London: Chapman and Hall, 1850), 217.

35. *the University of Heidelberg.:* Gustave Koerner, *Memoirs of Gustave Koerner, Volume I* (Cedar Rapids, Ia.: The Torch Press, 1909), 28.

35. *some written exclusively in German.:* "History of St. Clair County, Illinois," St. Clair County Genealogical Society, www.stclair-ilgs.org/1876hist.htm.

35. *wild frontier from Virginia.: Belleville Weekly Advocate,* October 21, 1881.

35. *became county sheriff soon after.:* Illinois Adjutant General's Office, "Record of the Services of Illinois Soldiers in the Black Hawk War."

36. *the Illinois state legislature.:* Alvis Louis Nebelsick, *A History of Belleville* (Belleville, Ill.: Township High School and Junior College, 1951), 26.

36. *made him look even taller.:* Description from Wilson Baltz. *Millstadt Enterprise,* March 13, 1974.

36. *he considered an honor.: Belleville Weekly Advocate,* October 21, 1881.

36. *in Charleston, South Carolina.:* Koerner, *Memoirs,* 81.

36. *of siege or revolution.":* Frederick Law Olmsted, *A Journey in the Seaboard Slave States* (New York: Dix and Edwards, 1856), 404.

37. *boys not to enlist.:* Belleville Public Library, card catalogue, May 6, 1864.

37. *at a high shine. Always.:* My description of Sheriff James W. Hughes largely comes from Wilson Baltz. *Millstadt Enterprise,* March 13, 1974.

37. *served as a sheriff's deputy.:* Based on analysis of 1870 US Census, St. Clair County, Illinois, and 1880 US Census, St. Clair County, Illinois.

37. *call upon his troops.":* Description from Wilson Baltz. *Millstadt Enterprise,* March 13, 1974.

38. *found the townspeople in a panic.:* St. Louis Daily Times, March 22, 1874.

38. *and followed Hughes.:* Ibid.

38. *to speak with Ben.:* Millstadt Enterprise, March 13, 1974.

39. *"flame, smoke, and faces.":* Description from Wilson Baltz. *Millstadt Enterprise,* March 13, 1974.

39. *blood and "congealed gore.":* St. Louis Daily Globe, March 22, 1874.

39. *"sad scene of confusion.":* St. Louis Dispatch, March 21, 1874.

40. *concealed inside the house.:* St. Louis Democrat, March 22, 1874.

40. *had discovered the bodies.:* This legend grew throughout the decades after the murders.

40. *heard of," Hughes exclaimed.:* St. Louis Daily Globe, March 22, 1874.

40. *the murders were committed?":* Ibid.

41. *or give an alarm.":* Ibid.

41. *has left none of them.":* Ibid.

41. *bleeding and to treat wounds.:* Ann Charlton, "Medicinal Uses of Tobacco in History," *Journal of the Royal Society of Medicine* 97, no. 6 (2004): 292–96. www.ncbi.nlm.nih.gov/pmc/articles/PMC1079499/.

Chapter 6: Demonism!

43. Demonism, *St. Louis Daily Globe,* March 22, 1874; Wholesale Human Slaughter, *St. Louis Democrat,* March 21, 1874; A Crime Unparalleled in a Century, *St. Louis Daily Globe,* March 22, 1874; One of the Darkest Deeds Ever Recorded, *St. Louis*

Daily Globe, March 22, 1874; THE ILLINOIS HORROR, *St. Louis Daily Times,* March 22, 1874.

43. *New York, San Francisco, Chicago.: New York Times,* March 22, 1874; *San Francisco Daily Morning Call,* April 2, 1874; *Chicago Daily Tribune,* March 21, 1874.

43. *night of March 20, 1874.: St. Louis Daily Globe,* March 21, 1874.

43. *bold headline:* A BLOODY TRAGEDY.*:* Ibid.

44. *been sometime this morning.":* Ibid.

44. *the arrival of the officers.":* Ibid.

44. *Denver, and everywhere else.: Indianapolis Journal,* March 23, 1874; *Daily Rocky Mountain News,* March 21, 1874; *Daily Arkansas Gazette,* March 24, 1874.

44. *headlined the* Chicago Daily Tribune.*: Chicago Daily Tribune,* March 21, 1874.

44. *"like a seven-foot pirate.":* Donald A. Ritchie, *American Journalists: Getting the Story* (New York: Oxford University Press, 1997), 99.

45. *United States at age eleven.:* Ibid.

45. *pleased and yet frightened me.":* Theodore Dreiser, *Newspaper Days: An Autobiography* (Santa Rosa, Calif.: Black Sparrow Press, 2000), 107.

45. *old enough to vote.:* Ritchie, *American Journalists,* 99.

45. *whittling pieces of wood.":* Ibid., 101.

45. *their* Chicago Republican *newspaper.:* Charles C. Clayton, *Little Mack: Joseph B. McCullagh of the St. Louis Globe-Democrat* (Carbondale, Ill: Southern Illinois University Press, 1969), 68.

46. *everything he owned.:* Ibid.

46. *headed to a new upstart.:* Ibid., 72.

46. *new in the field.":* Ibid.

46. *hell will break loose next.":* J. Cutler Andrews, *The North Reports the Civil War* (Pittsburgh: University of Pittsburgh Press, 1955), 165.

46. *soon be on the story.:* Ritchie, *American Journalists,* 103.

46. *headed to the crime scene:* St. Louis Democrat, March 21, 1874.

47. *and simply reprinting it.:* Clayton, *Little Mack.*

47. *at the panicked farm.:* St. Louis Dispatch, March 21, 1874.

47. *certainty," the* Dispatch *wrote.:* Ibid.

47. GRAUENHAFTER MORD *punched one headline.:* Stern des Westens, March 21, 1874, translation by Annerose Romer.

48. *the body," the* Stern *wrote.:* Ibid.

48. *the judge to try them.":* Ibid.

48. *and heartless murderers committed.":* Stern des Westens, March 23, 1874, translation by Annerose Romer.

48. *"the scene of blood.":* St. Louis Daily Globe, March 22, 1874.

48. *than the first announcement.":* Ibid.

49. *fire "already burning white.":* Ibid.

49. *the way to Saxtown.:* Ibid.

49. *a* Globe *reporter noted.:* Ibid.

49. *the* Globe *reporters observed·* Ibid.

49. *"rolled slowly toward the house.":* Ibid.

49. *the* Globe *reporters remembered.:* Ibid.

49. *details," the* Globe *wrote.:* Ibid.

50. *conviction of the murderers.":* Stern des Westens, March 21, 1874.

50. *gained admittance," they wrote.:* St. Louis Daily Globe, March 22, 1874.

50. *the* Globe *reporters, entered.":* Ibid.

50. *"Oh my God!":* Ibid.

Chapter 7: The Crime Scene

51. *stoutest heart stand still.":* St. Louis Daily Globe, March 22, 1874.

51. *the bodies had been found.:* Ibid. The *Globe* reporters arrived on Saturday morning. Their account appeared in the newspaper the next day.

51. *big puddle of red muck.:* Ibid.

52. *had lodged in his head.:* Ibid.

52. *assassin's instrument of death.":* Ibid.

52. *a human being looked upon.":* Ibid.

52. *his head was crushed.:* Ibid.

53. *noticeable in his locks.":* Ibid.

53. *heart rending scene of all.":* Ibid.

53. *then all was over.":* Ibid.

54. *stockings were hung neatly.:* Ibid.

54. *the* Daily Globe *wrote.:* Ibid.

54. *the time the murderer was at work.":* Ibid.

54. *caught?" the newspapermen wondered.:* Ibid.

54. *catch any new details.:* Ibid. The *Daily Globe* ran two separate accounts that day, one from the St. Louis reporters and the other from a "Belleville correspondent."

54. *Saxtonites performed their own investigation.:* Ibid. The *Daily Globe* reported that "there are a number of rumors flying around the country in regard to the persons suspected of being implicated in the crime."

55. *brother-in-law, Fred Boeltz.:* Fred Boeltz was identified by several spellings of his last name. Most newspapers, all court records, and the Stelzriedes' chattel mortgage used the spelling Boeltz. The 1870 US Census used the spelling Baltz. And in later years it became Boelts.

55. *Faint drops of blood.:* St. Louis Daily Globe, March 22, 1874.

Chapter 8: Wanted

57. *the screed of Sheriff James W. Hughes.:* Illinois State Archives, John Lourie Beveridge Correspondence, 1873–1877, Springfield, Illinois.

57. *and made off with up to six thousand dollars.:* Ted P. Yeatman, *Frank and Jesse James* (Nashville: Cumberland House Publishing, 2003), 21. Newspapers generally disagree on the amount netted from the heist. Some reported it at twelve thousand, while others reported lower. I have relied on scholars who have looked at the heist more closely.

58. *discarded with three bullet wounds.:* St. Louis Dispatch, March 16, 1874.

58. *to anyone who could help solve it.:* St. Louis Republican, March 22, 1874.

58. *staggering sum of one thousand dollars.:* Stern des Westens, March 21, 1874. A one thousand dollar reward was publicly offered and reported by newspapers as early as March 21, 1874, the day after the bodies were discovered.

58. *and no stranger to blood or death.:* Description is based on personal characteristics listed in Illinois Civil War Detail Report, Illinois State Archives. Beveridge served in the Eighth and Seventeenth Cavalries.

58. *wanted to bury the former president.:* "Construction of the Capitol," The Illinois State Capitol, last modified October 1, 2010, www .ilstatehouse.com/construction.htm.

59. *as does a wax figure in the museum.":* Emanuel Hertz, *The Hidden Lincoln* (New York: Blue Ribbon Books, 1940), 151.

59. *steps at a stride," Volk later remembered.:* Henry C. Whitney, *Life on the Circuit with Lincoln* (Boston: Estes and Lauriat, 1892). http:// lincoln.lib.niu.edu/file.php?file=whitney.html.

60. *with the plaster and made his eyes water...":* Ibid.

60. *by the time he was honorably discharged.:* Beveridge was said to have initiated the call for battle at Gettysburg, although there are conflicting accounts.

60. *Major Beveridge in the Army of the Potomac.":* Jeriah Bonham, *Fifty Years' Recollections* (Peoria, Ill: J.W. Franks and Sons, 1883), 134.

60. *which made it harder to sell alcohol.:* Andrew J. Jutkins, *Handbook of Prohibition* (Chicago: Lever Print, 1885), 128.

61. *for the office had been always defeated.":* Gustave Koerner, *Memoirs of Gustave Koerner, Volume 2* (Cedar Rapids, Ia.: The Torch Press, 1909), 577.

61. *so I can get out my bills. Don't delay.":* Illinois State Archives, John Lourie Beveridge Correspondence, 1873–1877, Springfield, Illinois.

61. *not consented to reprieve Rafferty.":* Inter Ocean, February 22, 1874.

62. *no appropriations made for such cases.":* Stern des Westens, March 25, 1874.

62. *seemed to suspect each other.:* Belleville Advocate, March 27, 1874.

62. *even more so than when he had left.:* St. Louis Daily Globe, March 22, 1874.

62. *on his train the morning of the murders.:* St. Louis Dispatch, November 14, 1877.

62. *reverted to this unknown passenger.":* Ibid.

62. *among "ten thousand convicts.":* Ibid.

Chapter 9: The Inquest

63. *stepped outside a lunatic asylum.":* St. Louis Daily Globe, March 22, 1874.

63. *to have shown little concern—for anyone.:* Children based on 1870 and 1880 US Census.

63. *to the crime scene. They had refused.:* St. Louis Daily Globe, March 22, 1874. Boeltz was told twice that his in-laws had been killed and he pleaded sick, saying he couldn't look upon them because under no circumstances "could he look upon a dead man."

63. *the "lamest of excuses.":* St. Louis Republican, March 22, 1874.

63. *dead man—much less five of them.:* St. Louis Daily Globe, March 22, 1874.

64. *to the house and attend to matters.":* Ibid.

64. *and former hired hand of the Stelzriedes.:* St. Louis Times, March 23, 1874.

64. *have been in an intense conversation.:* Belleville Zeitung, April 2, 1874.

64. *time to go to the murder scene.:* St. Louis Times, March 22, 1874.

64. *and discussing the case's sordid details.:* St. Louis Daily Globe, March 22, 1874.

64. *crowd numbered three hundred and growing.:* Ibid.

65. *asked him to pay his debt.:* Illinois Regional Archives, Carbondale, Illinois, Chattel Mortgage Record Books.; St. Louis Times, March 23, 1874.

65. *never gave a specific reason as to why.:* St. Louis Daily Globe, March 22, 1874.

65. *placed Fred in an unenviable light.":* Ibid.

65. *stamping across the Stelzriede lawn.:* Ibid.

65. *German friends of the murdered family!":* Ibid.

66. *leading Boeltz to the crime scene.:* Ibid.

66. *"he would never be hung!":* Ibid.

66. *you mean?" the reporter asked.:* Ibid.

66. *sufficient punishment for the brute.":* Ibid.

66. *I will be absent on business.":* Ibid.

66. *started to gather around Boeltz..:* Ibid.

66. *I'll bet my life upon it!":* Ibid.

66. *that man's house," Hughes said.:* Ibid.

67. *murmur" ran through the crowd.:* St. Louis Daily Globe, March 23, 1874.

67. *Bloodstained clothes. Bloody weapons.:* Ibid.

67. *when in the vicinity," the reporters remarked.:* Ibid.

67. *or the smallest drop of blood.:* Ibid.

68. *entered it," a* Daily Globe *reporter remembered.:* Ibid.

68. *had swelled to over five hundred people.:* Ibid.

68. *about two o'clock from East St. Louis.: St. Louis Times,* March 22, 1874.

68. *which accentuated his buggy eyes.:* My description of Coroner John Ryan comes from Wilson Baltz, who changed Ryan's name to Coroner Doyle in his a fictional account. *Millstadt Enterprise,* March 13, 1974,

68. *a physician who practiced in Millstadt.: St. Louis Republican,* March 22, 1874.

69. *nail prints," the investigators deduced.: Stern des Westens,* March 23, 1874.

69. bearing in a criminal trial should one be held.": Quote of inquest reading comes from Wilston Baltz. *Millstadt Enterprise,* March 27, 1974.

69. *in order to get some potato seedlings.": Anzeiger des Westens,* March 23, 1874.

69. *the justice of the peace, Isaiah Thomas.:* Ibid.

69. *were found just as he had described.:* Ibid.

70. *Afken "kept wonderfully cool.": St. Louis Daily Globe,* March 23, 1874.

70. *did the blood "mantle his face.":* Ibid.

70. *man put up for murder or stratagem.":* Ibid.

70. *and he has a meek expression.":* Ibid.

70. *knew that. He taught Sunday school.: Stern des Westens,* March 23, 1874.

70. *religious fanaticism," the* Daily Globe *reported.: St. Louis Daily Globe,* March 23, 1874.

71. *had suffered an "unnatural death.": St. Louis Daily Globe,* March 22, 1874.

71. *answers incoherent," the* Daily Globe *reported.:* Ibid.

71. *fear that they themselves would faint.:* Ibid.

71. *in a pool of blood. So he was forced.:* Ibid.

71. *shrank from the ghastly sight as if from a snake.":* Ibid.

71. *a look of anger or a look of sorrow.":* Ibid.

71. *vacant stare," the* Globe *reported.:* Ibid.

71. *Boeltz showed "terrible fear.": Stern des Westens,* March 23, 1874.

72. *the sheriff had conducted, showed no wounds.:* Ibid.

72. *no longer a reason to be suspicious.:* Ibid.

72. *head. All by unknown hands.:* Ibid.; *Anzeiger des Westens,* March 23, 1874, reported that the inquest ended shortly before eleven thirty at night.

72. *to bring the suspects to justice.":* Ibid.

72. *witnessed in the house of the Stelzriedes in Saxtown.":* Ibid.

73. *and then use the other weapon.":* Ibid.

73. *time to be brought to light.": Stern des Westens,* March 23, 1874.

Chapter 10: Saxtown

75. *jumping through Southern Illinois that Sunday.: St. Louis Daily Globe,* March 24, 1874.

75. *of him anymore," the* Stern des Westens *wrote.: Stern des Westens,* March 23, 1874.

76. *more than one person may have killed the family.: Anzeiger des Westens,* March 23, 1874.

76. *to make the coffins and bury the dead.:* Michael Brinkman, *Quincy, Illinois Immigrants from Munsterland* (Westminster, Maryland: Heritage Book, 2010), 178.

76. *turned up nearly a dozen corpses.:* St. Louis Daily Globe, March 22, 1874.

76. *horse-drawn wagon toward Fort Scott, Kansas.:* New York Times, May 13, 1873.

76. *the Leavenworth, Lawrence, and Galveston Railroad.:* Weekly Kansas Chief, May 15, 1873.

77. *headed from Fort Scott to Cherryvale.:* New York Times, April 19, 1874.

77. *beautiful, red-faced woman named Kate.:* New York Times, May 13, 1873.

77. *Blindness. Fits. Deafness. Dumbness.:* Ibid.

77. *that once belonged to the Osage Indians.:* St. Louis Post-Dispatch, August 2, 1908.

77. *rude inn," the* St. Louis Post-Dispatch *reported.:* Ibid.

78. *They flocked to the Bender farm.:* New York Times, May 13, 1873.

78. *It was a trapdoor.:* Ibid.

78. *a well six feet deep and five feet wide.:* Ibid.

78. *their fingers," the* Weekly Kansas Chief *newspaper reported.:* Weekly Kansas Chief, May 15, 1873.

78. *clammy, sticking blood," the newspaper said.:* Ibid.

78. *German garden: tomatoes, beets, apples, cherries.:* St. Louis Post-Dispatch, August 2, 1908. In later years people uprooted the garden and sold "Bender beets" and "Bender apples" and "Bender cherries."

78. *Dr. York!" someone among the crowd exclaimed.:* Ibid.

79. *buried on the first dark night.":* Ibid.

79. *and proved false.":* Ibid.

79. *remembering the whole bloody Bender affair.:* St. Louis Daily Globe, March 22, 1874.

79. *to their homeland of Germany.:* New York Times, December 19, 1873; St. Louis Post-Dispatch, August 2, 1908.

79. *Missouri, and quite frequently in Illinois.:* The October 31, 1889, St. Louis Post-Dispatch even reported on some of the alleged Bender clan passing through St. Louis (from Illinois) to Kansas for interrogation.

79. *blood of the second," the newspaper wrote.:* St. Louis Daily Globe, March 22, 1874.

80. *and to help investigate the case.:* St. Louis Democrat, March 22, 1874.

80. *of social discrimination and religious persecution.:* Steven Ozment, *A Mighty Fortress* (New York: HarperCollins, 2004), 5.

80. *attracted by a spring, a pasture, or a grove.":* S. Baring-Gould, *The Nations of the World: Germany* (New York: Peter Fenelon Collier, 1898), 72.

81. *land of "spires, turrets, and towers.":* Simon Winder, *Germania: In Wayward Pursuit of the Germans and Their History* (New York: Farrar, Straus and Giroux, 2010), 129.

81. *eating grass, clover, and potato peelings.":* David Blackbourn, *The Long Nineteenth Century* (New York : Oxford University Press, 1998), 138–39.

81. *a farm town in northern Germany.:* Brinkman, *Illinois Immigrants,* 161.

81. *very miserable and by far incomparable.":* Ibid., 161.

81. *fights with wolves; women were haggard.:* Saxtown residents frequently dealt with roving packs of wolves. By 1900 things got so bad that a man, who was young when the Stelzriedes were murdered, killed a wolf in a physical fight. St. Louis Post-Dispatch, January, 18, 1900.

81. *the language of the rural and uneducated.*: Brinkman, *Illinois Immigrants*, 97.

82. *roofs surrounded by an eighteenth-century castle.*: Dieter Buse, *Regions of Germany* (Westport, Conn.: Greenwood Press, 2005),121. Census records and various government documents showed that Boeltz listed his previous home as Oldenburg.

82. *"rise (and fall) of little people."*: Buse, *Regions of Germany,* 128.

82. *good through the moralistic stories of Wilhem Busch.*: Ibid., 128.

82. *compounded by his own financial failures.*: St. Louis Republican, March 22, 1874.

82. *may have known each other in the Old World.*: The 1870 US Census shows that Afken listed his birthplace as Oldenburg. It is unknown whether the two knew each other. The news accounts and limited court records never addressed the issue or picked up on their shared home.

83. *to arrest Boeltz and Afken.*: St. Louis Times, March 22, 1874.

83. *mourned at the Stelzriede family funeral.*: St. Louis Daily Globe, March 23, 1874.

Chapter 11: The Funerals

85. *them around," the* St. Louis Daily Globe *pleaded.*: St. Louis Daily Globe, March 24, 1874.

85. *pastor would read a short eulogy.*: Michael Brinkman, *Quincy, Illinois Immigrants from Munsterland* (Westminster, Maryland: Heritage Book, 2010), 178.

86. *heads were swollen and black.*: Description based on several accounts of the dead bodies, in particular *St. Louis Daily Globe,* March 22, 1874.

86. *Stelzriede family would never be seen again.*: Account from interview with Wilson Baltz, who based his description on conversations with those present at the time.

86. *death was linked to his growing legacy.:* "Pastor Jacob Knauss," Zion Evangelical Church, www.zionmillstadt.com/Zion/175/Photos /Pages/Cemetery_Walk_files/JacobKnauss.pdf.

86. *a plate-glass front," the* St. Louis Post-Dispatch *remembered.: St. Louis Post-Dispatch,* May 10, 1908.

86. *and often came with a nasty disease.: St. Louis Post-Dispatch,* July 18, 2010.

86. *swiftly, within hours of infection.:* "Cholera," Mayo Clinic, last modified March 30, 2011, www.mayoclinic.com/health/cholera/DS00579.

86. *"rice-water stool" from their bodies.: St. Louis Magazine,* July 2010.

87. *leaving the tubs full of wet clothes.":* Ellin Kelly, "The Vincentian Mission from Paris to the Mississippi: The American Sisters of Charity," *Vincentian Heritage Journal* 14, no. 1 (1993): 187.

87. *More than 120 died of cholera in April 1849.: St. Louis Post-Dispatch,* July 18, 2010.

87. *one in eleven souls living in St. Louis died.:* Ibid.

87. *battle "foul air," and converted schools into hospitals.:* Ibid.

87. *"established residents" blamed sauerkraut.: St. Louis Magazine,* July 2010.

87. *more land than enough to bury him.":* R.S. Elliott quote is from James Neal Primm, *Lion of the Valley* (St. Louis: Missouri Historical Society Press, 1998), 156.

87. *as the epidemic reached its peak.: St. Louis Post-Dispatch,* July 18, 2010.

88. *experience to us, and a terrible one.":* Gustave Koerner, *Memoirs of Gustave Koerner, Volume 1* (Cedar Rapids, Ia.: The Torch Press, 1909), 544.

88. *when the epidemic hit the farms of Saxtown.:* "Pastor Jacob Knaussk," Zion Evangelical Church, www.zionmillstadt.com/Zion/175 /Photos/Pages/Cemetery_Walk_files/JacobKnauss.pdf.

88. *the "Evangelical Pioneer in South Illinois.":* Zion Centennial 1835–1935 (Millstadt, Ill.: Enterprise Print, 1935), 9.

88. *once a month in Saxtown in 1835.*: Zion Evangelical Church, *Zion's Legacy 1835–1985* (Millstadt, Ill.: 150th Anniversary Historical Committee, 1985), 6.

88. *services were often held on Freivogel's lawn.*: Ibid.

88. *preached on the final judgement.*": Ibid.

88. *the sorrowing,*" *according to a Zion church history.*: Ibid, 7.

88. *scattered and small rural population.*: "Pastor Jacob Knauss," Zion Evangelical Church, www.zionmillstadt.com/Zion/175/Photos/Pages/Cemetery_Walk_files/JacobKnauss.pdf.

89. *cholera took her three-year-old son.*: Deaths are based on church records, cemetery records, and St. Clair County records.

89. *buried at Freivogel in unmarked graves.*: Freivogel Cemetery grave listings, Zion Evangelical Church.

89. *suspicion attaches,*" the St. Louis Daily Globe *reported.*: *St. Louis Daily Globe,* March 23, 1874.

90. *the appalling event had aroused.*": Ibid.

90. *to the cemetery,*" *reported the* St. Louis Democrat.: *St. Louis Democrat,* March 23, 1874.

90. *observed to* "*not have shed a tear.*": Ibid.

90. *hallowed be Thy name. Thy kingdom come . . .* ": My description of prayer is based on Wilson Baltz. *Millstadt Enterprise,* June 19, 1974.

91. *to do nothing until it was over.*: St. Louis Dispatch, March 25, 1874.

91. *This was no half-way butchery.*": St. Louis Daily Globe, March 23, 1874.

91. *placed into the three graves.*: Stern des Westens, March 23, 1874.

91. *covered the bodies,*" the Stern des Westens *wrote.*: Ibid.

91. *custody and then to jail in Belleville.*: St. Louis Daily Globe, March 23, 1874.

91. *deceased family,"* the Belleville Advocate *wrote.: Belleville Advocate,* March 27, 1874.

91. *over the question, "Who is the murderer?":* Belleville Zeitung, April 2, 1874.

92. *real criminals will not create surprise.":* St. Louis Daily Globe, March 23, 1874.

Chapter 12: Sweating

93. *and requested a Bible.:* St. Louis Dispatch, March 23, 1874.

93. *and the air in it was hardly fit for reptiles.":* Alvin Louis Nebelsick, *A History of Belleville* (Belleville, Ill.: Township High School and Junior College, 1951), 121.

93. *after being arrested miles away at the Stelzriede funeral.:* St. Louis Daily Globe, March 23, 1874.

93. *questions,"* the Waterloo Republic *wrote of Boeltz.:* Waterloo Republic, March 26, 1874.

93. *where he also taught Sunday school.:* St. Louis Times, March 26, 1874.

94. *he may yet be induced to squeal.":* Ibid.

94. *will force from him the story of his crime.":* Allan Pinkerton, *Bucholz and the Detectives* (New York: G. W. Carleton & Company, 1880), xiii.

94. *was "no clue to the assassins.":* New York Times, March 22, 1874.

94. *temperance movement in the United States.:* Ibid.

94. *their sisters in the West,"* the Times *wrote.:* Ibid.

94. *of the fiendish crime,"* the St. Louis Times *wrote.:* St. Louis Times, March 27, 1874.

95. *a term first used in the 1750s.:* Oxford English Dictionary.

95. *so shaken that he had to confess.:* Description of "sweating" is based on culture of the time and article on St. Louis police in *St. Louis Post-Dispatch,* January 12, 1896.

95. *choose to divulge it," the* St. Louis Times *wrote.: St. Louis Times,* March 24, 1874.

95. *confess it before you go to the gallows.": New York Times,* December 1, 1895.

96. *though my body would burst," Strang said.:* Jesse Strang, *The Confession of Jesse Strang* (Albany: John B. Van Steenbergh, 1827), 32.

96. *the fate of the finally impenitent," Strang said.:* Ibid, 34.

96. *committed here,) in the world of spirits.":* Ibid, 34.

96. *by heaven's redeeming gleam.":* Ibid, 34.

97. *the position in which he is placed.": Belleville Advocate,* March 27, 1874.

97. *along some religious tracts and papers.: St. Louis Democrat,* March 25, 1874.

97. *This is altogether a mistake.":* Ibid.

97. *in cases like that," the* Stern des Westens *wrote.: Stern des Westens,* March 25, 1874.

97. *and was "mum as an oyster.": St. Louis Times,* March 24, 1874.

97. *will not come from him," the* St. Louis Times *reported.:* Ibid.

97. *"strenuous" efforts to secure their release.: St. Louis Times,* March 25, 1874.

97. *there is no proof for anything.": Anzeiger des Westens,* March 25, 1874.

98. *its first "Police School of Instruction.":* Allen Wagner, *Good Order and Safety: A History of the St. Louis Metropolitan Police* (Columbia, Mo.: University of Missouri Press, 2008), 78.

98. *his freedom unless the original owner appeared.":* Nebelsick, *History of Belleville,* 219.

98. *his iron determination and his tireless activity.":* James Cox, *Old and New St. Louis* (St. Louis: Central Biographical Publishing, 1894), 389.

98. *where was he?" Nebelsick wrote of the frontier justice system.*: Nebelsick, *History of Belleville*, 112.

99. *they offered an additional reward of one thousand dollars.*: St. Louis *Times*, March 24, 1874.

99. *are still unrewarded," the* Belleville Advocate *wrote.*: *Belleville Advocate*, March 27, 1874.

100. *a real detective should avoid at all times.".* Thomas Furlong, *Fifty Years a Detective* (St. Louis: For sale by C.E. Barnett, 1912), 6.

100. *balance of the work is usually easy.".* Ibid.

100. *to say the least, doubtful moral character.".* St. Louis *Post-Dispatch*, May 15, 1884.

100. *thoroughly that we can do nothing.".* Ibid.

101. *fingers seemed to have been bitten almost off.".* Stern des Westens, March 25, 1874.

101. *"vicious and murderous countenance.".* St. Louis *Dispatch*, March 23, 1874.

101. *there was no evidence against him.*: Ibid. *Dispatch* wrote: "[Afken] may possibly prove himself innocent . . ."

101. *not at home on the night of the murders.*: St. Louis *Times*, March 26, 1874. News reports at the time erroneously reported Boeker's last name as "Becker."

Chapter 13: Bloody Evidence

103. *get away with this gruesome crime.".* Stern des Westens, March 24, 1874.

103. *They were found secreted in a stove.".* St. Louis *Democrat*, March 25, 1874.

104. *Attorney R. A. Halbert corroborated the story.*: Ibid.

104. *reportedly large with an iron handle.*: St. Louis *Democrat*, March 26, 1874.

104. *perpetrators of the bloody deed," the* Democrat *reported.:* Ibid.

104. *they would be housed in the local jail.: St. Louis Democrat,* March 25, 1874.

104. *knives were placed on the stove, he said.: St. Louis Democrat,* March 26, 1874.

104. *press seeking to feed anything to their readers.: Belleville Advocate,* March 27, 1874. The Belleville newspaper was quick to criticize its German rival.

104. *told and eagerly devoured," the* Belleville Advocate *wrote.:* Ibid.

105. *will probably be released in a few days.":* Ibid.

105. *displaying the "utmost unconcern.":* Ibid.

105. *when he went to the murder scene.: St. Louis Times,* March 27, 1874. Newspapers wrongly referred to Jacob Becker as "Birker."

105. *which helped keep the dust in check.: St. Louis Dispatch,* March 26, 1874.

105. *remained there for the rest of the night.: St. Louis Times,* March 27, 1874.

105. *knowing anything about it.":* Ibid.

106. *taken to Belleville as evidence.:* Ibid.

106. *nothing suspicious other than the bloodstains.:* Ibid.

Chapter 14: Next of Kin

107. *Charles didn't attend his relatives' funeral.:* Charles Stelzriede was born in 1817 in Hille, Germany. Age comes from the 1870 US Census.

107. *indignation of everyone," the* St. Louis Daily Globe *reported.: St. Louis Daily Globe,* March 23, 1874.

107. *bad blood within the Stelzriede family?: St. Louis Times,* March 25, 1874.

107. *man capable of doing desperate things.": St. Louis Daily Globe,* March 23, 1874.

108. *649 Washington Street in the Greenwich Village neighborhood.:* New York City Directory, p. 371. The directory lists Charles F. Stelzriede as a grocer, and living at the same address as his brother, Frederic W. Stelzriede.

108. *not far from the Hoboken ferry.:* 1842 New York map, David Rumsey Map Collection, www.davidrumsey.com/luna/servlet/s/2v1f98.

108. *walked by beer gardens and brothels.:* My descriptions of the neighborhood are based on the Greenich Village Historic District Designation Report, May 2, 2006; and Greenwich Village Historic District Designation Report, 1969.

108. *and was committed for ten days.: New York Times,* July 27, 1855.

108. *saloon owner's name: Patrick Farrell.:* Ibid.

109. *shop and appeared to have avoided the debauchery.:* Directory lists the same address as their store, which was common during this time and in Greenwich Village.

109. *Martin in 1851. And William in 1854.:* US Census records show the birthplaces and years of the three sons.

109. *with various paintings and large prints.": New York Times,* March 9, 1855.

109. *Especially the "papists.": The New Yorker,* March 20, 1954.

110. *betray the trust received from Heaven.":* Ibid.

110. *Fillmore won the party's presidential nomination.):* Millard Fillmore was soundly defeated by James Buchanan.

110. *determined to ship all her poorest class here.'": Startling Facts for Native Americans called "Know-Nothings"* (New York: 128 Nassau Street, 1855), 52.

110. *biting, brawling, gouging—at any moment.: New York Times,* March 9, 1855.

110. *Irish son of a bitch!" the Butcher shouted.:* The New Yorker, March 20, 1954.

111. *American son of a bitch!" Morrissey responded.:* Ibid.

111. *Butcher in the heart. The men fled.:* Ibid.

111. *I've been murdered by a set of Irish.":* New York Times, March 9, 1855.

111. *were brought in requisition," the* New York Times *wrote.:* New York Times, March 12, 1855.

111. *"I die a true American.":* Ibid.

111. *labeled it the "Stanwix Hall Tragedy.":* Ibid.

111. *headed halfway across the country to Illinois.:* St. Clair County Property records show the Stelzriedes arrived in the fall of 1855.

111. *became a liquor store and distillery.:* Description based on New York City directories from the 1860s.

112. *a pig, some oxen. No horses.:* 1860 US Agricultural Census.

112. *nor a last will and testament.:* New York court papers said Stelzriede died intestate.

112. *tracked down "were utterly irresponsible.":* New York, Probate Records, 1629–1863.

112. *near the Washington County line.:* US Census, Township 2 Range 1, Jefferson, Illinois. Records show the property was in Jefferson County but close to Washington County.

112. *local one-room school, and games of checkers.:* Continental Historical Bureau, "History of Jefferson County, Illinois," 1962.

113. *remains unclear if Charles permitted it.:* Albert Meyer, "Memories: Recollections of the Life, Times and Activities of Albert F. Meyer," http://stelzriede.net/pafg09.htm.

113. *world around them, including St. Louis.:* Illinois Railroad Map, 1874.

113. *by about fifteen hundred dollars.: St. Louis Daily Globe,* March 23, 1874.

113. *not visited each other for some time.":* Ibid.

113. *Charles had vowed to seek revenge.: Anzeiger des Westens,* March 25, 1874.

113. *always refused," the* St. Louis Dispatch *reported.: St. Louis Dispatch,* March 25, 1874.

113. *seen the day after near Fred Boeltz's farm.: Anzeiger des Westens,* March 25, 1874.

113. *had to be wounded," the* Anzeiger des Westens *reported.:* Ibid.

114. *Henry, Martin, and William—had been arrested but quickly released.: St. Louis Democrat,* March 26, 1874. The brothers were arrested by different parties but all released.

114. *railroad employee in Washington County.:* Illinois State Archives, Illinois Statewide Marriage Index.

114. *stories are afloat as to who the perpetrators are.": St. Louis Democrat,* March 26, 1874.

114. *McCullagh, the editor of the* St. Louis Daily Globe.: *St. Louis Daily Globe,* March 26, 1874.

115. *the article referred to of the 23rd.":* Ibid.

116. *late Stelzriede murder in St. Clair County, Illinois.":* Ibid.

116. *succession to Fred and Margaret Boeltz.: St. Louis Daily Globe,* March 23, 1874.

116. *fixed by the statutes," the* St. Louis Times *reported.: St. Louis Times,* March 31, 1874.

116. *with a jacket in his hand.: Belleville Zeitung,* April 2, 1874.

117. *shot Lincoln, play Shakespeare's Hamlet.: St. Louis Times,* March 26, 1874.

117. *provided a note from his doctor.: St. Louis Times,* March 27, 1874.

117. *sick for nearly a year," the* St. Louis Times *reported.:* Ibid.

117. *unacquainted with Afken," an observer reported.:* Ibid.

118. *the arrest and conviction of the murderers.:* St. Louis Daily Globe, April 9, 1874.

118. *1869 and built out from East St. Louis.:* L. U. Reavis, *The Railway and River Systems of St. Louis* (St. Louis: Woodward, Tiernan, and Hale, 1879), 244.

118. *St. Clair County the morning of the murders.:* St. Louis Post-Dispatch, November 14, 1877.

Chapter 15: Cursed

119. *sun shone cheerfully above the Saxtown skies.:* St. Louis Dispatch, April 1, 1874. Weather report stated the "sun shone out brightly this morning and gave a cheering aspect . . ."

119. *preferred shorter skirts to "demi-trains.":* St. Louis Republican, March 29, 1874.

119. *an "excellent state of cultivation.":* St. Louis Times, March 31, 1874.

120. *alive with chickens," someone observed.:* Ibid.

120. *wouldn't go away without a coat of paint.:* Ibid.

120. *three times the value of the Stelzriede land and stock.:* 1870 Non-Population Census, St. Clair County, Illinois, Agriculture.

120. *ten children—most of them boys.:* 1870 and 1880 US Census, St. Clair County, Illinois.

120. *a ten dollar bounty for every wolf skin:* St. Louis Post-Dispatch, January 18, 1900.

120. *air and howled into the big sky.:* Ibid.

120. *The fight was over.:* Ibid.

120. *ten dollars "without question.":* Ibid.

121. *murderers to a swift and speedy justice.":* Belleville Advocate, March 27, 1874.

121. *strangely when the bodies were first discovered.:* No evidence exists that Hughes ever investigated Killian, George Schneider, or George Fritzinger.

121. *perpetrators have all escaped," the article noted.:* Belleville Advocate, March 27, 1874.

122. *a device that ushered in modern life.:* Robert V. Bruce, *Bell: Alexander Graham Bell and the Conquest of Solitude* (Ithaca, New York: Cornell University Press, 1990), 181.

122. *but he had footwear impressions.:* St. Louis Daily Globe, April 9, 1874.

122. *and made outside travel nearly impossible.:* St. Louis Dispatch, April 6, 1874.

122. *said to have "dissolute character.":* Belleville Advocate, April 10, 1874.

122. *correspond exactly with the feet of these men.":* St. Louis Daily Globe, April 9, 1874.

122. *for what he called a "square deal.":* Illinois State Historical Society, "Papers in Illinois History and Transactions for the Year," 1920.

123. *bond that was secured by his father.:* Belleville Advocate, April 17, 1874.

123. *for a supposed criminal matter.":* St. Clair County Circuit Clerk's file.

123. *he was told that he might get released.:* St. Louis Daily Globe, April 26, 1874.

123. *which was agreed to by the state's attorney.:* Ibid.

123. *"completely overcome" with emotion.:* Ibid.

123. *born just two years after Illinois became a state.:* St. Clair County Circuit Clerk's file.

123. *to release them for lack of evidence.:* Ibid.

124. *best known lawyers in Belleville, to defend him.:* Belleville Weekly Advocate, June 5, 1874.

124. *knives found at the Stelzriede murder scene.*: St. Louis Democrat, March 25, 1874.

124. *innocent persons on the barest suspicion.*": Belleville Weekly Advocate, June 5, 1874.

124. *out" over and over in hushed conversations.*: St. Louis Dispatch, May 11, 1876.

124. *Hughes, though severely injured, is not fatally hurt.*": St. Louis Dispatch, May 11, 1874.

125. *at their Belleville home and broke her leg.*: Ibid.

125. *by a pair of runaway horses.*: St. Louis Daily Globe, May 13, 1874.

Chapter 16: Deathbed Confessions

127. *Daniel Webster were repeated in the Saxtown case.*: St. Louis Daily Globe, March 23, 1874.

127. *in the Saxtown case. Or so said a developing legend.*: This legend was reported and repeated in the decades following the murders.

127. *created a tableau of distrust.*: St. Louis Dispatch, May 11, 1876.

128. A CLUE AT LAST TO THE STELZRIEDE MURDER.": Ibid.

128. *and under what circumstances it was prompted.*": Ibid.

128. *before the letter was delivered to Orp.*: Ibid.

128. *since the night of the butchery," the* Dispatch *reported.*: Ibid.

128. *description had been found drowned in Memphis.*: Ibid. The *Dispatch* said a "floater" matched Gretting's description.

128. *allegedly hired him to kill the Stelzriedes.*: Ibid.

129. *had killed the murderous Bender family.*: St. Louis Post-Dispatch, August 2, 1908.

129. *tracked the Benders as they escaped justice.*: Ibid.

129. *she "liked to see the blood come.*": Ibid.

129. *the extermination of the murderous family.*": Ibid.

129. *"something about a murder" without giving a location.:* St. Louis *Dispatch,* November 14, 1877.

129. *and to get a good look at him.:* Ibid.

130. *illness he had been in a "morose disposition.":* Ibid.

130. *and that haunting shadow of a crime.":* Ibid.

130. *murder that stains the annals of Illinois.":* Ibid.

130. *was found and taken for treatment.:* St. Louis Republican, March 8, 1882.

130. *the secrets of the Stelzriede murders.:* Ibid.

Chapter 17: The Feuds

131. *Isaiah Thomas couldn't let it go.:* St. Louis Post-Dispatch, March 7, 1882.

131. *forever changed his tiny corner of the world.:* Belleville Advocate, March 10, 1882. My description of Thomas is based on multiple lawsuits that were filed against him. He went to extreme measures to accuse people of the murders, and it was written that he spent most of his spare time in those pursuits.

131. *setting the mousetraps when the days were done.:* "One-room School-teachers," Sherri Dagel, Iowa Pathways, "*The Goldfinch* 16," no. 1, (Fall 1994), Iowa City: State Historical Society of Iowa. www.iptv.org /iowapathways/mypath.cfm?ounid=ob_000254. I've used this descrip-tion to help inform school life in the neighboring state of Illinois.

131. *rural children didn't have to attend school.:* Ibid.

132. *stonemasons, coal diggers.:* 1880 US Census, St. Clair County, Illinois.

132. *Saxtown farm to nearby Millstadt.:* Ibid.

132. *elected president after losing the popular vote.:* Ibid. Records show that Isaiah Thomas was born in Ohio.

132. *named her Minnie.:* Ibid.

132. *then killed himself in Memphis, Tennessee.: St. Louis Dispatch*, May 11, 1876.

132. *but never indicted for the murders.:* Fred Boeltz, John Afken, William Stelzriede, Martin Stelzriede, Jacob Petrie, and Frederick Eckert Jr. had all been arrested but ultimately released.

133. *neighborhood," the* Belleville Advocate *wrote.: Belleville Advocate*, March 10, 1882.

133. *had incurred his suspicions.":* Ibid.

133. *who murdered the Stelzriede family.:* Ibid.

133. *although it normally roamed the farmstead.: St. Louis Daily Globe-Democrat*, March 8, 1882.

134. *Thomas in St. Clair County court for defamation.:* St. Clair County Circuit Court, case no. 55, roll 394, seq. 61.

134. *Republican politician hired to represent Schneider.:* Ibid.

134. *are the murderers of Stelzriede.":* Ibid.

135. *the tracks showed two people running.:* Ibid.

135. *"we would have been hung long ago.":* Ibid.

135. *murder of the Stelzriede family was done.":* Ibid.

135. *One witness had died.:* Ibid.

135. *without ever making an indictment.: St. Louis Post-Dispatch*, October 3, 1897.

136. *Thomas Jefferson–designed Virginia State Capitol.:* St. Clair County Genealogical Society, "The Fifth St. Clair County Courthouse: Neoclassicism on the Prairie," 2004.

136. *found later on the stone basement floor.: East St. Louis Herald*, October 22, 1881.

136. *twenty-five feet to the slab stone floor below.: St. Louis Daily Globe*, October 21, 1881.

136. *had been erected to the Stelzriede family.*: *Belleville Weekly Advocate*, October 21, 1881.

136. *believed that Hughes had been pushed.*: The story has been preserved in the oral tradition. Author interview with Mark Westhoff, former director of the St. Clair County Historical Society.

Chapter 18: The Case Reopens

137. *eight years after the crime.*: *Belleville Advocate*, March 10, 1882.

137. *between the busy Olive and Locust Streets.*: *St. Louis Post-Dispatch*, June 21, 1882.

137. *connect factories and hotels and railroad depots.*: *St. Louis Post-Dispatch*, February 25, 1882.

138. *unknown," the* St. Louis Post-Dispatch *wrote.*: *St. Louis Post-Dispatch*, September 20, 1882.

138. *Edison told the New York Board of Fire Underwriters in an 1881 letter.*: *St. Louis Globe-Democrat*, May 10, 1881.

138. *would "surely kill a man.".*: *New York Times*, July 24, 1889.

138. *dying men allegedly confessing to the crime.*: Description comes from previous events discussed, including the confessions related to Christian Orp and George Killian.

138. *West," the* St. Louis Post-Dispatch *remarked in 1882.*: *St. Louis Post-Dispatch*, September 5, 1889.

139. *Democratic politician looking to make a splash.*: Frederic Crossley, *Courts and Lawyers of Illinois* (Chicago: The American Historical Society, 1916), 1010– 11.

139. *No one was there to do it for him.*: Ibid.

139. *impressed nearly everyone he met.*: Ibid.

139. *bragging about her brushes with death.*: *St. Louis Post-Dispatch*, March 2, 1882.

140. *Thomas had destroyed his reputation.*: St. Louis Republican, March 8, 1882.

140. *being unable to hold his liquor.*: Ibid. Various accounts discuss Killian's inability to hold his alcohol.

140. *tell the story," the* St. Louis Daily Globe-Democrat *observed*: St. Louis Daily Globe-Democrat, March 8, 1882.

140. *he will divulge it remains to be seen.*": St. Louis Post-Dispatch, March 15, 1882.

141. *Thomas was unfazed by the verdict.*: St. Louis Daily Globe-Democrat, March 8, 1882.

141. *murder him for telling what he has told.*": Ibid.

141. *enacted it," the* St. Louis Republican *newspaper wrote.*: St. Louis Republican, March 7, 1882.

141. *to Killian and took him into custody.*: Ibid.

141. *in Belleville before going to jail.*: St. Louis Republican, March 8, 1882.

142. *available and was able to furnish.*: Ibid.

142. *was still fresh at the end of his term.*: History of St. Clair County, Illinois (Philadelphia: Brink, McDonough & Company, 1881), 90.

142. *to come was high theater.*: Chicago Daily Tribune, March 9, 1882.

142. *German family of Saxtown,*": St. Louis Republican, March 7, 1882.

142. *they shared near the Stelzriede farm.*: St. Louis Daily Globe-Democrat, March 8, 1882.

142. *they were "prospecting" for coal.*: Ibid.

143. *in the ground," the* St. Louis Post-Dispatch *wrote.*: St. Louis Post-Dispatch, October 3, 1897.

143. *disappeared two days* before *the murders.*: St. Louis Daily Globe-Democrat, March 8, 1882.

143. *the misfortune of living near Thomas.*: 1880 US Census, St. Clair County, Illinois.

143. *told," the* St. Louis Daily Globe-Democrat *reported.: St. Louis Daily Globe-Democrat,* March 8, 1882.

143. *murderers are, but I won't tell."*: Ibid.

143. *he wouldn't give them away.*: Ibid.

143. *stolen loot to keep quiet.*: Ibid.

144. *George is a butcher."*: Ibid.

144. *all that I can say at present to you."*: St. Louis Republican, March 8, 1882.

144. *alleged was the property of Killian."*: St. Louis Daily Globe-Democrat, March 8, 1882.

144. *"hollow back of the Stelzriede house."*: St. Louis Post-Dispatch, October 3, 1897.

144. *boots," the* St. Louis Daily Globe-Democrat *reported.: St. Louis Daily Globe-Democrat,* March 8, 1882.

144. *his brother wore big or small shoes.*: Ibid.

145. *that eye is sticking out yet."*: Ibid.

145. *going on," State's Attorney Holder said.: St. Louis Republican,* March 8, 1882.

145. *at the farmhouse of neighbor John Schellhouse.*: St. Louis Daily Globe-Democrat, March 8, 1882.

145. *to prevent him from following them."*: Ibid.

145. *sold the dog to the Stelzriedes.*: Ibid.

145. *the murders of the Stelzriedes than you do."*: Ibid.

145. *say a good deal when he is drunk."*: Ibid.

146. *or was connected to the horror.*: St. Louis Republican, March 8, 1882.

146. *he hit and punched his wife.*: Ibid.

146. *her husband might be locked up.*: Ibid.

146. *something he had done in St. Clair County.*: Ibid.

147. *conspiracy that involved four people.:* Ibid.

147. *to do that job, and you can say so.":* Ibid.

147. *on the morning after the tragedy,":* St. Louis Post-Dispatch, March 15, 1882.

Chapter 19: Hounded by Suspicion

149. *Stelzriede family," Killian said in 1897.:* St. Louis Post-Dispatch, October 3, 1897.

149. *sue them and make them shut up.":* Ibid.

150. *husband,"* the St. Louis Post-Dispatch *reported.:* Ibid.

150. *word of mouth and shrugging of shoulders.":* Ibid.

150. *"It won't do him any good.":* Ibid.

150. *Killian should want to get at me.":* Ibid.

150. *had beaten and threatened to leave.:* Ibid.

151. *and there is no mirth in his laugh.":* Ibid.

151. *and did not leave it," Killian said.:* Ibid.

151. *accused Killian of murdering the Stelzriede family.:* Millstadt Enterprise, June 16, 1899.

151. *"dangerous knife wounds.":* Ibid.

152. *himself from vile slurs and insinuations.":* Ibid.

152. *was charged with attempted murder.:* St. Clair County Circuit Clerk, case no. 307, roll 60, seq. 51 (1907).

Chapter 20: Land of the Free

153. *Boeltz planned his escape.:* One such sleuth was Christian Orp (see chapter 16). He had moved to Saxtown by 1876 and said he received a letter from a suicidal man claiming to have committed the murders for hire. It gave no other specifics and was quickly discounted. *St. Louis Dispatch*, May 11, 1876.

153. *a few seconds," the document concluded.:* "History of St. Clair County, Illinois," July 4, 1876, www.stclair-ilgs.org/1876hist.htm.

154. *cash but not the farmland.:* Stelzriede estate papers, St. Clair County Circuit Clerk's office, Belleville, Illinois.

154. *had been accused of murder.:* Land Entry Case Files: Homestead Final Certificates, National Archives.

154. *never seen in St. Clair County or Illinois again.:* US Homestead documents.

155. *rough, uncouth, and uncivilized people.":* "Central City—Merrick County," University of Nebraska–Lincoln, www.casde.unl.edu /history/counties/merrick/centralcity.

155. *and Missouri River Railroad depot.:* Merrick County Land Ownership Maps, 1899, roll no. 105.

155. *and an eight-by-ten-foot windmill.:* US Homestead documents; testimony of witness, July 15, 1893.

156. *valued at three thousand dollars.:* Ibid.

156. *It was now "Boelts.":* The last name had many variations through the years. For most of his early years in St. Clair County, he went by Boeltz. At times, it was recorded as Boeltz, but never as Boelts. Immigrants were often recorded as the person documenting their name could spell it phonetically. Until Boeltz applied for citizenship, he used the Boeltz spelling in land documents, news articles, and a chattel mortgage.

156. *sons, John, Gustav, Henry, and Fred Jr.:* Merrick County, Nebraska, Land Ownership Maps, 1917, roll no. 105.

156. *daughter Tillie became schoolteachers.:* US Census, Merrick County, Nebraska, 1900.

156. *marked grave etched with the last name B-O-E-L-T-S.:* Archer Evangelical Community Cemetery photos.

Chapter 21: Gone, but Not Forgotten

157. *East St. Louis & Carondelet Rail Way.:* Belleville, Illinois, City Directory, 1891, p. 466.

158. *before it,"* the New York Times *wrote.: New York Times,* May 29, 1896.

158. *were killed at one depot alone.:* St. Louis Post-Dispatch, May 28, 2011.

158. *pockets of the dead and injured.:* Ibid.

158. *heart of stone," wrote one account.:* Julian Curzon, ed., *The Great Cyclone at St. Louis and East St. Louis* (St. Louis: Cyclone Publishing Company, 1896), 214.

158. *Thirteen people there were killed.:* St. Louis Post-Dispatch, May 29, 1896.

159. *erroneously reported to have died.: The Belleville Weekly Advocate,* January 4, 1878.

159. *Hannah, died later that year.:* Centreville Cemetery, Millstadt, Illinois.

159. *St. Clair County Poor Farm and Hospital.: Belleville Weekly Advocate,* November 11, 1887.

159. *is now a hundred-fold a mystery.":* St. Louis Post-Dispatch, October 3, 1897.

159. *killed Peter. The case was dropped.: Belleville Advocate,* April 14, 1882.

160. *an order prohibiting any removal.: Belleville News-Democrat,* January 18, 1971.

160. *many more years on his farm near Richview.:* US Census, Perry County, Illinois, 1880.

160. *which by 1897 had gone "neglected.":* St. Louis Post-Dispatch, October 3, 1897.

160. *the tardiness of justice," it was observed.:* St. Louis Post-Dispatch, October 24, 1902.

160. *Friends disputed that account.:* St. Louis Post-Dispatch, October 24, 1902.

160. *Murat Halstead and Charles Dana belong."*: Charles C. Clayton, *Little Mack: Joseph B. McCullagh of the St. Louis Globe-Democrat* (Carbondale, Ill.: Southern Illinois University Press, 1969), 234.

160. *saloons, and easy transportation.*: St. Louis Post-Dispatch, August 6, 1911.

161. *the finished appearance of a modern city."*: Ibid.

161. *and disability caused his retirement."*: Millstadt Enterprise, June 24, 1927.

161. *his stories contributed to the growing lore.*: Author interview with Wilson Baltz, who attended the Millstadt School during the years Ben Schneider was a janitor.

161. HALF CENTURY AGO STILL A MYSTERY.: *Millstadt Enterprise*, March 21, 1924.

161. *his left hand," the* Millstadt Enterprise *reported.*: Ibid.

161. *contracted it while preaching a funeral.*: "Pastor Jacob Knauss," Zion Evangelical Church, www.zionmillstadt.com/Zion/175/Photos /Pages/Cemetery_Walk_files/JacobKnauss.pdf.

161. *no money, and so we are safe."*: St. Louis Post-Dispatch, October 3, 1897.

162. *misdirected blows of a murderous hammer."*: Ibid.

162. *never seen any of them around here."*: Ibid.

162. *yard," Percy later told the* Belleville News-Democrat.*: Belleville News-Democrat*, March 20, 1988.

163. *man "may have been the murderer."*: Ibid.

163. *auction before he was murdered.*: Ibid.

163. *hanging, but the money was gone."*: Ibid.

163. *to Jessie and Leslie Jines in 1945.*: St. Clair County, Illinois, property records.

163. *hunted down and punished as he deserves."*: St. Louis Globe-Democrat, July 7, 1875; *St. Louis Globe-Democrat*, July 10, 1875.

164. *feet bound and a gunny sack over his head.*: St. Louis Post-Dispatch, April 12, 1921.

164. *a family feud over his estate.:* St. Louis Post-Dispatch, May 5, 1921.

164. *Kolter had buried money on his farm.:* St. Louis Post-Dispatch, March 16, 1922.

164. *got the Stelzriede family's name wrong.:* St. Louis Post-Dispatch, April 15, 1922.

Chapter 22: Ghosts

165. *Stelzriede murder was committed.":* Millstadt Enterprise, August 19, 1954.

165. *which large portions of human kind will eagerly admit.":* St. Louis Daily Globe, March 29, 1874.

165. *the apparition of departed friends.":* St. Louis Daily Globe, March 29, 1874.

166. *worked for the M & O Motor Company.:* East St Louis, Illinois, City Directory, 1930.

166. *murder mystery" eighty years after it began.:* Millstadt Enterprise, August 19, 1954.

166. *in the house until she died in 1985.:* St. Clair County land records.

166. *shivering, shaking. Scared to death.:* Author interview with Randy Eckert.

167. *walking up the steps in our basement.":* Author interview with Chris Nauman.

167. *magazine article on the Saxtown murders.:* Suzanne Hutcherson, "The Ghosts of Saxtown Road," Ghosts of the Prairie 25 (Spring 2007): 14.

168. *crime that, now, only God can bestow.":* Ibid.

168. *None was ever found.:* Author interview with Randy Eckert.

168. *be talking in German?" he asked.:* Ibid.

Chapter 23: Whodunit

169. *fingers," said Terry Buecher, who played Fritz.:* Millstadt Community Times, October 8, 2010.

169. *sign that our troubles were over.":* Ibid.

170. *1974 for the weekly* Millstadt Enterprise. *"Forever.": Millstadt Enterprise,* June 26, 1974.

170. *protect the privacy of living relatives.":* Ibid.

170. *knows what really happened there.": Belleville News-Democrat,* March 20, 1988.

170. *to blame the guy who found the bodies.":* Ibid.

171. *say who he suspected," Eckert said.: Belleville News-Democrat,* March 20, 1988.

171. *just family members overreacting.":* Author interview with Mark Westhoff.

171. *when he come to investigate," Luckherdt said.: Belleville News-Democrat,* March 20, 1988.

172. *than you'll find written," Westhoff said.:* Author interview with Mark Westhoff.

172. *Oldenburg in Lower Saxony.:* Census records show that both Boeltz and Afken claimed Oldenburg as their place of origin.

172. *found wet the day after the murders.: Missouri Republican,* March 22, 1874.

173. *noticed something odd about Afken.:* Author interview with Mark Westhoff.

173. *thought belonged to Carl Stelzriede.:* Ibid.

173. *attacker's hair as he fought for his life.:* Ibid.

173. *freckled Afken had red hair.:* Afken's light complexion was reported by a variety of newspapers in 1874. Those who knew him said he had red hair.

INDEX

About the Author

A reporter at the *St. Louis Post-Dispatch,* Nicholas J. C. Pistor has broken stories on some of the biggest crimes in the Midwest and has been a consultant for CBS News's *48 Hours Mystery.* He has appeared on nearly every major national news network, including NBC's *Today Show,* CBS, Fox News, MSNBC, C-Span, and CNN's *Nancy Grace. St. Louis Magazine* named him the city's "best Twitterer." He grew up a few miles from the Saxtown murder scene, where talk of the century-old crime kept him awake as a boy. He currently lives in downtown St. Louis, Missouri. You can send the author a tweet at @nickpistor, e-mail him at npistor@gmail.com, or visit his website at nickpistor.com.